VISUAL QUICKSTART GUIDE

Mac OS 8

Maria Langer

 Peachpit Press

Visual QuickStart Guide

Mac OS 8

Maria Langer

Peachpit Press
2414 Sixth Street
Berkeley, CA 94710
510/548-4393
510/548-5991 (fax)

Find us on the World Wide Web at: http://www.peachpit.com

Peachpit Press is a division of Addison Wesley Longman

Editors: Roslyn Bullas, Jeremy Judson
Technical Editor: Stu Gitlow
Indexer: Maria Langer
Cover Design: The Visual Group
Production: Maria Langer, Kate Reber

Colophon

This book was produced with Adobe® PageMaker® 6.5 on a Power Macintosh 7100/66, a Power Macintosh 8500/180, and a PowerBook 3400/180. The fonts used were Charlotte, Charlotte Sans, and Corinthian Bold from Letraset.

Notice of Rights

Notice of Liability

ISBN 0-201-69645-2

9 8 7 6 5 4 3 2

Printed and bound in the United States of America.

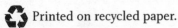 Printed on recycled paper.

Dedication

To Guy Kawasaki
and the rest of the Apple Evangelists

Thanks!

To Roslyn Bullas, for helping me meet an impossible deadline. To Jeremy Judson, for leaving the country and handing me off to Ros. ;-)

To the rest of the folks at Peachpit Press for doing what they do so well—and being so nice about it!

To Stu Gitlow, for applying his expert knowledge of Mac OS to the manuscript to make sure it was right.

To the folks at Apple Computer, Inc., especially Nathalie Welch and Peter Lowe who helped me get the material and information I needed to get this book done.

And to Mike, for the usual collection of reasons.

http://www.intac.com/~gilesrd

TABLE OF CONTENTS

Table of Contents

Table of Contents

Table of Contents

Table of Contents

Table of Contents

Table of Contents

Table of Contents

INTRODUCTION TO MAC OS 8

Introduction

Mac OS 8 is the latest version of the computer operating system that put the phrase *graphic user interface* in everyone's vocabulary. With Mac OS, you can point, click, and drag to work with files, applications, and utilities. Because the same intuitive interface is utilized throughout the system, you'll find that a procedure that works in one program works in virtually all the others.

This Visual QuickStart Guide will help you learn Mac OS 8 by providing step-by-step instructions, plenty of illustrations, and a generous helping of tips. On these pages, you'll find everything you need to know to get up and running quickly with Mac OS 8—and more!

This book was designed for page flipping. Use the thumb tabs, index, or table of contents to find the topics for which you need help. If you're brand new to Mac OS, however, I recommend that you begin by reading at least the first two chapters. In them, you'll find basic information about techniques you'll use every day with your computer.

If you're interested in information about new Mac OS features and the components of Mac OS 8, be sure to browse through this **Introduction**. It'll give you a good idea of what you can expect to see on your computer.

Start Here

New Features in Mac OS 8

About New Features in Mac OS 8

Mac OS 8 adds many new features to the Mac OS Finder and system. You can see many of them in **Figure 1**. Here's a list:

New appearance features

■ Set appearance options with the Appearance control panel.

■ Put your favorite picture on the Desktop with the Desktop Pictures control panel.

■ Enhanced appearance includes platinum color scheme, new icons, and new system font.

New Finder window features

■ Move a window by dragging its border.

■ Collapse a window to its title bar.

■ View items as icons, buttons, or lists.

■ Keep icon view and button view items sorted.

■ Use pop-up windows to keep items handy, but out of the way.

■ Use spring-loaded folders to automatically open and close folders as you file items.

■ Enable Simple Finder to limit Finder menu options.

■ Get details about items being copied in the enhanced copy status window.

New Finder menu features

■ Use sticky menus to keep menus open by clicking.

■ Display contextual menus with commands for items you click.

■ Use the Move to Trash command to place selected items in the trash.

■ Access online help from the Help menu.

New performance features

■ See the contents of a window scroll when you drag the scroll box.

■ Perform multiple Finder operations at the same time.

New Internet features

■ Use the Internet Setup Assistant to configure an Internet connection.

■ Connect to an ISP via modem with the Internet Dialer.

■ Open icons on the Desktop to access the World Wide Web and e-mail.

■ Use the Connect To command to quickly connect to any location on the Internet.

■ Browse the World Wide Web with Netscape Navigator.

■ Exchange e-mail with Claris Emailer Lite.

■ Set up your own Web site with Personal Web Sharing.

Window border

Platinum appearance, new icons, new system font

Collapse box

Enhanced copy status window

Internet access from Desktop

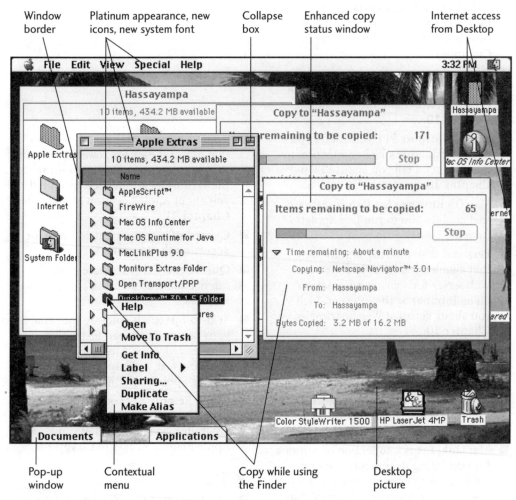

Pop-up window

Contextual menu

Copy while using the Finder

Desktop picture

Figure 1. *This view of a Finder Desktop illustrates many of the new features in Mac OS 8.*

New Features in Mac OS 8

About Mac OS 8 Components

Mac OS 8 includes the following software components:

- **Mac OS 8** is the primary collection of system software files, including the System file, Finder file, control panels, and extensions. This is the foundation of Mac OS 8; its various parts are covered throughout this book.

- **Mac OS Info Center** is a collection of files that provide information about Mac OS 8 and links to the Internet for getting more information. I tell you about Mac OS 8 Info center in **Chapter 13**.

- **Internet Access** is the software you need to connect to the Internet. I tell you about accessing the Internet in **Chapter 10**.

- **Open Transport PPP** is software you need to establish a PPP connection to the Internet. I tell you about PPP in **Chapter 10**.

- **Mac OS Runtime for Java** is software that enables you to run Java applets from the Finder.

- **Personal Web Sharing** is software that enables you to build your own Web server for sharing information on an Intranet or the Internet. I tell you about Personal Web Sharing in **Chapter 10**.

- **QuickDraw 3D** is software for working with three-dimensional graphics.

- **OpenDoc** is component software that enables you to build custom documents. I tell you a little about OpenDoc in **Chapter 5**.

- **MacLinkPlus** is a collection of software for translating documents from one application or computer platform to another. I tell you about MacLinkPlus in **Chapter 7**.

- **Apple Location Manager** is software that makes it easy for PowerBook users to maintain separate system settings for the various locations they visit. I tell you about Apple Location Manager in **Chapter 11**.

- **Cyberdog** is component software for accessing the Internet.

- **QuickDraw GX** is software that offers enhanced printing and preview features.

- **Text-to-Speech** is software that enables your computer to read text with a synthesized voice. I tell you about speaking text in **Chapter 5** and about setting Speech options in **Chapter 12**.

- **Apple Remote Access** is software that you can use to connect to a network or computer via modem. I tell you about Apple Remote Access in **Chapter 9**.

✔ Tip

- The Mac OS 8 installer, which I discuss in **Chapter 1**, enables you to install any combination of these components.

SETTING UP MAC OS 8

About Setting Up Mac OS 8

Before you can use Mac OS 8, you must install it on your computer and configure it to work the way you need it to. This is a three-step process:

1. Use the Mac OS 8 installer to install the components you want.

2. Restart your computer to load the Mac OS 8 software into RAM.

3. Use the Mac OS Setup Assistant, as well as other assistants, to configure the Mac OS 8 components you installed.

This chapter explains how to complete all three of these steps, so you can properly install and configure Mac OS 8 on your computer.

✔ Tips

■ Mac OS 8 offers many installation and configuration options—far too many to discuss in detail in this book. Although the figures and instructions in this chapter cover only the most common options, I think you'll find enough general information to help you complete virtually any combination of installation and configuration options.

■ I tell you how to use the Internet Setup Assistant, the ISP Registration Assistant, and the Internet Editor Assistant in **Chapter 10**.

About Setting Up Mac OS 8

About the Installer

Mac OS 8 comes with an installer application that makes software installation easy. Simply launch the installer and follow the instructions that appear on screen to select a destination disk, learn more about the software, agree to a license agreement, and select the Mac OS 8 components you want installed. The installer builds the System and Finder files for your computer and copies the software you specified to your hard disk.

The Mac OS 8 installer can perform two types of installations:

- **Standard Installation** - this lets you select the Mac OS 8 components you want installed. The installer copies all standard parts of each selected component to your hard disk.

- **Customized Installation** - this lets you select the Mac OS 8 components you want installed and then lets you select the individual parts of each component to be installed.

The first half of this chapter explains how to use the Mac OS 8 installer to perform both a standard and a customized installation.

✔ Tips

- The installation instructions in this chapter assume you know basic Mac OS techniques, such as pointing, clicking, double-clicking, dragging, and selecting items from a menu. If you're brand new to the Mac and don't know any of these techniques, skip ahead to **Chapter 2**, which discusses Mac OS basics.

- You can click the Go Back button at any time during installation to change options in a previous window.

- You can press Return or Enter to "click" a default button—a button with a dark border around it—such as the Continue button in **Figure 2**.

Mac OS Install

Figure 1.
To launch the Mac OS 8 installer, double-click its icon.

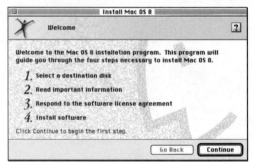

Figure 2. *The Mac OS 8 installer's Welcome window appears when you launch it.*

Figure 3. *Use the Select Destination window to select the disk on which to install Mac OS 8.*

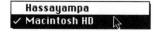

Figure 4. *Choose a disk from the Destination Disk pop-up menu.*

Figure 5. *The Select Destination window displays the currently installed Mac OS version, as well as disk space statistics.*

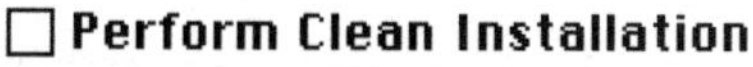

☐ **Perform Clean Installation**

Figure 6. *Turn on the Perform Clean Installation check box to create a brand new System folder for Mac OS 8.*

To launch the installer

1. Insert the Mac OS 8 CD-ROM disc or the Install Me First disk of the Mac OS 8 installation disk set.

2. Locate and double-click the Mac OS Install icon (see **Figure 1**).

3. After a moment, the installer's Welcome window appears (see **Figure 2**). Click Continue.

To select a destination disk

1. In the installer's Select Destination window (see **Figure 3**), use the Destination Disk pop-up menu (see **Figure 4**) to select the disk on which you want to install Mac OS 8.

2. Click Select.

✔ Tips

■ The destination disk is normally your internal hard disk, but can be any disk that is turned on at startup.

■ Only those hard disks and removable high-capacity media (such as Zip, Jaz, and SyQuest disks) that appear on your desktop are listed in the Destination Disk pop-up menu.

■ A status area beneath the Destination Disk pop-up menu indicates the version of Mac OS that is already installed on the disk, as well as the available disk space and the amount of disk space required for a basic installation (see **Figures 3** and **5**).

■ If you turn on the Perform Clean Installation check box (see **Figure 6**), the installer automatically creates a new System Folder for Mac OS 8 files. The old System folder is renamed "Previous System Folder" and should be deleted after non-Apple control panels, extensions, and preferences files have been moved to their proper locations in the new System Folder.

To read important information about Mac OS 8

1. Read the contents of the installer's Important Information window (see **Figure 7**). Click the down arrow on the vertical scroll bar to scroll through the entire document.

2. When you have finished reading the information, click Continue.

✔ Tips

■ Read the information in this window carefully! It provides important, late-breaking news about Mac OS and its installation, including compatibility information and special installation instructions not included in this book.

■ To save a copy of the information for future reference, click the Save button. Then use the Save As dialog box that appears to select a disk location and enter a name for the file. Click Save to complete the save. I tell you more about the Save As dialog box in **Chapter 5**.

■ To print a copy of the information for reference, click the Print button. Then click Print in the Print dialog box that appears to send the document to your printer. I tell you about printing and using the Print dialog box in **Chapter 8**.

Figure 7. *The Important Information window contains late-breaking news about Mac OS 8 and its installation.*

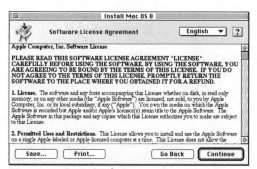

Figure 8. *The Software License Agreement tells you exactly what you're allowed to do with Mac OS 8 software.*

Figure 9. *To complete the installation of Mac OS 8, you must click Agree in this dialog box.*

To read and agree to the Software License Agreement

1. If desired, choose a language from the pop-up menu at the top-right of the Software License Agreement window (see **Figure 8**).

2. Read the contents of the window. Click the down arrow on the vertical scroll bar to scroll through the entire document.

3. When you have finished reading the agreement, click Continue.

4. A dialog box appears, informing you that you must agree to the terms of the agreement you just read in order to continue (see **Figure 9**). Click Agree.

✔ Tips

■ To save a copy of the license agreement for future reference, click the Save button. Then use the Save As dialog box that appears to select a disk location and enter a name for the file. Click Save to complete the save. (I tell you more about the Save As dialog box in **Chapter 5**.)

■ To print a copy of the license agreement for reference, click the Print button. Then click Print in the Print dialog box that appears to send the document to your printer. (I tell you about printing and using the Print dialog box in **Chapter 8**.)

■ If you click Disagree in step 4, the installer returns you to its Welcome window (see **Figure 2**).

Reading the License Agreement

About Standard Installations

The quickest and easiest way to install Mac OS 8 on your computer is with a standard installation. You simply select the components you want installed, click the Start button, and let the Mac OS 8 installer do the rest. A dialog box requiring your attention won't appear until the installation is done.

To select Mac OS components for installation

1. Follow the steps on previous pages to select a destination disk, read important information about Mac OS 8, and read and agree to the Software License Agreement.

2. In the Install Software window (see **Figure 10**), click the check boxes so only those for the components you want to install are turned on. Be sure to click the down arrow at the bottom of the vertical scroll bar to view all the options.

✔ Tips

■ The Mac OS basic system, which is automatically installed, includes Mac OS, Mac OS Info Center, Internet Access, and Open Transport PPP.

■ I tell you about the individual components of Mac OS 8 in the **Introduction** of this book.

■ If desired, you can customize the installation. I tell you how later in this chapter.

Figure 10. *Use the Install Software window to select the Mac OS components you want to install.*

Figure 11. *To prevent the installer from automatically updating the disk driver on a non-Apple hard disk, turn off this check box.*

■ By default, the installer automatically attempts to update the hard disk driver of the destination disk. Although it can only update the driver for Apple-branded disks, it will not harm a disk from another manufacturer. To disable this feature, click the Options button in the Install Software window (see **Figure 10**) to display a dialog box like the one in **Figure 11**. Turn off the Update Apple Hard Disk Drivers check box and click OK.

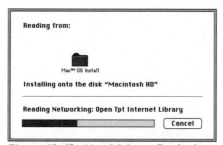

Figure 12. *The Mac OS 8 installer displays a progress window as it works. If you're installing from disks, disk icons appear in this window.*

Figure 13. *A dialog box like this appears when the installation is complete.*

To complete the installation

1. In the Install Software window (see **Figure 10**), click the Start button.

2. The installer performs some maintenance tasks, then begins installing the software you selected. A progress window like the one in **Figure 12** appears to show you how it's doing. If you're installing Mac OS 8 from disks, follow the instructions that appear on screen to insert each disk as it is needed.

3. When the installation is complete, a dialog box like the one in **Figure 13** appears. Click Quit.

✔ Tips

■ The amount of time it takes to install Mac OS 8 depends on the number of components you selected, the speed of your computer's CPU, and the speed of your CD-ROM drive (if applicable). A basic installation of the default options can easily take 20 minutes or more.

■ To perform additional Mac OS 8 installations, click the Continue button in the dialog box that appears when installation is complete (see **Figure 13**). This returns you to the Install Software window (see **Figure 10**).

Completing a Standard Installation

About Customized Installations

A customized installation lets you specify which parts of each Mac OS 8 component you want installed. Rather than install all the software at once, it launches an installer for each component of Mac OS 8 that you want to install. You can then do an easy installation of the component or specify exactly which parts should be installed. This feature, which gives you greater control over installation options, is designed primarily for expert users.

✔ Tips

- To successfully use the Customize option, you must be familiar with all components you want installed.

- Performing a custom installation is generally more time consuming than performing a standard installation because you must select options that appear in dialog boxes thoughout the installation process.

To customize an installation

1. Follow the steps earlier in this chapter to select a destination disk, read important information about Mac OS 8, and read and agree to the Software License Agreement.

2. In the Install Software window (see **Figure 10**), click the Customize button. The window changes to the Custom Installation and Removal window (see **Figure 14**), which displays additional installation options.

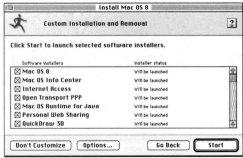

Figure 14. *Use the Custom Installation and Removal window to select Mac OS 8 components for a custom installation.*

To select Mac OS components for a custom installation

In the Custom Installation and Removal window (see **Figure 14**), click the check boxes so only those for the components you want to install are turned on. Be sure to click the down arrow at the bottom of the vertical scroll bar to view all the options.

✔ Tips

■ I tell you about the individual components of Mac OS 8 in the **Introduction** of this book.

■ By default, the installer automatically attempts to update the hard disk driver of the destination disk. Although it can only update the driver for Apple-branded disks, it will not harm a disk from another manufacturer. To disable this feature, click the Options button in the Install Software window (see **Figure 10**) to display a dialog box like the one in **Figure 11**. Turn off the Update Apple Hard Disk Drivers check box and click OK.

■ If you change your mind about making a custom installation, click the Don't Customize button (see **Figure 14**) to go back to the Install Software window (see **Figure 10**).

Selecting Custom Install Components

To complete the custom installation

1. In the Custom Installation and Removal window (see **Figure 14**), click the Start button.

2. The installer performs some maintenance tasks, then launches the first installer. (**Figure 15** shows the splash screen for the Mac OS 8.0 installer.) Click Continue.

3. An installer window appears next (see **Figure 16**). Chose an installation option from the pop-up menu at the top-left of the window (see **Figure 17**):

   ▲ Easy Install (see **Figure 16**) installs the basic parts of the component you are installing.

   ▲ Custom Install (see **Figure 18**) lets you select the parts of the component you are installing. To use this option, turn on the check boxes to the left of each item you want. Click the triangle to the left of a check box to display individual items within a part (see **Figure 19**).

   ▲ Custom Remove lets you select previously installed parts of a component to remove. It works just like the Custom Install option, but removes (rather than installs) software. You can only use this option if part of the component has already been installed.

4. Click the Install button.

5. The active installer begins installing the software you selected. A progress window like the one in **Figure 12** appears to show you how it's doing. If you're installing Mac OS 8 from disks, follow the instructions that appear on screen to insert each disk as it is needed.

(continued on next page)

Figure 15. *The Mac OS 8 installer's splash screen appears when it is launched.*

Figure 16. *The Easy Install window installs the basic parts of the component you are installing.*

Figure 17. *Choose an installation type from this pop-up menu.*

Figure 18. *The Custom Install window lets you select the parts of the component you are installing.*

Completing a Custom Installation

Figure 19. *Clicking a triangle to the left of an item displays individual items within it.*

Figure 20. *When you click an item's "i" button, a window full of information about the item appears.*

Figure 21. *To restart your computer, choose Restart from the Special menu.*

(continued from previous page)

6. When the installation of the active installer's component is complete, the next installer launches. Follow steps 3 through 5 to select options and complete the installation process for each subsequent installer that appears.

7. When the last installation is complete, a dialog box like the one in **Figure 13** appears. Click Quit.

✔ Tip

■ When performing a custom install of a Mac OS component, you can click the info icon (or "i" button) to the right of an item to learn more about it (see **Figure 20**). Click OK to dismiss the information dialog box.

About Restarting Your Computer

To configure and use your newly installed Mac OS 8 software, you must restart your Macintosh. This loads the new software into the computer's RAM and, if necessary, launches the Mac OS Setup Assistant.

To restart your computer

Choose Restart from the Special menu (see **Figure 21**).

✔ Tips

■ Do not restart your computer by turning off power and then turning it back on! This can cause file corruption. I tell you other ways to restart your computer in **Chapter 2**.

■ If you have more than one disk with Mac OS software installed on it, you may have to use the Startup Disk control panel to specify which disk's operating system should be loaded at startup. I tell you about the Startup Disk control panel in **Chapter 12**.

About the Mac OS Setup Assistant

When you restart your computer after installing Mac OS 8, the Mac OS Setup Assistant automatically appears (see **Figure 22**). This program uses a simple question and answer process to get information about you and the way you use your computer. The information you provide is automatically entered into the appropriate control panels to configure Mac OS 8.

✔ Tips

- ■ Your computer may automatically rebuild the Desktop file for attached disks when you restart after installing Mac OS 8. If so, a dialog box like the one in **Figure 23** appears. Do not stop this process. When it is finished, the dialog box will automatically disappear.

- ■ Depending on your computer model, other items may launch before the Mac OS Setup Assistant. For example, on my Power Macintosh 8500/180, an Energy Saver window appears first (see **Figure 24**). If a message like this appears, simply close it to continue.

- ■ If the Mac OS Setup Assistant does not automatically appear at startup, you can launch it by opening the Mac OS Setup Assistant icon in the Assistants folder on your hard disk. I tell you how to work with files and folders in **Chapter 3**.

- ■ I tell you about control panels and how you can use them to customize Mac OS in **Chapter 12**.

Figure 22. *The Mac OS Setup Assistant offers an easy way to configure Mac OS 8.*

Figure 23. *When you first start your computer after installing Mac OS 8, it may automatically rebuild the invisible desktop files on attached disks.*

Figure 24. *On some computer models, a message like this one may appear before the Mac OS Setup Assistant launches.*

To use the Mac OS Setup Assistant

1. Read the information in each Mac OS Setup Assistant window (see **Figure 22**). Enter information or make selections when prompted.

2. Click the right arrow button or press Page Down to continue.

   or

   Click the left arrow button or press Page Up to go back and make changes in previous windows.

✔ Tip

■ The next few pages explain exactly how to enter information in each window that appears.

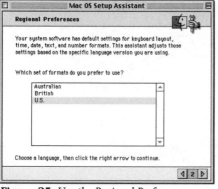

Figure 25. *Use the Regional Preferences window to select your language version.*

To select regional preferences

1. If you haven't already done so, click the right arrow button in the Introduction window of the Mac OS Setup Assistant (see **Figure 22**).

2. Read the information in the Regional Preferences window (see **Figure 25**) to learn how Mac OS 8 uses your language version.

3. Click the language you prefer once to select it.

4. Click the right arrow button.

✔ Tips

■ The languages that appear in this dialog box will vary depending on the language supported by your copy of Mac OS 8.

■ You can set the keyboard layout for a language in the Keyboard control panel, which I discuss in **Chapter 12**.

Selecting Regional Preferences

To enter your name & organization

1. Read the information in the Name and Organization window (see **Figure 26**) to learn how Mac OS 8 uses your name and company.

2. Enter your name in the What is your name? edit box.

3. Press ⎣Tab⎦ or click in the What is your company or organization? edit box to position the blinking insertion point.

4. Enter the name of your company or organization.

5. Click the right arrow button.

✔ Tips

■ You must enter a name in the What is your name? box. You may, however, leave the What is your company or organization? box empty if desired.

■ You can also enter your name in the File Sharing control panel, which I tell you about in **Chapter 9**.

Figure 26. *Enter your name and organization in these edit boxes.*

Figure 27. *Use the Time and Date window to check and, if necessary, change the time or date.*

Figure 28. *To change the time (or date), click an incorrect number in* *the sequence to select it and then click the up or down arrow until the right number appears.*

To set the time & date

1. Read the information in the Time & Date window of the Mac OS Setup Assistant (see **Figure 27**) to learn how Mac OS 8 uses the time and date.

2. If daylight savings time is currently in effect, select the Yes radio button by clicking it.

3. If the time in the What time is it? box is not correct, change it. To do this, click an incorrect number in the time sequence to select it (see **Figure 28**) and either type in the correct number or click the up or down arrow button buside the time until the correct number appears.

4. If the date in the What is today's date? box is not correct, change it. To do this, click an incorrect number in the date sequence to select it and either type in the correct number or click the up or down arrow button buside the date until the correct number appears.

5. Click the right arrow button.

✔ Tips

■ The time and date, which are tracked by your computer's internal clock, may already be correct. If so, no changes will be necessary.

■ You can also set the time and date in the Date and Time control panel, which I tell you about in **Chapter 12**.

To select your geographic location

1. Read the information in the Geographic Location window of the Mac OS Setup Assistant (see **Figure 29**) to learn how Mac OS 8 uses your location.

2. Click the up or down arrow on the scroll bar until the name of a city in your time zone (preferably near you) appears. Click it once to select it.

3. Click the right arrow button.

✔ Tip

■ You can also set your geographic location or time zone in the Date and Time control panel and the Map control panel, which I tell you about in **Chapter 12**.

To set Finder preferences

1. Read the information in the Finder Preferences window of the Mac OS Setup Assistant (see **Figure 30**) to learn about the difference between the standard Finder and Simple Finder.

2. If you want fewer menu commands in the Finder, click the Yes radio button to select it.

3. Click the right arrow button.

✔ Tips

■ The standard Finder—*not* Simple Finder—is used throughout this book.

■ I illustrate both standard Finder and Simple Finder menus in **Appendix A**.

■ You can also set Finder preferences in the Preferences dialog box, which I tell you about in **Chapter 4**.

Figure 29. *The Geographic Location window lists cities all over the world—including one near you.*

Figure 30. *Use the Finder Preferences window to turn Simple Finder on or off.*

Figure 31. *The Local Network Introduction window tells you a little about networks.*

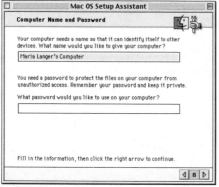

Figure 32. *Use this window to enter a name for your computer and a password to protect your files from unauthorized network users.*

Figure 33. *Use this window to set up a shared folder—if you want one.*

To set network options

1. Read the information in the Local Network Introduction window of the Mac OS Setup Assistant (see **Figure 31**) to learn more about networks.

2. Click the right arrow button.

3. Read the information in the Computer Name and Password window (see **Figure 32**) to learn how Mac OS uses your computer's name and password.

4. To change the default name that the Mac OS Setup Assistant has assigned to your computer, type it in the top edit box. (The name should be selected as shown in **Figure 32** so it is not necessary to click in the box first; simply type to overwrite the contents of the edit box.) Then press [Tab] or click in the bottom edit box to position the insertion point there.

   or

   To accept the default name that the Mac OS Setup Assistant has assigned to your computer, just press [Tab] or click in the bottom edit box to position the insertion point there.

5. In the bottom edit box, enter a password you want to use to protect your computer from unauthorized access by other network users.

6. Click the right arrow button.

7. Wait while the Mac OS Setup Assistant validates the computer name and password.

8. Read the information in the Shared Folder window (see **Figure 33**) to learn what a shared folder is and how it is used.

(continued on next page)

Setting Network Options

(continued from previous page)

9. If you do not want a shared folder on the network, select the No radio button by clicking it. Then skip to step 11.

10. To change the default name that the Mac OS Setup Assistant has assigned to your shared folder, type it in the edit box. (The name should be selected as shown in **Figure 33** so it is not necessary to click in the box first; simpy type to overwrite the contents of the box.)

11. Click the right arrow button.

✔ Tips

■ You must go through these steps even if your computer is not connected to a network.

■ You must provide both a name and password for your computer.

■ You can also set network settings in the File Sharing control panel, which I tell you about in **Chapter 9**.

Setting Network Options

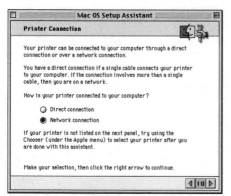

Figure 34. *Use the Printer Connection window to tell the Mac OS Setup Assistant how your printer is connected.*

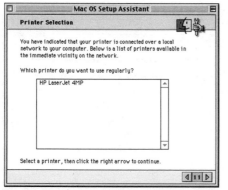

Figure 35. *If your printer is connected to your computer through a network connection, select it from this window.*

Figure 36. *If your printer is directly connected to your computer, select the type of printer you have from this window.*

To set printer options

1. Turn on your printer and, if necessary, let it warm up.

2. Read the information in the Printer Connection window of the Mac OS Setup Assistant (see **Figure 34**) to learn the difference between a direct connection and a network connection.

3. Select the appropriate connection type by clicking its radio button.

4. Click the right arrow button.

5. If you selected Network Connection in step 2, wait while the Mac OS Setup Assistant searches the network for connected printers. Then, in the Printer Selection window that appears (see **Figure 35**), select the printer you use most often by clicking its name.

   or

   If you selected Direct Connection in step 2, the Printer Type window appears (see **Figure 36**). Select the type of printer connected to your computer by clicking its name in the list. Then select the port to which the printer is connected by clicking the Printer Port of Modem Port radio button.

6. Click the right arrow button.

✔ Tips

- You can also select a printer in the Chooser, which I tell you about in **Chapter 8**.

- If the type of printer you use does not appear in the Printer Type window (see **Figure 36**), you may have to install a printer driver for it. I tell you about that in **Chapter 8**, too.

Setting Printer Options

To complete the setup process

1. Click the Go Ahead button in the Conclusion window of the Mac OS Setup Assistant (see **Figure 37**).

2. Wait while the Mac OS Setup Assistant configures your system. The Conclusion window changes to indicate the configuration progress (see **Figure 38**). When the configuration is complete, the Conclusion window tells you that the Mac OS Setup Assistant is done (see **Figure 39**).

3. To stop configuring your computer, click the Quit button.

    or

    To go on to the Internet Setup Assistant, click the Continue button.

✔ Tips

■ To check your settings one last time before they're written to your computer's configuration files, click the Show Details button (see **Figure 37**). The Conclusion window changes to list all configuration options you entered or selected.

■ If you have not installed the Internet Connection component of Mac OS 8, the Continue button in the Conclusion window (see **Figure 39**) will not appear.

■ I tell you how to use the Internet Setup Assistant in **Chapter 10**.

Figure 37. *When the Mac OS Setup Assistant is finished asking for information, it displays this window.*

Figure 38. *The Conclusion window also indicates the configuration progress.*

Figure 39. *Finally, the Conclusion window tells you when the configuration is done.*

Figure 1. The Finder is the program that provides a graphic user interface for working with files.

Finder

About the Finder & Desktop

The *Finder* (see **Figure 1**) is a program that is part of Mac OS. It launches automatically when you start your computer.

The Finder provides a graphic user interface called the *Desktop* (see **Figure 2**) that you can use to open, copy, delete, list, organize, and perform other operations on computer files.

This chapter provides important instructions for using the Finder and items that appear on the Mac OS Desktop. It's important that you understand how to use these basic Finder techniques, since you'll use them again and again every time you work with your computer.

Menu bar   Window   Desktop   Icons

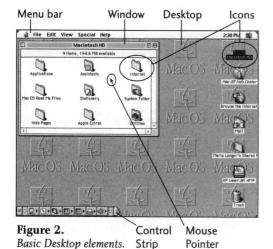

Figure 2.   Control   Mouse
Basic Desktop elements.   Strip   Pointer

✔ Tips

- Do *not* delete the Finder! Doing so will prevent your computer from operating properly.

- You never have to manually launch the Finder; it always starts automatically.

- Under normal circumstances, you cannot Quit the Finder.

- If you're new to Mac OS, don't skip this chapter. It provides the basic information you'll need to use your computer successfully.

About the Finder & Desktop

About the Mouse

Mac OS, like most graphic user interface systems, uses the mouse as an input device. There are several basic mouse techniques you must know to use your computer:

- **Point** to a specific item on screen.
- **Click** an item to select it.
- **Double-click** an item to open it.
- **Drag** to move an item or select multiple items.

✔ Tips

- Some computers use either a trackball or a trackpad instead of a mouse.
- You can customize the way the mouse works with the Mouse control panel, which I tell you about in **Chapter 12**.

To point

1. Move the mouse on the work surface or mouse pad.

   or

   Use your fingertips to move the ball of the trackball.

   or

   Move the tip of one finger (usually your forefinger) on the surface of the trackpad.

   The mouse pointer, which usually looks like an arrow (see **Figure 3**), moves on your computer screen.

2. When the tip of the mouse pointer's arrow is on the item to which you want to point (see **Figure 4**), stop moving it.

✔ Tips

- The tip of the mouse pointer is its "business end."
- When using a trackpad, use only one finger to manipulate the mouse pointer.

Figure 3. *The mouse pointer usually looks like an arrow pointer when you are working in the Finder.*

System Folder

Figure 4. *Move the mouse pointer so the arrow's tip is on the item to which you want to point.*

Figure 5.
*Click to select
an icon...*

Figure 6. *...or an item in a list.*

Figure 7.
*Drag to move
items like
folders.*

To click

1. Point to the item on which you want to click.

2. Press (and release) the mouse button once. The item on which you clicked becomes selected (see **Figures 5** and **6**).

To double-click

1. Point to the item on which you want to double-click.

2. Press (and release) the mouse button twice quickly. The item on which you double-clicked opens.

✔ Tip

■ It is vital that you keep the mouse pointer still while double-clicking. If you move the mouse pointer during the double-click process, you may move the item instead of double-clicking it.

To drag

1. Point to the item you want to drag.

2. Press the mouse button down.

3. While holding the mouse button down, move the mouse pointer. The item you are dragging moves (see **Figure 7**).

Using the Mouse

About Menus

The Finder—and just about every other Mac OS-compatible program—offers menus full of options. There are four types of menus in Mac OS 8:

- A **pull-down menu** appears on the menu bar at the top of the screen (see **Figure 8**).

- A **submenu** appears when a menu option with a right-pointing triangle is selected (see **Figure 9**).

- A **pop-up menu**, which displays a double-pointed triangle, appears within a window (see **Figures 10** and **11**).

- A **contextual menu** appears when you hold down Control while clicking on an item (see **Figure 12**).

✔ Tips

- A menu option followed by an ellipse (…) (see **Figure 8**) will display a dialog box when chosen. I tell you about dialog boxes in this **Chapter 5**.

- A menu option that is dimmed or gray (see **Figure 8**) cannot be chosen.

- A menu option preceded by a check mark (see **Figure 9**) is selected or "turned on."

- A menu option followed by a series of keyboard characters (see **Figure 8**) has a keyboard command. I tell you about keyboard commands later in this chapter.

- Contextual menus only display options that apply to the item to which you are pointing.

- Depending on how menu preferences are set, a menu option should blink when chosen. You can set menu blinking preferences in the General Controls control panel, which I discuss in **Chapter 12**.

Figure 8.
The menu bar offers pull-down menus.

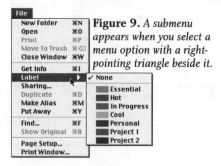

Figure 9. *A submenu appears when you select a menu option with a right-pointing triangle beside it.*

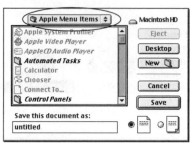

Figure 10. *Pop-up menus can appear within dialog boxes.*

Figure 11.
To display a pop-up menu, click it.

Figure 12.
A contextual menu appears when you hold down Control *while clicking.*

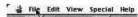

Figure 13. *Point to the menu name.*

Figure 14. *Hold down the mouse button or just click to display the menu.*

Figure 15. *Drag to or just click the menu option you want.*

To use a menu

1. Point to the name of the menu (see **Figure 13**).
2. Press and hold down the mouse button. The menu opens, displaying its options (see **Figure 14**).
3. Drag to select the menu option you want (see **Figure 15**).
4. Release the mouse button to choose the selected option. The menu disappears.

✔ Tip

■ This is the standard way to choose an option from a menu. This method works in all versions of Mac OS.

To use a sticky menu

1. Point to the name of the menu (see **Figure 13**).
2. Click. The menu opens, displaying its options (see **Figure 14**).
3. Point to the menu option you want (see **Figure 15**).
4. Click to choose the selected option. The menu disappears.

✔ Tips

■ This method of choosing a menu option works in Mac OS version 8 and later only.

■ To close a sticky menu without choosing an option, click outside the menu.

■ A sticky menu will close automatically by itself if no option is chosen after a few seconds.

Using Menus

To use a contextual menu

1. Point to the item on which you want to act (see **Figure 16**).

2. Press and hold down (Control).

3. Press and hold down the mouse button.

   or

   Click.

   A contextual menu appears at the item (see **Figure 17**).

4. Drag to select the menu option you want (see **Figure 18**). Then release the mouse button to choose the option.

   or

   Click the menu option you want (see **Figure 18**).

To use a keyboard command

1. Hold down the modifier key(s) in the sequence. This is usually (⌘), but can be (Option), (Control), or (Shift).

2. Press the letter, number, or symbol key in the sequence.

For example, to choose the Open command, which can be found under the File menu (see **Figure 15**), hold down (⌘) and press (O).

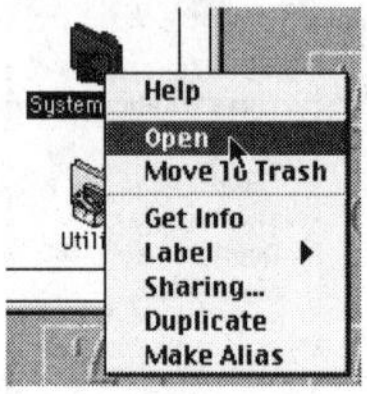

✔ Tips

■ You can learn keyboard commands by observing the key sequences that appear to the right of some menu commands (see **Figure 8**).

■ Some commands include more than one modifier key. You must hold all modifier keys down while pressing the letter, number, or symbol key for the keyboard command.

■ I provide a list of all Finder keyboard commands in **Appendix A**.

Figure 16.
Point to the item on which you want to act.

Figure 17.
A contextual menu appears where you click.

Figure 18.
Drag or click to select the option you want.

SimpleText   PageMaker® 6.5   MoviePlayer

Figure 19. *Application icons.*

Read Me   About Mac OS 8   Introduction

Figure 20. *Document icons, including two different SimpleText documents and a PageMaker document.*

Internet   Utilities   System Folder

Figure 21. *Folder icons.*

Apple CD-ROM   Appearance   LaserWriter 8

Figure 22. *Icons for System files including an extension, a control panel, and a printer driver (or Chooser extension).*

Macintosh HD   nstaller Disk   untitled   Mac OS 8

Figure 23. *Four different disk icons: hard disk, Mac OS diskette, PC diskette, and CD-ROM disc.*

HP LaserJet 4MP   Trash   Trash

Figure 24. *A desktop printer icon and the Trash icon when the Trash is empty and full.*

About Icons

Mac OS uses icons to graphically represent files and other items on the Desktop or within Finder windows:

■ **Applications** (see **Figure 19**) are programs you use to get work done. I tell you more about working with applications in **Chapters 5** and **6**.

■ **Documents** (see **Figure 20**) are the files created by applications. I tell you more about working with documents in **Chapter 5**.

■ **Folders** (see **Figure 21**) are used to organize files. I tell you more about using folders in **Chapters 3** and **4**.

■ **System files** (see **Figure 22**), such as control panels, extensions, and drivers, are used by Mac OS to add capabilities to your computer and operate peripherals. I tell you about various System files in **Chapter 12** and elsewhere throughout this book.

■ **Disks** (see **Figure 23**) are used to store files. I tell you about working with disks in **Chapter 3**.

■ **Desktop printers** (see **Figure 24**) let you print documents from the Finder and check the status of documents scheduled to be printed. I tell you about printing in **Chapter 8**.

■ The **Trash** (see **Figure 24**) is for discarding items you no longer want.

✔ Tip

■ Icons can appear in two different sizes, as smaller icons in lists, or as various sized buttons, depending on the view chosen for a window. I tell you about windows later in this chapter and about views in **Chapter 3**.

To select an icon

Click the icon that you want to select. The icon darkens and its name becomes highlighted (see **Figure 25**).

To deselect an icon

Click anywhere in the window or on the Desktop other than on the selected icon.

✔ Tips

■ If you deselect an icon by clicking another icon, the originally selected icon is deselected and the icon you clicked becomes selected instead.

■ I tell you more about windows later in this chapter.

To select multiple icons by clicking

1. Click the first icon that you want to select.

2. Hold down [Shift] and click on another icon that you want to select (see **Figure 26**).

3. Repeat step 2 until all icons that you want to select have been selected.

✔ Tip

■ Icons that are part of a multiple selection must be in the same window. I tell you about windows later in this chapter.

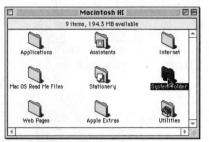

Figure 25. *To select an icon, click it.*

Figure 26. *Hold down* [Shift] *while clicking other icons to add them to a multiple selection.*

Figure 27. *Position the mouse pointer above and to the left of the first icon that you want to select.*

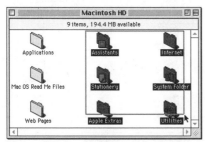

Figure 28. *Drag to draw a selection box around the icons that you want to select.*

Figure 29. *Release the mouse button to complete the selection.*

Figure 30. *Choose Select All from the Edit menu.*

To select multiple icons by dragging

1. Position the mouse pointer slightly above and to the left of the first icon in the group that you want to select (see **Figure 27**).

2. Press the mouse button down and drag diagonally across the icons you want to select. A gray border appears to indicate the selection area and the items within it become selected (see **Figure 28**).

3. When all the icons that you want to select are included in the selection area, release the mouse button (see **Figure 29**).

✔ Tip

■ To select multiple icons by dragging, the icons must be adjacent.

To select all icons in a window

Choose Select All from the File menu (see **Figure 30**).

or

Press ⌘Ⓐ.

All icons in the active window are selected.

✔ Tip

■ I tell you more about windows, including how to activate them, later in this chapter.

To deselect one icon in a multiple selection

Hold down Shift while clicking the icon that you want to deselect. That icon is deselected while the others remain selected.

Selecting & Deselecting Icons

To move an icon

1. Position the mouse pointer on the icon that you want to move (see **Figure 31**).

2. Press the mouse button down and drag the icon to the new location. As you drag, a shadowy image of the icon moves with the mouse pointer (see **Figure 32**).

3. Release the mouse button when the icon is in the desired position. The icon moves (see **Figure 33**).

✔ Tips

■ You can only move icons in windows set to icon view. I tell you about views in **Chapter 3**.

■ You move icons to rearrange them in a window or on the Desktop or to copy or move the items they represent to another folder or disk. I discuss copying and moving items in **Chapter 3**.

■ You can also move multiple icons at once. Simply select the icons first, then position the mouse pointer on one of the selected icons and follow steps 2 and 3 above. All selected icons move together.

Figure 31. *Point to the icon that you want to move.*

Figure 32. *Drag the icon to the new location.*

Figure 33. *When you release the mouse button, the icon moves.*

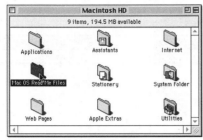

Figure 34. *Select the icon.*

Figure 35.
*Choose Open
from the File
menu.*

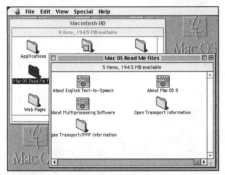

Figure 36. *Opening a folder icon opens a window that displays the contents of the folder.*

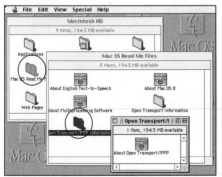

Figure 37. *Open folder icons appear shaded.*

To open an icon

1. Click the icon once to select it (see **Figure 34**.

2. Choose Open from the File menu (see **Figure 35**) or press ⌃⌘O.

or

Double-click the icon that you want to open.

✔ Tips

■ What happens when you open an icon depends on the type of icon you open. For example:

▲ Opening a folder icon opens a new Finder window that displays the contents of that folder (see **Figure 36**). I tell you about windows later in this chapter.

▲ Opening an application icon launches the application so that you can work with it. I tell you about working with applications in **Chapters 5** and **6**.

▲ Opening a document icon launches the application that created that document and displays the document so you can view or edit it. I tell you about working with documents in **Chapter 5**.

▲ Opening a desktop printer icon displays a list of files waiting to be printed so you can reschedule them or remove them from the print queue. I tell you about printing in **Chapter 8**.

▲ Opening the Trash displays items that will be deleted when you empty the Trash. I tell you about emptying the Trash later in this chapter.

■ You can identify an open disk, folder, or application icon by its shaded appearance in a Finder window (see **Figure 37**).

Opening Icons

About Windows

Mac OS makes extensive use of windows for displaying icons and other information in the Finder and documents in other applications. **Figures 38** and **39** show examples of Finder windows.

Each window includes a variety of controls you can use to manipulate it:

- The **title bar** displays the name of the window and can be used to move the window.

- The **close box** lets you close the window.

- The **zoom box** lets you toggle the window between full size and a custom size.

- The **collapse box** lets you toggle the window between collapsed and expanded views.

- The **size box** lets you resize the window by dragging.

- **Scroll bars** let you scroll the contents of the window into view.

- The **header** indicates the number of items in the window and the amount of space available on the disk.

- **Column headings** (in list view only) display the names of the columns and let you quickly sort by a column.

✔ Tip

- I tell you about views in **Chapter 3**.

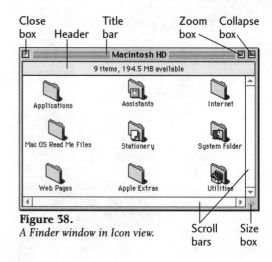

Close box   Header   Title bar   Zoom box   Collapse box

Figure 38.
A Finder window in Icon view.

Scroll bars   Size box

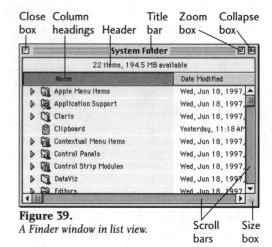

Close box   Column headings   Header   Title bar   Zoom box   Collapse box

Figure 39.
A Finder window in list view.

Scroll bars   Size box

About Windows

Figure 40. *The active window always has horizontal lines on its title bar.*

Figure 41. *Position the mouse pointer on the title bar.*

Figure 42. *As you drag, an outline of the window moves with the mouse pointer.*

Figure 43. *When you release the mouse button, the window moves.*

To activate a window

Click anywhere in or on the window.

✔ Tips

- It's important to make sure that the window with which you want to work is open and active *before* using commands that work on the active window—like Print Window, Select All, and View menu options.

- You can distinguish between the active window and inactive windows by the appearance of their title bars; the active window's title bar always has horizontal lines (see **Figure 40**).

- When two or more windows overlap, the active window will always be on top of the stack (see **Figure 40**).

To move a window

1. Position the mouse pointer on the window's title bar (see **Figure 41**).

   or

   Position the mouse pointer on the border of the window.

2. Press the mouse button down and drag the window to a new location. As you drag, an outline of the window moves along with your mouse pointer (see **Figure 42**).

3. When the outline of the window is in the desired position, release the mouse button. The window moves (see **Figure 43**).

✔ Tip

- If you move a window to the very bottom of the screen, it becomes a pop-up window. I tell you about pop-up windows in **Chapter 4**.

To resize a window

1. Position the mouse pointer on the window's size box (see **Figure 44**).

2. Press the mouse button down and drag. As you drag, dotted lines indicating the right and bottom borders of the window move with the mouse pointer (see **Figure 45**).

3. When the dotted lines indicate the desired borders for the window, release the mouse button. The window resizes (see **Figure 46**).

✔ Tips

■ The larger a window is, the more you can see inside it.

■ By resizing and repositioning windows, you can see inside more than one window at a time. This comes in handy when moving or copying the icons for files and folders from one window to another. I tell you about moving and copying files and folders in **Chapter 3**.

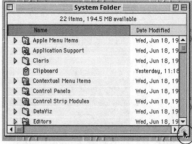

Figure 44. *Position the mouse pointer on the size box.*

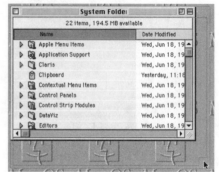

Figure 45. *As you drag, a dotted border moves with the mouse pointer.*

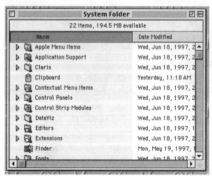

Figure 46. *When you release the mouse button, the window resizes.*

Figure 47. *Click the window's zoom box...*

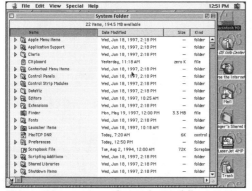

Figure 48. *...to zoom the window to full size.*

Figure 49.
*Click on the
collapse box...*

Figure 50.
*...to collapse
the window so only its title bar shows.*

To zoom a window

Click the window's zoom box (see F**igure 47**).

✔ Tips

- Each time you click the zoom box, the window's size toggles between full size (see **Figure 48**) and the custom size you specified with the size box (see **Figure 47**).

- The actual size of a window zoomed to full size varies based on its content. If a window contains only a few icons, zooming the window to full size will make it only as large as it needs to be to display the items it contains (see **Figure 49**).

To collapse a window

Click the window's collapse box (see **Figure 49**).

or

Double-click the window's title bar.

✔ Tips

- Each time you click the collapse box, the window either collapses to display just its title bar (see **Figure 50**) or expands to display its contents (see **Figure 49**).

- A collapsed window can be moved around the screen like any other window.

To collapse all open windows

Hold down (Option) while clicking the active window's collapse box (see **Figure 49**).

or

Hold down (Option) while double-clicking the active window's title bar.

Zooming & Collapsing Windows

To scroll a window's contents

Click one of the scroll bar arrows (see **Figure 51**) as follows:

- To scroll the window's contents up, click the down arrow on the vertical scroll bar.

- To scroll the window's contents down, click the up arrow on the vertical scroll bar.

- To scroll the window's contents to the left, click the right arrow on the horizontal scroll bar.

- To scroll the window's contents to the right, click the left arrow on the horizontal scroll bar.

✔ Tips

- If you have trouble remembering which scroll arrow to click, think of it this way:

  - ▲ Click down to see down.
  - ▲ Click up to see up.
  - ▲ Click right to see right.
  - ▲ Click left to see left.

- You can also scroll a window's contents by either clicking in the scroll bar between the scroll box and a scroll arrow or by dragging the scroll box to a new position on the scroll bar.

- If all of a window's contents are displayed, you will not be able to scroll the window. A window that cannot be scrolled will have flat or empty looking scroll bars without scroll boxes (see **Figure 49**).

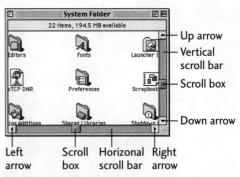

Figure 51. *Scroll bars, scroll bar arrows, and scroll boxes.*

Up arrow
Vertical scroll bar
Scroll box
Down arrow
Left arrow
Scroll box
Horizontal scroll bar
Right arrow

Scrolling a Window's Contents

Figure 52. *Click in the window's close box.*

Figure 53. *Choose Close Window from the File menu.*

To close a window

Click the window's close box (see **Figure 52**).

or

Choose Close Window from the File menu (see **Figure 53**).

or

Press ⌘W.

To close all open windows

Hold down Option while clicking the active window's close box (see **Figure 52**).

or

Hold down Option while choosing Close Window from the File menu (see **Figure 53**).

or

Press ⌘ Option W.

To close the active window automatically when you open an icon within it

1. Select the icon that you want to open.

2. Hold down Option while choosing Open from the File menu (see **Figure 35**).

   or

   Press ⌘ Option O.

or

Hold down Option while double-clicking the icon that you want to open.

About Sleeping, Restarting, & Shutting Down

The Special menu (see **Figure 54**) offers several options that change the work state of your computer:

- **Sleep** puts the computer into a state where it uses very little power. The screen goes blank and the hard disk may stop spinning.

- **Restart** instructs the computer to shut down and immediately start back up.

- **Shut Down** closes all open documents and programs, clears memory, and either cuts power to the computer or tells you that it's safe to turn off the power switch.

✔ Tips

- You can view a dialog box with buttons for Restart, Sleep, and Shut Down commands (see **Figure 55**) by pressing the Power key (the one with the triangle carved into it). This feature, however, does not work with all Mac OS-computer models.

- The Energy Saver control panel, which I tell you about in **Chapter 12**, can automatically put a computer to sleep or shut it down after a specific period of inactivity.

- Do *not* restart or shut down a computer by simply flicking off the power switch. Doing so prevents the computer from properly closing files, thus possibly resulting in file corruption and related problems.

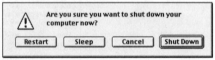

Figure 55. *Pressing the Power key on some Mac OS computers displays a dialog box like this one.*

About Sleep, Restart, & Shut Down

To put your computer to sleep

Choose Sleep from the Special menu (see **Figure 54**).

or

1. Press the Power key.
2. In the dialog box that appears (see **Figure 55**), click Sleep.

✔ Tips

■ Not all computers support sleep mode. If your computer does not support sleep mode, the Sleep command will not appear on the Special menu.

■ When you put your computer to sleep, everything in memory is preserved. When you wake the computer, you can quickly continue working where you left off.

■ Sleep mode is an effective way to conserve the battery life of a PowerBook without turning it off. I tell you more about special PowerBook considerations in **Chapter 11**.

To wake a sleeping computer

Press any keyboard key (except [Caps Lock]). Expect to wait from 10 to 30 seconds for the computer to fully wake.

✔ Tip

■ It's much quicker to wake a sleeping computer than to restart a computer that has been shut down.

Putting the Computer to Sleep

To restart your computer

Choose Restart from the Special menu (see **Figure 54**).

or

1. Press the Power key.
2. In the dialog box that appears (see **Figure 55**), click Restart.

✔ Tips

■ Restarting the computer clears memory and reloads the System, Finder, and all system files.

■ It's a good idea to restart your computer after a program bombs so your computer's memory can start fresh.

To shut down your computer

Choose Shut Down from the Special menu (see **Figure 54**).

or

1. Press the Power key.
2. In the dialog box that appears (see **Figure 55**), click Shut Down.

   or

   Press (Return) or (Enter).

✔ Tip

■ On most computers, the Shut Down command will cut power to the computer as part of the shut down process. If it doesn't, a dialog box will appear on screen, telling you it's safe to turn off your computer. You can then use the power switch to cut power to the computer.

FILE MANAGEMENT

About File Management

In Mac OS, you use the Finder to organize and manage your files.

- View the contents of your disks in windows in a variety of ways.
- Automatically sort items by name, kind, creation date, or other criteria.
- Assign colored labels to items.
- Rename items.
- Create folders to store related items.
- Move items on disk to organize them so they're easy to find and back up.
- Copy items to other disks to back them up or share them with others.
- Delete items you no longer need.
- Mount and eject disks.
- Format and erase floppy disks.

✔ Tip

- If you're brand new to Mac OS, be sure to read the information in Chapter 2 before working with this chapter. That chapter contains information and instructions about techniques that are used throughout this chapter.

About Views

Every Finder window's contents can be viewed a variety of ways:

- As **Icons** displays the window's contents as small or large icons (see **Figure 1**).
- As **Buttons** displays the window's contents as clickable buttons (see **Figure 2**).
- As **List** displays the window's contents as a sorted list (see **Figure 3**).

In addition to setting a specific view for a Finder window, you can use the View Options dialog box (see **Figures 6**, **7**, and **9**) to specify view options that fine tune the view.

✔ Tip

- Button view works a little differently than icon and list views. I tell you about working with button view a little later in this chapter.

To change a window's view

1. Activate the window whose view you want to change.
2. Choose the view option you want from the View menu (see **Figure 4**). The view of the active window changes.

✔ Tips

- Commands on the View menu (see **Figure 4**) work on the active window only.
- A check mark appears to the left of the name of the window's currently selected view on the View menu (see **Figure 4**).
- You can set the view for each window individually.

Figure 1.
You can display a window's contents as icons...

Figure 2.
...clickable buttons...

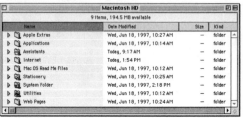

Figure 3. *...or a list.*

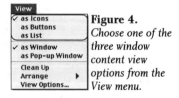

Figure 4.
Choose one of the three window content view options from the View menu.

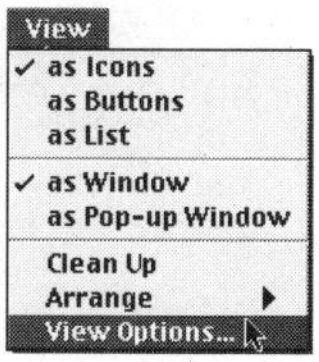

Figure 5.
*Choose View
Options from
the View menu.*

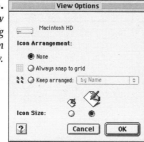

To set View Options for icon or button view

1. Activate a window displayed in icon view (see **Figure 1**) or button view (see **Figure 2**).

2. Choose View Options from the View menu (see **Figure 5**). The View Options dialog box for icon view (see **Figure 6**) or button view (see **Figure 7**) appears.

3. Select an Icon Arrangement or Button Arrangement option:

   ▲ To remove any automatic icon or button arrangement, click the None radio button.

   ▲ To force icons or buttons to snap to an invisible grid within the window, click the Always snap to grid radio button.

   ▲ To automatically keep icons or buttons arranged in a certain order, turn on the Keep arranged radio button. Then choose an option from the pop-up menu beside it (see **Figure 8**).

4. Select an Icon Size or Button Size option by clicking the radio button beneath the size you want.

5. Click OK to accept your changes.

Figure 6.
*The View
Options dialog
box for an icon
view window.*

✔ Tips

■ You can set grid spacing options in the Preferences window, which I tell you about in **Chapter 4**.

■ I provide more details about working with dialog boxes in **Chapter 5**.

Figure 7.
*The View
Options dialog
box for a button
view window.*

Figure 8.
*Use the Keep arranged
pop-up menu to
choose an automatic
arrangement option.*

To set View Options for list view

1. Activate a window displayed in list view (see **Figure 3**).

2. Choose View Options from the View menu (see **Figure 5**). The View Options dialog box for list view appears (see **Figure 9**).

3. To display the date in relative terms (i.e., using the words "today" and "yesterday"), make sure the Use relative date check box is turned on.

4. To display the total disk space occupied by the contents of folders in the list, make sure the Calculate folder sizes check box is turned on.

5. Select the columns you want to appear in list view by turning Show Columns check boxes on or off:

   ▲ **Date Modified** is the date and time an item was last changed.

   ▲ **Date Created** is the date and time an item was first created.

   ▲ **Size** is the amount of disk space the item occupies.

   ▲ **Kind** is the type of item. I tell you about types of icons in **Chapter 2**.

   ▲ **Label** is the label assigned to the item. I tell you about labels later in this chapter.

   ▲ **Comments** is the information you entered in the comments field of the Info window. I tell you about the Info window in **Chapter 4**.

   ▲ **Version** is the item's version number.

6. Select an Icon Size option by clicking the radio button beneath the size that you want.

7. Click OK to accept your changes.

Figure 9.
The View Options dialog box for a list view window.

✔ Tips

■ Turning on the Calculate folder sizes check box in step 4 could slow down the opening of list view windows.

■ I provide more details about working with dialog boxes in **Chapter 5**.

Figure 10.
*Point to the
name of the
button.*

Figure 11.
*When you click,
the button is
selected.*

Figure 12. *Drag a button's name to move it.*

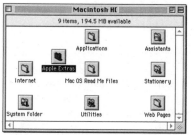

Figure 13. *When you release the mouse button, the button moves to its new position.*

Figure 14.
*Choose Open
from the File
menu.*

About Button View

Designed for novices and to give the Finder a more user-friendly look, button view works a bit differently from icon and list views. Here's a summary of the differences.

To select a button

Click the name of the button (see **Figure 10**). The button becomes selected and an edit box appears around the button name (see **Figure 11**).

To move a button

1. Position the mouse pointer on the button name (see **Figure 10**).

2. Press the mouse button down and drag the button to a new position. As you drag, the shadow of the button moves with the mouse pointer (see **Figure 12**).

3. Release the mouse button to complete the move (see **Figure 13**).

To open a button

Click the button once.

or

1. Select the button that you want to open (see **Figure 11**).

2. Choose Open from the File menu (see **Figure 14**).

   or

   Press ⌘O.

Working with Button View

About Cleaning Up & Arranging Icons & Buttons

Even if you're not a neat freak, you'll like the automatic clean-up and arrangement features that are part of Mac OS 8's Finder.

■ The **Clean Up** command neatly arranges icons or buttons in the window's invisible grid.

■ The **Arrange** options let you specify the order in which icons or buttons should appear in the window.

To clean up a window

1. Activate the window that you want to clean up (see **Figure 15**).

2. Choose Clean Up from the View menu (see **Figure 16**). The icons move into empty slots in the window's invisible grid (see **Figure 17**).

✔ Tips

■ To have an icon you are moving automatically move into an empty grid slot, hold down ⌘ as you drag it. When you release the mouse button, the icon's position adjusts automatically.

■ You can set the grid spacing in the Preferences window, which I tell you about in **Chapter 4**.

To arrange a window's contents

1. Activate the window whose contents you want to arrange (see **Figure 17**).

2. Choose an option from the Arrange submenu under the View menu (see **Figure 18**). The icons are sorted by the option you selected (see **Figure 19**).

✔ Tip

■ You can specify a default arrangement order for the window in the View Options dialog box, which I tell you about earlier in this chapter.

Figure 15. *Start with a messy window like this one…*

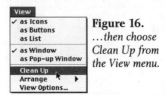

Figure 16. *…then choose Clean Up from the View menu.*

Figure 17. *The window's icons are moved into empty slots of the window's invisible grid.*

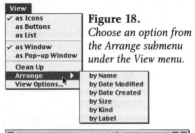

Figure 18. *Choose an option from the Arrange submenu under the View menu.*

Figure 19. *These icons are arranged by name.*

Figure 20. *A window sorted by Name.*

Figure 21. *Point to the heading for the column by which you want to sort.*

Figure 22. *A window sorted by Kind.*

About Sorting List Views

A window in list view can be sorted by any of its columns.

✔ Tip

■ A list view window automatically remains in the order in which it is sorted, even if new items are added to it.

To sort a window's contents

1. Activate the window that you want to sort (see **Figure 20**).

2. Click the column heading for the column by which you want to sort (see **Figure 21**). The list is sorted by that column (see **Figure 22**).

✔ Tips

■ You can always identify the column by which a list is sorted because it's column heading is dark and its column is shaded (see **Figures 20** and **22**).

■ To properly sort folders in a window sorted by size, you should turn on the Calculate folder sizes check box in the View Options dialog box (see **Figure 9**) for that window. Otherwise, a folder has no size and is sorted to the bottom of the list.

Sorting List Views

About Labels

The label feature of Mac OS lets you assign a colored label to each icon. This makes it possible to do two things:

- Visually identify items based on the color assigned.
- Arrange or sort items based on the label assigned.

✔ Tips

- You can use labels to organize icons by project or importance.
- I tell you how to arrange icon and button view windows and how to sort list view windows earlier in this chapter.

To assign a label to an icon

1. Select the icon to which you want to assign a label (see **Figure 23**).
2. Choose the label that you want from the Labels submenu under the File menu (see **Figure 24**).

✔ Tips

- To see the color assigned to the selected icon, deselect the icon (see **Figure 25**).
- As shown in **Figures 23** and **25**, you can assign a color or label to more than one icon at a time.
- You can use the Preferences window to change the labels that are associated with each color in the Labels submenu. I tell you how in **Chapter 4**.

To remove a label from an icon

1. Select the icon from which you want to remove a label.
2. Choose None from the Labels submenu under the File menu (see **Figure 26**).

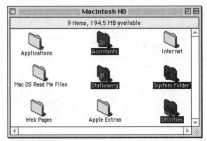

Figure 23. *Select the icon(s) to which you want to apply a color or label.*

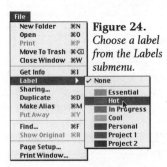

Figure 24. *Choose a label from the Labels submenu.*

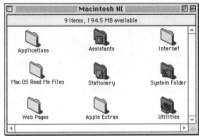

Figure 25. *The color of the selected icon(s) changes.*

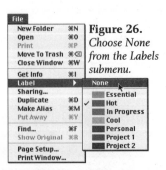

Figure 26. *Choose None from the Labels submenu.*

Figure 27.
*Point to
the name of
the icon.*

About Icon Names

Mac OS is very flexible when it comes to names for files, folders, and disks.

■ A file or folder name can be up to 31 characters long. A disk name can be up to 27 characters long.

■ A name can contain any character except a colon (:).

This makes it easy to give your files, folders, and disks meaningful names that make sense to you.

Figure 28.
*When you click, an
edit box appears
around the name.*

✔ Tips

■ Normally, you name documents when you save them. I tell you how to save documents in **Chapter 5**.

■ No two documents in the same window can have the same name.

■ I tell you more about disks later in this chapter.

Figure 29.
*Type a new
name for the
icon.*

To rename an icon

1. Point to the name of the icon (see **Figure 27**) and click. After a brief pause, an edit box appears around the name and the name becomes highlighted (see **Figure 28**).

2. Type the new name. The text you type automatically overwrites the highlighted text (see **Figure 29**).

Figure 30.
*When you press
Return, the
name changes.*

3. Press Return or Enter or click anywhere else in the window or on the desktop. The icon is renamed (see **Figure 30**).

✔ Tip

■ If you prefer, you can use standard editing techniques to change the name of the icon. I tell you about editing text in **Chapter 5**.

Renaming Icons

About Folders

Mac OS uses folders to organize files and other folders on disk. You can create a folder, give it a name that makes sense to you, and move files and other folders into it. It's a lot like organizing paper files and folders in a file cabinet.

✔ Tips

- ■ A folder can contain any number of files and other folders.

- ■ It's a very good idea to use folders to organize the files on your hard disk. Imagine a file cabinet without file folders—that's how your hard disk would appear if you never used folders to keep your files tidy.

To create a folder

1. Choose New Folder from the File menu (see **Figure 31**).

   or

   Press ⌘N.

   A new untitled folder (see **Figure 32**) appears in the active window.

2. While the edit box appears around the new folder's name (see **Figure 32**), type a name for it (see **Figure 33**) and press Return.

✔ Tips

- ■ You can rename a folder the same way you rename any other icon. I tell you how on the previous page.

- ■ I tell you more about windows, including how to activate them, in **Chapter 2**.

Figure 31.
Choose New Folder from the File menu.

Figure 32.
A new folder appears.

Figure 33.
Enter a name for the folder while the edit box appears around it.

About Moving & Copying Items

In addition to moving icons around within a window or on the desktop, which I discuss in **Chapter 2**, you can move or copy items to other locations on disk or to other disks by dragging them:

- When you drag an item to a location on the same disk, the item is moved to that location.

- When you drag an item to a location on another disk, the item is copied to that location.

- When you hold down (Option) while dragging an item to a location on the same disk, the item is copied to that location.

I provide instructions for all these techniques, as well as instructions for duplicating items, on the next few pages.

✔ Tips

- You can move or copy more than one item at a time. Begin by selecting all the items you want to move or copy, then drag any one of them to the destination. All items will be moved or copied.

- You can continue working with the Finder—even start more copy jobs— while a copy job is in progress.

About Moving & Copying Items

To move an item to another location on the same disk

1. Drag the icon for the item that you want to move as follows:

   ▲ To move the item into a specific folder on the disk, drag the icon to the icon for the folder. The icon becomes highlighted when the mouse pointer moves over it (see **Figure 34**).

   ▲ To move the item into a specific window on the disk, drag the icon into the window (see **Figure 35**).

2. Release the mouse button. The item moves.

✔ Tip

■ If the destination location is on another disk, the item you drag will be copied rather than moved. You can always delete the original after the copy is made. I tell you how to delete items later in this chapter.

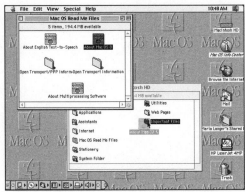

Figure 34. *Drag the icon onto the icon for the folder to which you want to move it...*

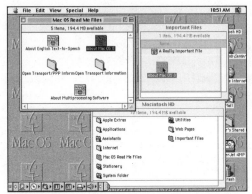

Figure 35. *....or drag the icon into the window in which you want to move it.*

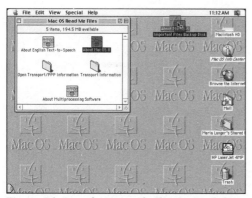

Figure 36. *Drag the icon to the destination disk's icon…*

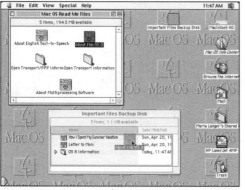

Figure 37. *…or to an open window on the destination disk…*

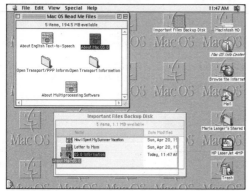

Figure 38. *…or to a folder icon in a window on the destination disk.*

Figure 39.
A window like this indicates copy progress.

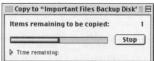

To copy an item to another disk

1. Drag the icon for the item that you want to copy as follows:

   ▲ To copy the item to the top (or root) level of a disk, drag the icon to the icon for the destination disk (see **Figure 36**).

   ▲ To copy the item into a specific window on the disk, drag the icon into the window (see **Figure 37**).

   ▲ To copy the item into a folder on the disk, drag the icon to the icon for the folder on the destination disk (see **Figure 38**).

   When the mouse pointer on the item you are dragging moves on top of the destination location a plus sign appears beside it. If the destination is an icon, the icon becomes highlighted.

2. Release the mouse button. A Copy status window like the one in **Figure 39** appears. When it disappears, the copy operation is complete.

✔ Tips

■ You can expand the Copy status window (see **Figure 39**) to show more information (see **Figure 40**). Simply click the right-pointing triangle near the bottom of the window. You can collapse the window by clicking the triangle again.

■ You cannot copy items to a disk that is write protected. I tell you about write-protecting disks later in this chapter.

Figure 40.
You can expand the Copy window to show more information.

To copy an item to another location on the same disk

1. Hold down [Option] while dragging the icon for the item that you want to copy onto a folder icon (see **Figure 41**) or into a window (see **Figure 42**).

   When the mouse pointer on the item you are dragging moves on top of the destination location a plus sign appears beside it. If the destination is an icon, the icon becomes highlighted.

2. Release the mouse button. A Copy status window like the one in **Figure 39** appears. When it disappears, the copy operation is complete.

✔ Tips

■ When copying an item to a new location on the same disk, you *must* hold down [Option]. If you don't the item will be moved rather than copied.

■ You can expand the Copy status window (see **Figure 39**) to show more information (see **Figure 40**). Simply click the right-pointing triangle near the bottom of the window. You can collapse the window by clicking the triangle again.

To duplicate an item

1. Select the item that you want to duplicate.

2. Choose Duplicate from the File menu (see **Figure 43**).

   or

   Press [⌘][D].

or

Hold down [Option] while dragging the item that you want to duplicate to a different location in the same window.

A copy of the item you duplicated appears beside the original. The word *copy* appears at the end of the file name (see **Figure 44**).

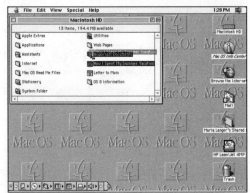

Figure 41. *Hold down* [Option] *while dragging the item onto a folder...*

Figure 42. *...or into a window on the same disk.*

Figure 43. *Choose Duplicate from the File menu.*

Figure 44. *A duplicate appears beneath the original.*

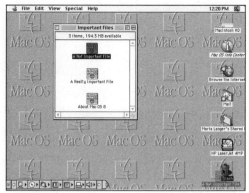

Figure 45. *To move an item to the Trash, drag it there…*

Figure 46.
…or select the item and choose Move to Trash from the File menu.

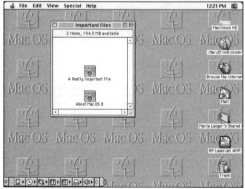

Figure 47. *When an item has been moved to the Trash, the Trash icon looks full.*

About the Trash & Deleting Items

The Trash is a special place on your hard disk where you place items you want to delete. Items in the Trash remain there until you empty the Trash, which permanently deletes them.

To move an item to the Trash

1. Drag the icon for the item you want to delete to the Trash icon on the Desktop.

2. When the mouse pointer moves over the Trash icon, the Trash icon becomes selected (see **Figure 45**). Release the mouse button.

or

1. Select the item that you want to delete.

2. Choose Move to Trash from the File menu (see **Figure 46**).

   or

   Press ⌃⌘ Delete.

✔ Tips

■ The Trash icon's appearance indicates its status:

  ▲ If the Trash is empty, the Trash icon looks like a covered trash can (see **Figure 45**).

  ▲ If the Trash is not empty, the Trash icon looks like an open trash can filled with papers (see **Figure 47**).

■ You can delete more than one item at a time. Begin by selecting all the items you want to delete, then drag any one of them to the Trash. All items will be moved to the Trash.

■ Moving a disk icon to the trash does not delete or erase it. Instead, it ejects or unmounts it. I tell you more about working with disks later in this chapter.

Moving Items to the Trash

To move an item out of the Trash

1. Open the Trash using one of these techniques:
   - Double-click the Trash icon.
   - Click the Trash icon once to select it and choose Open from the File menu (see **Figure 14**) or press ⌘O.

   A Trash window opens (see **Figure 48**).

2. Drag the item from the Trash window to the Desktop or another window on your hard disk.

   or

   Select the item and choose Put Away from the File menu (see **Figure 49**) or press ⌘Y.

✔ Tip

- The Put Away command automatically moves a selected icon from the Desktop or Trash to the folder in which it was located before being moved to the Desktop or Trash.

To empty the trash

1. Choose Empty Trash from the Special menu (see **Figure 50**).

2. A Trash warning dialog box like the one in **Figure 51** appears. Click OK to permanently remove all items that are in the Trash.

✔ Tips

- You can disable the Trash warning dialog box by turning off the Warn before emptying check box in the Trash Info window (see **Figure 52**). I tell you about the Info window in **Chapter 4**.

- Technically speaking, it may be possible to recover accidently deleted items using utility software such as Norton Utilities for Macintosh. File recovery software is not included with Mac OS 8.

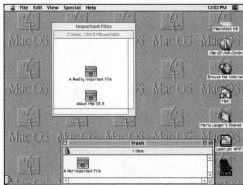

Figure 48. *Opening the Trash displays the Trash window.*

Figure 49. *Choose Put Away from the File menu.*

Figure 50. *Choose Empty Trash from the Special menu.*

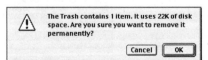

Figure 51. *The Trash warning dialog box asks you to confirm that you really do want to delete the items in the Trash.*

Figure 52. *You can disable the Trash warning dialog box by turning off the Warn before emptying check box in the Trash Info window.*

Term	Abbreviation	Size
byte	byte	1 character
kilobyte	KB	1,024 bytes
megabyte	MB	1,024 KB
gigabyte	GB	1,024 MB

Table 1. *Terms for storage media capacity.*

Figure 53. *The header in a disk window indicates how much space is available on the disk and whether the disk is write protected or locked.*

✔ Tips

- Don't confuse storage media with memory. The term *memory* usually refers to the amount of RAM in your computer, not hard disk space. I tell you about RAM in **Chapter 5**.

- At a minimum, most Mac OS computers come with a hard disk, floppy disk, and CD-ROM disc drives.

- Disk and other storage media drives can be internal (inside your computer) or external (attached to your computer by a cable).

- External storage devices must be properly connected and turned on *before* you start your computer or your computer may not recognize the device.

- Disk storage media capacity is specified in terms of bytes, kilobytes, megabytes, and gigabytes (see **Table 1**).

About Disks & Other Storage Media

A Mac OS-compatible computer can read and/or write to data on a wide range of storage media, including:

- **Hard disks** – high capacity magnetic media.

- **Diskettes or "floppy" disks** – low capacity, removable magnetic media.

- **CD-ROM discs** – high capacity, read-only, removable optical media.

- **Zip, Jaz, EZFlyer, SyQuest or other disks or cartridges** – high capacity, removable magnetic media.

To use storage media, it must be:

- **Mounted** – inserted, attached, or otherwise accessible to your computer.

- **Formatted** or **initialized** – specially prepared for use with your computer.

I tell you about all these things on the following pages.

- You can tell how much space is available on a disk by checking the header in any of the disk's windows (see **Figure 53**).

- If a floppy diskette is *write-protected* or *locked,* files cannot be saved or copied to it. To write protect a disk, move the plastic tab on the back of the disk so it exposes the square hole beneath it. To unlock a disk, move the plastic tab on the back of the disk so it covers the square hole.

- All windows for a write protected or locked disk display a padlock icon in the upper left corner (see **Figure 53**).

- Unless you have a special recordable CD-ROM (CDR) drive and recording software, you cannot write data to a CD-ROM disc.

About Mounting Disks

You mount a disk by inserting it in the disk drive so it appears on the Mac OS Desktop.

✔ Tips

- ■ You must mount a disk to use it.

- ■ To learn how to mount disks that are not specifically covered in this book, consult the documentation that came with the disk drive.

- ■ If you cannot successfully mount a CD-ROM disc or Zip disk by following these instructions, check to be sure the appropriate driver software has been installed and loaded. I tell you about driver software in **Chapter 12**.

To mount a floppy disk

Insert the disk in the computer's floppy disk drive, label side up, metal side in. The disk's icon appears on the desktop (see **Figure 54**).

To mount a CD-ROM disc

1. Follow the manufacturer's instructions to open the CD-ROM disc tray or eject the CD-ROM caddy.

2. Place the CD-ROM disc in the tray or caddy, label side up.

3. Gently push the tray or caddy into the CD-ROM drive. After a moment, the CD-ROM disc icon appears on the desktop (see **Figure 54**).

To mount a Zip disk

Insert the disk in the Zip drive, label side up, metal side in. After a moment, the Zip disk icon appears on the desktop (see **Figure 54**).

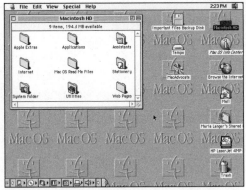

Figure 54. *Here's a Desktop with a hard disk, floppy disk, Zip disk, and CD-ROM disc mounted.*

Figure 55.
*Drag the
disk icon to
the Trash…*

About Ejecting Disks

When you eject a disk, the disk is physically removed from the disk drive and its icon disappears from the Desktop.

✔ Tip

■ When the disk's icon disappears from the desktop, it is said to be *unmounted*.

To eject a disk

1. Drag the disk's icon to the Trash.
2. When the mouse pointer moves over the Trash icon, it becomes highlighted (see **Figure 55**). Release the mouse button.

or

1. Click the disk's icon once to select it.
2. Choose Eject from the Special menu (see **Figure 56**).

   or

   Press ⌘E.

   or

   Choose Put Away from the File menu (see **Figure 49**).

   or

   Press ⌘Y.

Figure 56.
*or select the disk
and then choose
Eject from the
Special menu.*

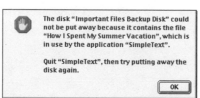

The disk "Important Files Backup Disk" could not be put away because it contains the file "How I Spent My Summer Vacation", which is in use by the application "SimpleText".

Quit "SimpleText", then try putting away the disk again.

OK

Figure 57. *A dialog box like this appears if you try to eject a disk that contains open files.*

✔ Tip

■ If you try to eject a disk that contains one or more files that are in use by your computer, a dialog box like the one in **Figure 57** appears. Click OK or press Return or Enter to dismiss the dialog box, then quit the open application. You should then be able to eject the disk. I tell you more about working with applications in **Chapter 5**.

About Formatting Disks

To use a floppy disk or other magnetic media, it must be *formatted* or *initialized* for the computer on which it will be used. A Mac OS computer can format disks for three different computer platforms:

- **Mac OS** – for Macintosh and Macintosh-compatible computers.

- **MS-DOS** – for Intel-based computer systems, including systems running Microsoft Windows and OS/2.

- **Pro-DOS** – for old Apple II computers.

✔ Tips

- The terms *formatting* and *initializing* are sometimes used interchangeably. Although these two words don't mean exactly the same thing, they're close enough for our purposes.

- Nowadays, most floppy disks come preformatted. If you buy preformatted disks, make sure they are formatted for Macintosh computers. Otherwise, you'll have to reformat them for use with your Mac OS system.

- Formatting or initializing a disk erases all the information on the disk. If the disk is brand new, however, it probably doesn't have any information on it anyway.

- Higher capacity magnetic media like hard disks, Zip disks, and SyQuest cartridges must be formatted using special software that comes with the device drive. For example, you format an Apple hard disk with Drive Setup. For more information, consult the documentation that came with the drive. I tell you about Drive Setup in **Chapter 6**.

- You cannot format a write-protected or locked disk.

Figure 58. *When you insert a brand new unformatted disk, a dialog box like this appears.*

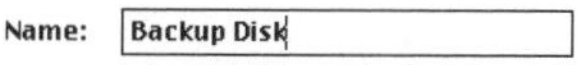

Figure 59. *Enter a name for the disk in the Name edit box.*

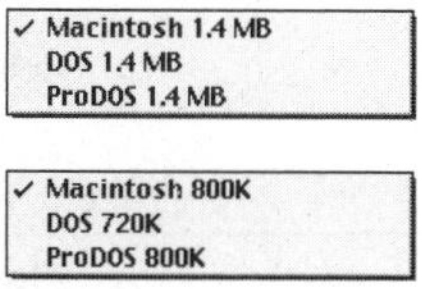

Figure 60a & 60b. *The options under the Format pop-up menu depend on the type of disk inserted: high density (top) or double-sided (bottom).*

Figure 61. *A warning dialog box like this appears when you format a disk.*

Figure 62. *Choose Erase Disk from the Special menu.*

Figure 63. *This dialog box appears when you use the Erase Disk command to erase a selected disk.*

To format a disk for the first time

1. Insert the disk into the disk drive. A dialog box like the one in **Figure 58** appears.

2. Type a name for the disk in the Name edit box (see **Figure 59**).

3. If desired, choose an option from the Format pop-up menu. As you can see in **Figures 60a** and **60b**, the options vary depending on the type of disk you inserted.

4. Click Initialize.

5. A warning dialog box like the one in **Figure 61** appears. If you're sure you want to initialize the disk, click Continue.

6. A status window appears while the disk is initialized and verified. Wait until it disappears. The icon for the formatted disk appears on the Desktop with the name you gave it.

To erase a disk

1. Insert the disk into the disk drive. If the disk is readable, its icon appears on the Desktop.

2. If necessary, click the disk icon once to select it.

3. Choose Erase Disk (see **Figure 62**) from the Special menu. A dialog box like the one in **Figure 63** appears.

4. If desired, type a new name for the disk in the Name edit box (see **Figure 59**).

5. If desired, choose an option from the Format pop-up menu (see **Figures 60a** and **60b**).

6. Click Erase.

7. A status window appears while the disk is erased and verified . Wait until it disappears. The icon for the disk appears on the Desktop with the name you gave it.

Formatting & Erasing Disks

ADVANCED FINDER TECHNIQUES

About Advanced Finder Techniques

In addition to the basic Finder and file management techniques covered in **Chapters 1** and **2**, Mac OS 8 offers more advanced techniques you can use to customize the Finder, work with windows, and manage files:

- Use the Preferences window to change the way the Finder looks and works.

- Use hierarchical outlines in list view windows.

- Use pop-up windows to keep frequently used windows handy but out of sight.

- Use spring-loaded folders to automatically open and then close multiple levels of folders while copying or moving items.

- Use aliases to make frequently used files easier to access without actually moving them.

- Search for files on your computer or the computers accessible by network.

- Use the Info window to learn more about an item or enter comments about it.

✔ Tips

- If you're brand new to Mac OS, be sure to read the information in **Chapters 2** and **3** before working with this chapter. Those chapters contain information and instructions about techniques that are used throughout this chapter.

- This chapter is especially useful for experienced Mac OS users since it goes beyond the basics with new or advanced Mac OS features.

About Finder Preferences

The Finder's Preferences window (see **Figure 1**) lets you customize some aspects of Finder appearance and operation:

- **Fonts for views** offers a pop-up menu to choose the font used in windows.

- **Simple Finder** simplifies Finder menus by reducing the number of options.

- **Spring-loaded folders** can automatically open and close folders when you drag an icon onto them.

- **Grid Spacing** specifies the amount of space between icons in icon and button view windows.

- **Labels** sets the name and color of options on the Label submenu under the File menu.

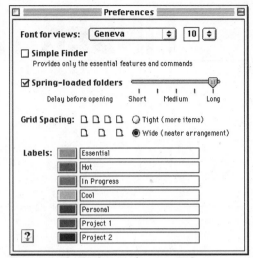

Figure 1. *The Finder's Preferences window.*

✔ Tip

- I tell you about more Mac OS 8 customization features in **Chapter 12**.

To open the Preferences window

Choose Preferences from the Edit menu (see **Figure 2**). The Preferences window appears (see **Figure 1**).

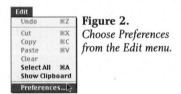

Figure 2.
Choose Preferences from the Edit menu.

To close the Preferences window

Click the Preferences window's close box.

or

1. Activate the Preferences window.

2. Choose Close Window from the File menu (see **Figure 3**).

   or

   Press ⌃⌘W.

Figure 3.
Choose Close from the File menu.

Figure 4. *Choose a font from the Font for views pop-up menu.*

To change the view font

1. Open the Preferences window (see **Figure 1**).

2. Choose a font from the Font for views pop-up menu (see **Figure 4**).

3. Choose a font size from the pop-up menu to the right of the Font for views pop-up menu (see **Figure 5**).

   or

   Enter the font size you want in the edit box to the right of the Font for views pop-up menu (see **Figure 6**).

4. Close the Preferences window.

Figure 5. *Choose a size from the pop-up menu to the right of the Font for views pop-up menu...*

Figure 6. *...or enter the exact size you want in the edit box to the right of the Font for views pop-up menu.*

✔ Tips

■ The Font for views pop-up menu lists all fonts properly installed in your system. I tell you about fonts in **Chapter 12**.

■ The Font for views options affect the names of icons and other text in Finder windows (see **Figure 7**).

To enable or disable Simple Finder

1. Open the Preferences window (see **Figure 1**).

2. To enable Simple Finder, turn on the Simple Finder check box.

   or

   To disable Simple Finder, turn off the Simple Finder check box.

3. Close the Preferences window.

✔ Tips

■ The illustrations throughout this book were created with Simple Finder disabled.

■ **Appendix A** illustrates both standard Finder and Simple Finder menus.

Figure 7. *Here's a Finder window with 12-point Charcoal font applied.*

Changing View Font, Enabling Simple Finder

To set spring-loaded folder options

1. Open the Preferences window (see **Figure 1**).

2. To enable the spring-loaded folders feature, turn on the Spring-loaded folders check box. Then use the slider bar beside it (see **Figure 8**) to set the delay from the time an item is dragged onto a folder to the time the folder opens.

   or

   To disable the spring-loaded folders feature, turn off the Spring-loaded folders check box.

3. Close the Preferences window.

✔ Tip

- I tell you how to use spring-loaded folders later in this chapter.

To set grid spacing

1. Open the Preferences window (see **Figure 1**).

2. For less space between icons or buttons in icon or button view windows (see **Figure 9**), turn on the Tight radio button.

   or

   For more space between icons or buttons in icon or button view windows (see **Figure 10**), turn on the Wide radio button.

3. Close the Preferences window.

✔ Tip

- Wide grid spacing yields a neater arrangement because file names are less likely to overlap (see **Figure 10**).

Figure 8. *Use the slider control to set the spring-loaded folder delay.*

Figure 9. *Tight spacing enables you to view more icons in less space.*

Figure 10. *Wide spacing offers a neater arrangement because names don't overlap.*

Figure 11. *Select the text of the label that you want to change...*

Figure 12. *...then type in the new label.*

Figure 13. *The new label appears in the Label submenu under the File menu.*

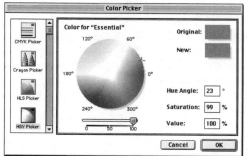

Figure 14. *The Color Picker dialog box lets you select a new color.*

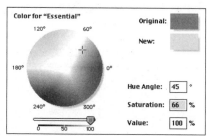

Figure 15. *Click anywhere in the color wheel to select a color. The new color appears in the New sample area.*

Essential

Figure 16. *The color you clicked in the Preferences window changes.*

To change the text of labels

1. Open the Preferences window (see **Figure 1**).

2. Drag the mouse pointer over the text in in the edit box that contains the label that you want to change. This selects the text (see **Figure 11**).

3. Type the text that you want to use as a label (see **Figure 12**).

4. Repeat steps 2 and 3 for each label that you want to change.

5. Close the Preferences window.

✔ Tip

■ The changes you make are reflected in the Labels submenu under the File menu (see **Figure 13**).

To change the color of labels

1. Open the Preferences window (see **Figure 1**).

2. Click the color you want to change. The Color Picker dialog box appears (see **Figure 14**).

3. Click in the color wheel to select a new color. The color appears in the New sample area (see **Figure 15**).

4. If desired, use the slider near the bottom of the dialog box to change the brightness of the color.

5. Click OK. The color you clicked in the Preferences window changes (see **Figure 16**).

6. Repeat steps 2 though 5 for each color that you want to change.

7. Close the Preferences window.

✔ Tip

■ The changes you make are reflected in the Labels submenu under the File menu and in the color of the icons which have labels applied.

Customizing Labels

About Outlines in List View

Windows displayed in list view have a
feature not found in icon or button views:
they can display the contents of folders
within the window as an outline (see
Figure 17).

✔ Tip

■ I tell you more about views in
Chapter 2.

To display a folder's contents

Click the right-pointing triangle beside the
folder (see **Figure 18**). The items within
that folder are listed below it, slightly
indented (see **Figure 19**).

✔ Tip

■ As shown in **Figure 17**, you can use this
technique to display multiple levels of
folders in the same window.

To hide a folder's contents

Click the down-pointing triangle beside
the folder (see **Figure 19**). The outline
collapses to hide the items in the folder
(see **Figure 18**).

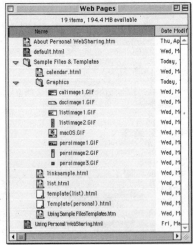

Figure 17. *The outline feature lets you display the contents of folders within the same list view window.*

Click here to expand the outline

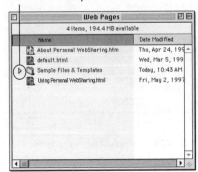

Figure 18. *The contents of a folder can be hidden...*

Click here to collapse the outline

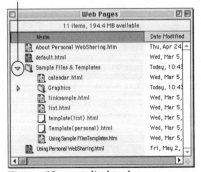

Figure 19. *...or displayed.*

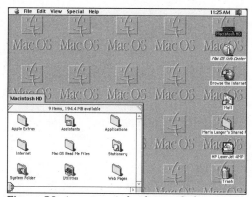

Figure 20. *A pop-up window has a tab that you can click...*

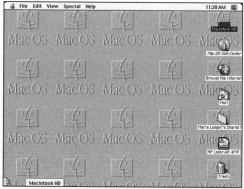

Figure 21. *...to hide the window at the bottom of the screen.*

About Pop-up Windows

Pop-up windows, a new feature of Mac OS, changes the appearance and functionality of a window's frame by adding a tab (see **Figure 20**) that you can click to instantly hide the window at the very bottom of the screen (see **Figure 21**). This makes it easy to keep frequently used windows handy without letting them clutter up the screen.

To turn a window into a pop-up window

1. Activate the window that you want to turn into a pop-up window.

2. Choose as Pop-up Window from the View menu (see **Figure 22**). The window changes to a pop-up window (see **Figure 20**).

   or

   Drag the window's title bar to the bottom of the screen. When a tab shape appears at the top of its gray outline (see **Figure 23**), release the mouse button. The window changes into a pop-up window tab (see **Figure 21**).

Figure 22. *Choose as Pop-up Window from the View menu.*

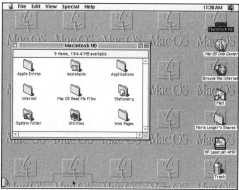

Figure 23. *Drag the window's title bar until a tab appears on its outline.*

To activate or deactivate a pop-up window

Click the tab at the top of the window.

If the window is active (fully visible) when you click its tab, it disappears, displaying only a tab at the bottom of the screen (see **Figure 21**).

If the window is inactive (displayed as a tab) when you click its tab, it appears (see **Figure 20**).

To resize a pop-up window

1. Position the mouse pointer on one of the top corners of the active pop-up window (see **Figure 24**).

2. Drag to make the window larger or smaller. As you drag, a dotted line border indicates the new edges of the window (see **Figure 25**).

3. Release the mouse button. The window resizes (see **Figure 26**).

To turn a pop-up window into a standard window

1. Activate the pop-up window that you want to turn into a standard window.

2. Choose as Window from the View menu (see **Figure 27**). The window changes to a standard window.

    or

    Position the mouse pointer on the tab of the pop-up window and drag up until the tab disappears from the gray outline of the window (see **Figure 28**). Release the mouse button. The window changes to a standard window.

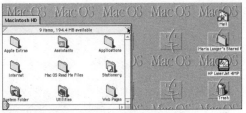

Figure 24. *A pop-up window has size boxes on the two upper corners of the active window.*

Figure 25. *As you drag a size box, a dotted-line border indicates the window's new borders.*

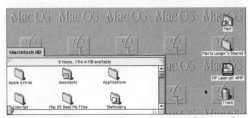

Figure 26. *When you release the mouse button, the window resizes.*

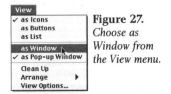

Figure 27. *Choose as Window from the View menu.*

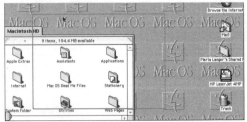

Figure 28. *Drag a pop-up window's tab up until the tab disappears from the gray outline.*

Working with Pop-up Windows

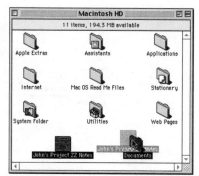

Figure 29. *Drag an icon onto a folder icon and wait…*

Figure 30. *…until the folder opens.*

About Spring-loaded Folders

Spring-loaded folders, a new feature of Mac OS, lets you move or copy items into folders deep within the file structure of your disk—without manually opening a single folder. Instead, you simply drag icons onto folders (see **Figures 29** and **31**) and wait as they're automatically opened (see **Figures 30** and **32**). When you drop the icon into the final window, all windows except the source and destination windows automatically close (see **Figure 33**).

✔ Tips

- The spring-loaded folders features is sometimes referred to as *spring-open folders*.

- Using the spring-loaded folders feature of Mac OS requires a steady hand, good mouse skills, and knowledge of the location of folders on your disk.

- To take advantage of the spring-loaded folders feature, the Spring-loaded folders check box must be turned on in the Preferences window (see **Figure 1**). You can also set the spring-loaded folder delay length in the Preferences window (see **Figure 8**). I tell you about Preferences at the beginning of this chapter.

- To use the spring-loaded folders feature to move or copy more than one item at a time, select the items first, then drag any one of them.

About Spring-loaded Folders

To move an item using spring-loaded folders

1. Drag the item you want to move onto the folder in which you want to move it (see **Figure 29**) but do not release the mouse button. After a moment, the folder blinks and opens (see **Figure 30**).

2. Without releasing the mouse button, repeat step 1. The destinationfolder becomes selected (see **Figure 31**), then blinks and opens (see **Figure 32**). Do this until you reach the final destination.

3. Release the mouse button to place the item into the final destination window (see **Figure 33**).

To copy an item using spring-loaded folders

Hold down (Option) while following the above steps.

✔ Tip

■ If the destination folder is on another disk, it is not necessary to hold down (Option) to copy items; they're automatically copied.

Figure 31. *Continue to drag the icon onto a folder in that window and wait...*

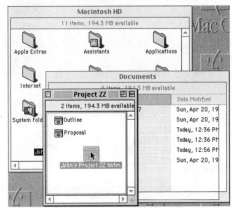

Figure 32. *...until that folder opens.*

Figure 33. *The icon appears in the final destination window.*

About Aliases

An *alias* is a pointer to an item. You can make an alias of an item and place it anywhere on your computer. Then, when you need to open the item, just open its alias.

✔ Tips

■ It's important to remember that an alias is not a copy of the item—it's a pointer. If you delete the original item, the alias will not open.

■ By putting aliases of frequently used items together where you can quickly access them—like on the Desktop, in a pop-up window, or in the Apple Menu Items folder—you make the items more accessible without actually moving them. I tell you about pop-up windows earlier in this chapter and about Apple Menu Items in **Chapter 6**.

■ You can make an alias for any item on your computer—including items accessible over a network. I tell you more about networking in **Chapter 9**.

■ You can name an alias anything you like, as long as you follow the file naming guidelines I discuss in **Chapter 3**. An alias's name does not need to include the word *alias*.

■ The alias for an item looks just like the item. Its name, however, appears in italic letters (see **Figure 34**).

■ You can move, copy, rename, open, and delete an alias just like any other file.

SimpleText   *SimpleText alias*

Figure 34. *The icon for an alias looks the same as the original's icon. But its name always appears in italic letters.*

To create an alias

1. Select the item for which you want to make an alias (see **Figure 35**).

2. Choose Make Alias from the File menu (see **Figure 36**).

    or

    Press ⌘M.

    The alias appears right beneath the original item (see **Figure 37**).

    or

    Hold down ⌘Option and drag the item for which you want to make an alias to a new location. The alias appears in the destination location.

✔ Tip

■ An alias's name is selected right after it is created (see **Figure 37**). If desired, you can immediately type in a new name to replace the default name.

To find an alias's original file

1. Select the alias's icon (see **Figure 38**).

2. Choose Show Original from the File menu (see **Figure 39**).

    or

    Press ⌘R.

    The original item appears selected in the window in which it resides on disk (see **Figure 40**).

Figure 35.
To create an alias, begin by selecting the item for which you want to make an alias.

Figure 36.
Choose Make Alias from the File menu.

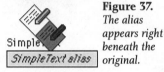

Figure 37.
The alias appears right beneath the original.

Figure 38.
Select the alias's icon.

Figure 39.
Choose Show Original from the File menu.

Figure 40.
The original item appears selected in its window.

Figure 41.
*The Info window
for a hard disk.*

Figure 42.
*The Info window
for a folder.*

Figure 43.
*The Info window
for an application.*

Figure 44.
*The Info window
for a document.*

About the Info Window

You can learn more about an item by opening its Info window (see **Figures 41** through **44**). Depending on the type of icon (disk, folder, application, document, alias, Trash, etc.), the window will provide some or all of the following information:

- **Icon** that appears in the Finder.
- **Name** of the item.
- **Kind** or type of item.
- **Capacity** of item (for disks only).
- **Available** space (for disks only).
- **Used** space (for disks only).
- **Size** of item or contents (for folders and files only).
- **Where** or location of item.
- **Contents** (for Trash only).
- **Created** date and time.
- **Modified** date and time.
- **Version** number or copyright date (for files only).
- **Original** location on disk (for aliases only).
- **Comments** entered by users (like you).
- **Memory Requirement** information (for applications only).
- **Locked** check box to prevent the file from being deleted or overwritten (for files only).
- **Stationery** check box to convert the file into a stationery format file (for documents only).
- **Warn before emptying** check box to toggle the Trash warning dialog box (for Trash only).

✔ Tip

- I tell you about application memory requirements and stationery documents in **Chapter 5**.

To open the Info window

1. Select the item for which you want to open the Info window (see **Figure 45**).

2. Choose Get Info from the File menu (see **Figure 46**).

   or

   Press ⌘ I.

   The Info window for that item appears (see **Figure 42**).

To close the Info window

Click the Info window's close box.

or

1. Activate the Info window.

2. Choose Close Window from the File menu (see **Figure 3**).

   or

   Press ⌘ W.

To enter comments in the Info window

1. Open the Info window for the item for which you want to enter comments.

2. Click in the Comment box to position the blinking insertion point there.

3. Type your comments (see **Figure 47**).

4. Close the Info window.

To lock an application or document

1. Open the Info window for the item you want to lock (see **Figure 43** or **44**).

2. Turn on the Locked check box.

3. Close the Info window.

✔ Tip

■ Locked items cannot be deleted or overwritten. They can, however, be moved.

Figure 45.
Select the item for which you want to open the Info window.

Figure 46.
Choose Get Info from the File menu.

Figure 47. *You can enter information about the item in the Comments box.*

USING APPLICATIONS

About Applications

Applications, which are often also known as *programs*, are software packages you use to get work done. Here are some examples:

- **Word processors** are used to write letters, reports, and other text-based documents. Examples include Simple-Text, Word, and MacWrite Pro.

- **Spreadsheets** are used to create number-based documents like work-sheets and charts. Calculation features are built-in, making them perfect for "what-if" style financial analysis. Examples include Excel.

- **Databases** are used to organize related information, like the names and ad-dresses of customers or the artists and titles in a record collection. Examples include FileMaker Pro and FoxBase Pro.

- **Graphics** and **presentation** programs are used to create and modify illustrations, presentations, and animations. Examples include ClarisDraw, Photoshop, Illustrator, PowerPoint.

- **Communications** programs are used to connect to other computers, including online services and the Internet. Examples include ZTerm, the Apple Internet Connection Kit, and Navigator.

- **Integrated** software combines stripped-down versions of most other types of software into one cost-effective package. Examples include ClarisWorks and Microsoft Works.

- **Utility** software performs computer-related tasks to help manage files or keep your computer in good working order. Examples include Disk First Aid, Drive Setup, and Norton Utilities for Macintosh.

✔ Tips

- Your Mac OS-compatible computer comes with some application software, most of which is discussed throughout this book.

- Unless you have a DOS compatibility card or SoftWindows installed in your computer, you should make sure the software you buy is Mac OS-compatible. I tell you more about working with PCs in **Chapter 7**.

About Using Applications & Creating Documents

You use an application by opening or *launching* it. It loads into the computer's memory or *RAM*. Its menu bar replaces the Finder's menu bar and offers commands that can be used only with that application. It may also display a document window and tools specific to that program.

Most applications create *documents*—files written in a format understood by the application. When you save documents, they remain on disk so you can open, edit, print, or just view them at a later date.

For example, you may use Microsoft Word to write a letter. When you save the letter, it becomes a document file that includes all the text and formatting you put into the letter, written in a format that Microsoft Word can understand.

Your computer keeps track of applications and documents. It automatically associates documents with the applications that created them. That's how your computer is able to open a document with the correct application if you open a document from the Finder.

✔ Tips

- You can launch an application by opening a document that it created.

- You can often tell which documents were created by a specific application just by looking at their icons. **Figure 1** shows some examples.

- A document created by an application that is not installed on your computer is sometimes referred to as an *orphan* document since no *parent* application is available. An orphan document often has a generic document icon (see **Figure 2**).

Microsoft Word   Document

FrameMaker 5   Document

Claris Home Page   Document

Acrobat™ Reader   Document

Figure 1. *Application and document icons often share elements that make them appear as part of a matched set.*

Figure 2.
An orphan document often has a generic document icon like this one.
Document

Figure 3.
Select the icon for the application that you want to open.

Figure 4.
Choose Open from the File menu.

Figure 5. *When you launch SimpleText by opening its application icon, it displays an empty document window.*

Figure 6.
Select the icon for the document that you want to open.

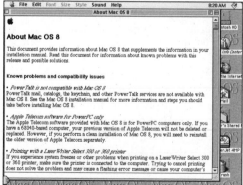

Figure 7. *When you launch SimpleText by opening one of its documents, it displays the document.*

To launch an application

Double-click the application's icon.

or

1. Select the application's icon (see **Figure 3**).

2. Choose Open from the File menu (see **Figure 4**).

   or

   Press ⌘O.

The application opens (see **Figure 5**).

To launch an application & open a document at the same time

Double-click the icon for the document that you want to open.

or

1. Select the icon for the document that you want to open (see **Figure 6**).

2. Choose Open from the File menu (see **Figure 4**).

   or

   Press ⌘O.

The application that created the document launches. The document appears in a window (see **Figure 7**).

✔ Tips

- If the application that created the document is already open, it does not launch again. Instead, it becomes active and displays the document in a window.

- If you try to open an orphan document, a dialog box will either tell you it can't open the document (see **Figure 10**) or will offer to open it with an installed application (see **Figure 9**). I tell you more about opening orphan documents on the next page.

Launching Applications

To open a document with drag & drop

1. Drag the icon for the document that you want to open onto the icon for the application with which you want to open it.

2. When the application icon becomes selected (see **Figure 8**), release the mouse button. The application launches and displays the document.

✔ Tips

- This is a good way to open a document with an application other than the one that created it.

- Not all applications can read all documents. Dragging a document icon onto the icon for an application that can't open it either won't launch the application or will display an error message.

To open an orphan document

Double-click the icon for the document that you want to open.

or

1. Select the icon for the document that you want to open.

2. Choose Open from the File menu (see **Figure 4**).

   or

   Press ⌃⌘O.

3. If a dialog box like the one in **Figure 9** appears, click once on the name of the application with which you want to try to open the document. Then click Open. The application you selected launches and attempts to open the document.

   or

   If a dialog box like the one in **Figure 10** appears, you don't have an application that will open the file. Click OK.

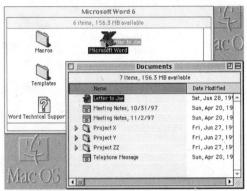

Figure 8. *Drag the document icon onto the application icon.*

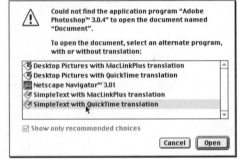

Figure 9. *A dialog box like this appears if you try to open an orphan document and have at least one program that can open it.*

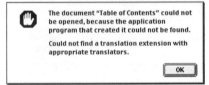

Figure 10. *If you don't have any programs that can open an orphan document, a dialog box like this appears.*

✔ Tips

- If you don't have a program that will open an orphan file, find someone who does, open it on his machine, and save it in a format you can open.

- Mac OS 8 comes with a limited number of MacLinkPlus translators. I tell you more about that and about using Mac OS Easy Open in **Chapter 7**.

About Multitasking & the Application Menu

Mac OS uses a form of *multitasking* that makes it possible for more than one application to be open at the same time. Only one application, however, can be *active*. The active application is the one whose menu bar appears at the top of the screen and whose windows are at the top of the stack of windows on your screen.

The Application menu at the far right end of the menu bar (see **Figure 11**) lets you do a number of things:

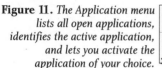

Figure 11. *The Application menu lists all open applications, identifies the active application, and lets you activate the application of your choice.*

- Identify the active application—the one with the check mark before its name; its icon also appears at the top of the application menu (see **Figure 11**).

- Make a different open application active.

- Hide the active application.

- Hide all applications except the active application.

- Show all open applications.

✔ Tips

- One application that is always open is the Finder, which I cover in detail in **Chapters 2** through **4**.

- The number of applications that can be opened at the same time depends on the amount of RAM installed in your computer. I tell you more about RAM later in this chapter.

- Hiding an application removes all its windows from the screen, thus reducing screen clutter.

To switch from one open application to another

Choose the application you that want from the Application menu (see **Figure 12**).

or

Click on a window of the application that you want (see **Figure 13**). You may have to move windows that are blocking your view.

To hide an application

1. If necessary, activate the application.

2. Choose Hide *Application* from the Application menu (see **Figure 14**). Although the wording of this command changes depending on the name of the application, it's always the first option on the Application menu.

✔ Tips

■ You cannot hide the active application if it is the only application that is open or if all the other open applications are already hidden.

■ The icon for a hidden application appears faded on the Application menu (see **Figures 15** and **16**).

To hide all applications except the active one

1. If necessary, activate the application that you don't want to hide.

2. Choose Hide Others from the Application menu (see **Figure 15**).

To unhide all applications

Choose Show All from the Application menu (see **Figure 16**).

✔ Tip

■ The Show All command is gray if all applications are already showing (see **Figure 14**).

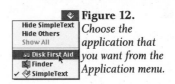

Figure 12.
Choose the application that you want from the Application menu.

Click here to activate this program.

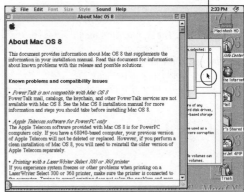

Figure 13. *In this example, SimpleText is the active application. Clicking on the Disk First Aid window sticking out behind it will activate Disk First Aid.*

Figure 14.
The first command under the Application menu hides the active application.

Figure 15.
The Hide Others command hides all applications except the active one.

Figure 16.
The Show All command shows all applications, including those that were hidden.

Switching & Hiding Applications

Figure 17a, 17b, & 17c. *The Quit command is always under the File menu. Here are three examples: SimpleText (top-left), Disk First Aid (bottom-left), and Microsoft Word (right).*

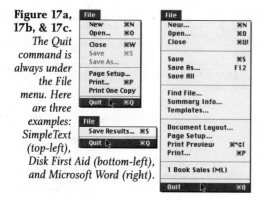

About Quitting

When you're finished using an application, you should properly Quit it. This completely clears the application out of RAM, freeing up RAM for other applications you may want to launch.

✔ Tip

■ Closing all of an applications open windows is not the same as quitting. An application is still running—and still taking up RAM—until you quit it.

To quit an application

1. If necessary, activate the application that you want to quit.

2. Choose Quit from the File menu (see **Figures 17a**, **17b**, and **17c**).

   or

   Press ⌘Q.

3. If unsaved documents are open, a dialog box like the one in **Figure 18** appears for each unsaved document.

   ▲ Click Save or press Return or Enter to save the document.

   ▲ Click Don't Save to quit without saving the document.

   ▲ Click Cancel or press Esc to return to the application without quitting.

   The application closes all windows, saves preference files (if applicable), and quits.

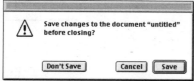

Figure 18. *If there are unsaved documents, a dialog box like this one appears for each one, giving you a last chance to save them.*

✔ Tip

■ I tell you more about saving documents later in this chapter.

Quitting

About Dialog Boxes

Mac OS-compatible applications use *dialog boxes* to tell you things (see **Figure 19**) and get information from you (see **Figures 20** through **23**). Think of it as the way your computer has a conversation—or dialog—with you.

Every application has its own set of dialog boxes, but there are some dialog boxes that are basically the same from one application to another:

■ **Open** dialog box (see **Figure 20**) lets you open a document from within an application (as opposed to opening it from the Finder).

■ **Save As** dialog box (see **Figure 21**) lets you save a document with the name and in the disk location you specify.

■ **Page Setup** dialog box (see **Figure 22**) lets you specify page and PostScript settings.

■ **Print** dialog box (see **Figure 23**) lets you specify print settings and print.

This part of the chapter explains how to use the standard parts of a dialog box—edit boxes, radio buttons, check boxes, scrolling lists, and push buttons—as well as how to use the Open and Save As dialog boxes.

✔ Tips

■ I tell you how to use the Page Setup and Print dialog boxes in **Chapter 8**.

■ It is often difficult to distinguish between windows and dialog boxes since Mac OS uses both to communicate with you. Throughout this book, a dialog box will refer to a window-like box that appears on screen and requires you to click a button to dismiss it. A window, on the other hand, can always be closed by clicking a close box or using the Close or Close Window command under the File menu.

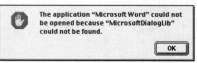

Figure 19. *This dialog box just gives you a message.*

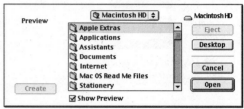

Figure 20. *Four SimpleText dialog boxes: the Open dialog box,…*

Figure 21. *…the Save As dialog box,…*

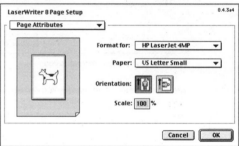

Figure 22. *…the Page Setup dialog box,…*

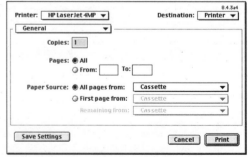

Figure 23. *…and the Print dialog box.*

Edit Scrolling Check   Pop-up Push
box list box   Tab   menu button

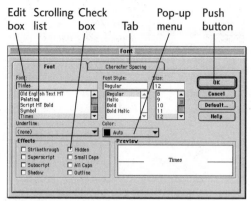

Figure 24. *One Microsoft Word dialog box illustrates most standard dialog box parts…*

Scrolling   Radio   Edit   Push
list   button   box   button

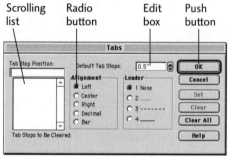

Figure 25. *…and another illustrates the rest.*

To use dialog box parts

■ Enter text or numbers into edit boxes (see **Figures 24** and **25**).

■ Use scroll bars to view the contents of scrolling lists (see **Figures 24** and **25**). Click once on a list item to select it.

■ Click a check box (see **Figure 24**) to turn it on or off.

■ Click a tab (see **Figure 24**) to view its options.

■ Click a pop-up menu (see **Figure 24**) to display its options. Drag through the menu to choose an option.

■ Click a push button (see **Figures 24** and **25**) to select it.

■ Click a radio button (see **Figure 25**) to select it.

✔ Tips

■ If an edit box has a pair of arrows or triangles beside it (see **Figure 25**) you can click the triangles to increase or decrease a value already in the edit box.

■ The default push button is the one with the dark border around it (see **Figures 24** and **25**). You can always select a default button by pressing ⎡Enter⎤ and often by pressing ⎡Return⎤.

■ You can usually select a Cancel button (see **Figures 24** and **25**) by pressing ⎡Esc⎤.

■ One and only one radio button in a group must be selected (see **Figure 25**). If you try to select a second button, the first button becomes deselected.

■ If you click the Cancel button in a dialog box (see **Figures 24** and **25**), any options you set are lost.

Using Dialog Boxes

To use the Open dialog box

1. Choose Open from the application's File menu (see **Figure 26**).

   or

   Press ⌘O.

   A dialog box similar to the ones in **Figures 20** and **27** appears.

2. Use these two techniques to navigate to the file you want to open:

   ▲ To open an item in a scrolling list, click it once and then click Open or double-click it.

   ▲ To back up out of the current folder to a previous folder in the file hierarchy, choose a folder from the pop-up menu above the scrolling list (see **Figures 28** and **29**).

3. Click the name of the file that you want to open once to select it and then click Open (see **Figure 30**) or press Return or Enter.

   or

   Double-click the name of the file that you want to open.

✔ Tips

■ To use this dialog box successfully, you must understand the file hierarchy. Remember that files reside in folders that are sometimes inside other folders.

■ To quickly view the items on the Desktop, click the Desktop button (see **Figures 20**, **27**, and **30**). This enables you to open other disks mounted on your Desktop.

■ Some Open dialog boxes, like the ClarisWorks one shown here (see **Figures 27** and **30**), offer pop-up menus that let you narrow down a file list by document and/or file type.

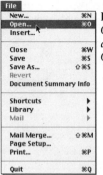

Figure 26.
Choose Open from the application's—in this case ClarisWorks'—File menu.

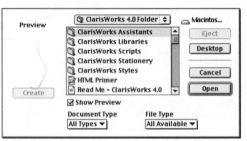

Figure 27. *The Open dialog box in ClarisWorks.*

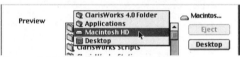

Figure 28. *Use the pop-up menu above the scrolling list to choose a different folder in the hierarchy...*

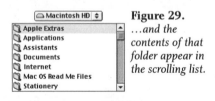

Figure 29.
...and the contents of that folder appear in the scrolling list.

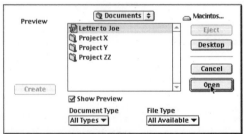

Figure 30. *Select the file's name and click Open to open it within the application.*

Figure 31. *Choose Save As from the application's—in this case, Microsoft Word's— File menu.*

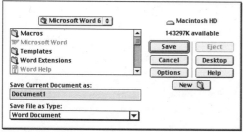

Figure 32. *The Save As dialog box in Microsoft Word.*

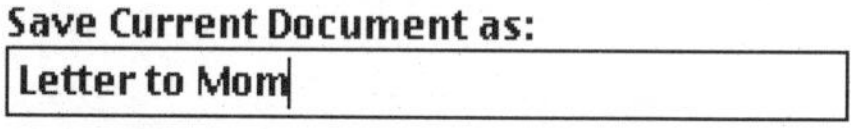

Save Current Document as:

Letter to Mom

Figure 33. *Enter a name for the document in the edit box.*

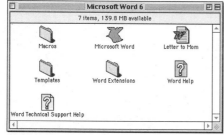

Figure 34. *An icon for the document you saved appears in the folder in which you saved it.*

Figure 35. *The name of the document appears in the title bar of the document window.*

To use the Save As dialog box

1. Choose Save As from the application's File menu (see **Figure 31**). A dialog box similar to the ones in **Figures 21** and **32** appears.

2. Use these two techniques to navigate to the folder in which you want to save the document:

   ▲ To open an item in a scrolling list, click it once and then click Open or double-click it.

   ▲ To back up out of the current folder to a previous folder in the file hierarchy, choose a folder from the pop-up menu above the scrolling list.

3. Enter the name that you want to give the document in the edit box beneath the scrolling list (see **Figure 33**).

4. Click Save or press Return or Enter.

The file is saved to disk in the destination you specified (see **Figure 34**). The name you gave it appears in the title bar of the document window (see **Figure 35**).

✔ Tips

■ If you have never saved the document, you can also choose Save from the application's file menu or press ⌘S to display the Save As dialog box.

■ The folder navigation techniques in the Save As dialog box work just like those in the Open dialog box discussed on the previous page.

■ To quickly view the items on the Desktop, click the Desktop button (see **Figures 21** and **32**). This enables you to open other disks mounted on your Desktop.

■ Some Save As dialog boxes, like the Microsoft Word one shown here (see **Figure 32**), offer a pop-up menu you can use to save a file in a specific file format.

Using the Save As Dialog Box

About SimpleText

SimpleText (see **Figure 36**) is a basic text editing application that comes with Mac OS. SimpleText lets you:

Figure 36.
The SimpleText application icon.

■ Create, open, edit, and print text documents, including the "Read Me" files that come with many applications.

■ Open and print PICT, GIF, and other graphic format documents and Quick-Time movies.

On the following pages, I tell you how to use SimpleText to create, edit, format, open, and save documents.

Figure 37.
A SimpleText Read Only document's icon.

✔ Tips

■ MoviePlayer, which also comes with Mac OS, offers more features than SimpleText for working with QuickTime movies. I tell you about QuickTime and MoviePlayer in **Chapter 6**.

Figure 38.
A standard SimpleText document's icon.

■ SimpleText read only documents, like those that come with Mac OS 8, cannot be edited. You can identify a SimpleText read only document by its icon, which looks like a newspaper (see **Figure 37**). A regular SimpleText document icon looks like a piece of paper with its corner folded down (see **Figure 38**).

■ Although SimpleText offers many of the basic features found in a word processing application, it falls far short of the feature list of word processors like Microsoft Word, Claris MacWrite Pro, and WordPerfect.

■ If you're new to Mac OS, don't skip this section. Not only does it explain how to use SimpleText, but if provides instructions for basic text editing skills—like text entry and the Copy, Cut, and Paste commands—that you'll use in all Mac OS-compatible applications.

Close box Title bar Zoom box Collapse box

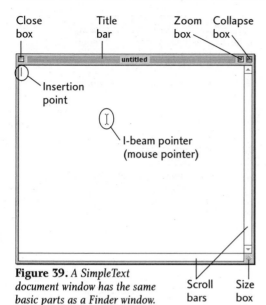

Insertion point

I-beam pointer (mouse pointer)

Figure 39. *A SimpleText document window has the same basic parts as a Finder window.*

Scroll bars Size box

Figure 40. *The text you type appears at the blinking insertion point.*

To launch SimpleText

Double-click the SimpleText application icon.

or

1. Select the SimpleText application icon (see **Figure 3**).

2. Choose Open from the File menu (see **Figure 4**).

   or

   Press ⌘O.

SimpleText launches. An untitled document window appears (see **Figures 5** and **39**).

✔ Tip

■ As illustrated in **Figure 39**, the Simple-Text document window has the same standard window parts found in Finder windows. I tell you how to use Finder windows in **Chapter 2**; SimpleText and other application windows work the same way.

To enter text

Type the text you want to enter. It appears at the blinking insertion point (see **Figure 40**).

✔ Tips

■ It is not necessary to press Return at the end of a line. When the text you type reaches the end of the line, it automatically begins a new line. This is called *word wrap* and is a feature of all word processors.

■ The insertion point moves as you type.

■ To correct an error as you type, press Delete. This key deletes the character to the left of the insertion point.

Launching SimpleText, Entering Text

To move the insertion point

Press ⬅, ➡, ⬇, or ⬆ to move the insertion point left, right, down, or up one character or line at a time.

or

1. Position the mouse pointer, which looks like an I-beam pointer, where you want the insertion point to appear (see **Figure 41**).

2. Click the mouse button once. The insertion point appears at the mouse pointer (see **Figure 42**).

✔ Tips

■ Since the text you type appears at the insertion point, it's a good idea to know where the insertion point is *before* you start typing.

■ When moving the insertion point with the mouse, you must click to complete the move. If you simply point with the I-beam pointer, the insertion point will stay right where it is (see **Figure 41**).

To insert text

1. Position the insertion point where you want the text to appear (see **Figure 43**).

2. Type the text that you want to insert. The text is inserted at the insertion point (see **Figure 44**).

✔ Tip

■ Word wrap changes automatically to accommodate inserted text.

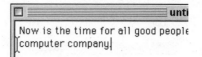

Figure 41. *Position the mouse pointer...*

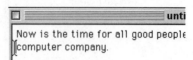

Figure 42. *...and click to move the insertion point.*

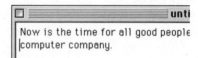

Figure 43. *Position the insertion point...*

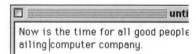

Figure 44. *...and type in the text that you want to appear.*

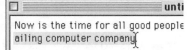

Figure 45. *Drag the mouse pointer over the text that you want to select.*

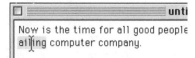

Figure 46. *Double-click the word that you want to select.*

Figure 47. *Choose Select All from the Edit menu.*

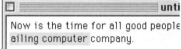

Figure 48. *Select the text that you want to delete.*

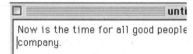

Figure 49. *When you press* [Delete]*, the selected text disappears.*

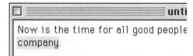

Figure 50. *Select the text that you want to replace.*

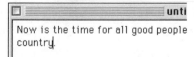

Figure 51. *The text you type replaces the selected text.*

To select text

To select any amount of text, drag the I-beam pointer over the text (see **Figure 45**).

or

To select a single word, double-click the word (see **Figure 46**).

or

To select the entire document, choose Select All from the Edit menu (see **Figure 47**) or press ⌃⌘A.

The text you select becomes highlighted (see **Figures 45** and **46**).

✔ Tips

■ There are other selection techniques in SimpleText and other applications. These are the basic techniques and they work in every application.

■ In some applications, double-clicking a word also selects the space after the word.

To delete text

1. Select the text that you want to delete (see **Figure 48**).

2. Press [Delete] or [Del]. The selected text disappears (see **Figure 49**).

✔ Tip

■ You can delete a character to the left of the insertion point by pressing [Delete]. You can delete a character to the right of the insertion point by pressing [Del].

To replace text

1. Select the text that you want to replace (see **Figure 50**).

2. Type the new text. The selected text is replaced by what you type (see **Figure 51**).

Selecting, Deleting, & Replacing Text

To apply a different font to text

1. Select the text to which you want to apply a different font (see **Figure 52**).

2. Choose a font from the Font menu (see **Figure 53**). The font you chose is applied to the selected text (see **Figure 54**).

✔ Tips

■ Generally speaking, a *font* is style of typeface.

■ The Font menu displays all fonts properly installed in your System.

■ A check mark appears on the Font menu beside the font currently applied to the selected text (see **Figure 53**).

■ I tell you more about fonts in **Chapter 12**.

To change the size of text characters

1. Select the text that you want to resize (see **Figure 54**).

2. Choose a size from the Size menu (see **Figure 55**). The size you chose is applied to the selected text (see **Figure 56**).

✔ Tips

■ The larger the text size, the less text appears on screen or on a printed page.

■ A check mark appears on the Size menu beside the size currently applied to the selected text (see **Figure 55**).

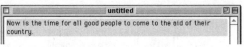

Figure 52. *Select the text to which you want to apply a different font.*

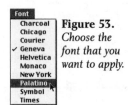

Figure 53. *Choose the font that you want to apply.*

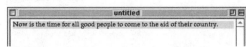

Figure 54. *The font you chose is applied.*

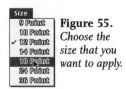

Figure 55. *Choose the size that you want to apply.*

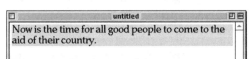

Figure 56. *The size you chose is applied.*

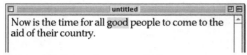

Figure 57. *Select the text to which you want to apply a style.*

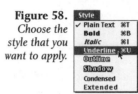

Figure 58. *Choose the style that you want to apply.*

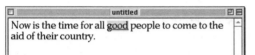

Figure 59. *The style you chose is applied.*

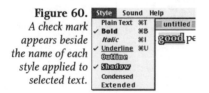

Figure 60. *A check mark appears beside the name of each style applied to selected text.*

To apply a different style to text

1. Select the text to which you want to apply a different style (see **Figure 57**).

2. Choose a style from the Style menu (see **Figure 58**). The style you chose is applied to the selected text (see **Figure 59**).

✔ Tips

■ You can apply more than one style to text (see **Figure 60**). Simply select each style that you want to apply.

■ A check mark appears on the Style menu beside each style applied to a selection (see **Figure 60**).

■ To remove an applied style, choose it from the Style menu again. (This works with all styles except Plain Text.)

■ The Plain Text style removes all other styles from text.

■ Some text styles can be applied with command keys:

▲ To apply Plain Text style, press ⌘T.

▲ To apply Bold style, press ⌘B.

▲ To apply Italic style, press ⌘I.

▲ To apply Underline style, press ⌘U.

Applying Styles

To undo the last action

Choose Undo from the Edit menu (see **Figure 61**).

or

Press ⌘Z.

The last thing you did is undone.

Figure 61. *Choose Undo from the Edit menu.*

✔ Tips

■ The Undo command is available in most applications and can always be found at the top of the Edit menu.

■ Although some programs, like Microsoft Word, offer multiple levels of undo, most programs let you undo only the very last thing you did.

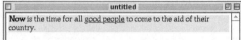

Figure 62. *Select the text you want to copy or cut.*

To copy text

1. Select the text that you want to copy (see **Figure 62**).

2. Choose Copy from the Edit menu (see **Figure 63**).

   or

   Press ⌘C.

   The text is copied to the Clipboard so it can be pasted elsewhere. The original remains in the document.

Figure 63. *To copy the selection to the Clipboard and keep it in the document, choose Copy from the Edit menu.*

To cut text

1. Select the text that you want to cut (see **Figure 62**).

2. Choose Cut from the Edit menu (see **Figure 64**).

   or

   Press ⌘X.

   The text is copied to the Clipboard so it can be pasted elsewhere. The original is removed from the document.

Figure 64. *To copy the selection to the Clipboard and remove it from the document, choose Cut from the Edit menu.*

Figure 65. *Choose Show Clipboard from the Edit menu.*

To view the Clipboard

Choose Show Clipboard from the Edit menu (see **Figure 65**).

Figure 66. *The Clipboard window displays the contents of the Clipboard.*

✔ Tips

- The Clipboard window (see **Figure 66**) displays the last thing you copied or cut.

- The Clipboard is shared by all applications. This makes it possible to copy something created in one document or application and paste it in another.

- Items remain on the Clipboard until you use the Cut or Copy commands again or shut off your computer.

Figure 67. *Choose Hide Clipboard from the Edit menu...*

Figure 68. *...or choose Close from the File menu.*

To close the Clipboard

Click the Clipboard window's close box (see **Figure 66**).

or

Choose Hide Clipboard from the Edit menu (see **Figure 67**).

or

1. If necessary, activate the Clipboard window.

2. Choose Close from the File menu (see **Figure 68**).

   or

   Press ⌘⌘W.

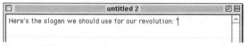

Figure 69. *Position the insertion point where you want the contents of the Clipboard to appear.*

Figure 70. *Choose Paste from the Edit menu.*

To paste Clipboard contents

1. Position the insertion point where you want the Clipboard contents to appear (see **Figure 69**).

2. Choose Paste from the Edit menu (see **Figure 70**).

   or

   Press ⌘⌘V.

   The Clipboard's contents are pasted into the document (see **Figure 71**).

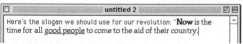

Figure 71. *The contents of the Clipboard are pasted into the document.*

To find text

1. Choose Find from the Edit menu (see **Figure 72**) or press ⌘F. The Find dialog box appears (see **Figure 73**).

2. Enter the text that you want to find in the edit box.

3. Click Find or press Return or Enter. The text that you are searching for is highlighted and the dialog box disappears.

To replace text

1. Choose Replace from the Edit menu (see **Figure 72**) or press ⌘R. The Replace dialog box appears (see **Figure 74**).

2. Enter the text that you want to find in the top edit box.

3. Enter the text that you want to replace it with in the bottom edit box.

4. To replace just the next occurrence of the text, click Replace or press Return or Enter. The text is replaced and the dialog box disappears.

   or

   To replace all occurrences of the text, click Replace All. Every occurrence of the text from the insertion point to the end of the document is replaced and the dialog box disappears.

✔ Find & Replace Tips

■ Once you've conducted a search, you can use the Find Again (⌘G) or Replace Again (⌘D) commands under the Edit menu (see **Figure 75**) to repeat the Find or Replace procedure with the same settings.

■ To find only those instances of the text that match the capitalization of the text you want to find, turn on the Case Sensitive check box (see **Figures 73** and **Figure 74**).

Figure 72.
You'll find the Find and Replace commands on the Edit menu.

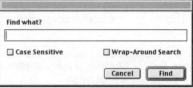

Figure 73. *Use the Find dialog box to enter the text that you want to find.*

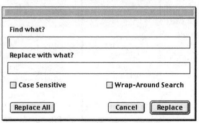

Figure 74. *Use the Replace dialog box to enter the text that you want to find and the text that you want to replace it with.*

Figure 75.
Once you're entered information in the Find or Replace dialog box, you can use the Find Again or Replace Again commands.

■ To continue the search at the beginning of the document, turn on the Wrap-Around Search check box (see **Figures 73** and **74**). Otherwise, the search begins at the insertion point and ends at the end of the document.

Finding & Replacing Text

Figure 76.
Choose the Speak Selection command to have your computer read selected text...

Figure 77.
...or choose the Speak All command to have your computer read all the text in the document.

Figure 78.
Choose Stop Speaking to shut your computer up.

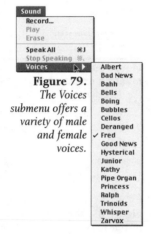

Figure 79.
The Voices submenu offers a variety of male and female voices.

Figure 80.
Choose Record from the Sound menu.

Figure 81. *Use the Recording dialog box to record and save a sound.*

Figure 82.
Once you've recorded a sound, you can use the Play and Erase commands.

To speak text

1. Select the text you want to hear.
2. Choose Speak Selection from the Sound menu (see **Figure 76**) or press ⌘J.

or

1. Make sure no text is selected.
2. Choose Speak All from the Sound menu (see **Figure 77**) or press ⌘J.

✔ Tips

■ You can stop text from being spoken by choosing Stop Speaking from the Sound menu (see **Figure 78**) or pressing ⌘. .

■ You can change the voice with which text is spoken by choosing a voice from the Voices submenu under the Sound menu (see **Figure 79**).

■ I tell you more about speaking text and alerts in **Chapter 12**.

To record & play a sounds

1. Choose Record from the Sound menu (see **Figure 80**).
2. Use the Recording dialog box that appears (see **Figure 81**) to record a sound.
3. Click Save to save the sound in the file.
4. Choose Play from the Sound menu (see **Figure 82**) to play back the sound.

✔ Tips

■ Your computer must have a microphone to record sounds.

■ I tell you how to use the Recording dialog box in **Chapter 6**.

■ You can only record one sound per SimpleText document.

■ To erase the sound, choose Erase from the Sound menu (see **Figure 82**).

Speaking Text & Recording Sounds

To save a document for the first time

1. Choose Save from the File menu (see **Figure 83**).

   or

   Press ⌘ ⌘ S.

   or

   Choose Save As from the File menu (see **Figure 83**).

2. Use the Save As dialog box that appears to enter a name and select a location for the file (see **Figure 84**).

3. Click Save or press Return or Enter.

The document is saved with the name you entered in the location you specified. The name of the document appears on the document's title bar (see **Figure 85**).

✔ Tip

■ I tell you how to use the Save As dialog box earlier in this chapter.

To save changes to an existing document

Choose Save from the File menu (see **Figure 83**).

or

Press ⌘ ⌘ S.

The document is saved. No dialog box appears.

✔ Tip

■ It's a good idea to save changes to a document frequently as you work with it. This helps prevent loss of data in the event of a system crash or power outage.

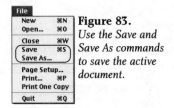

Figure 83.
Use the Save and Save As commands to save the active document.

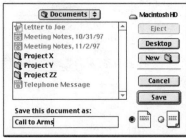

Figure 84. *Use the Save As dialog box to enter a name and select a location for the document.*

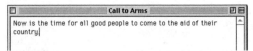

Figure 85. *The name of the document appears in its title bar.*

Figure 86. *Use the Save As dialog box to change the name or location (or both) for the file.*

Figure 87. *The document's new name appears in its title bar.*

Figure 88. *Choose Open from the File menu.*

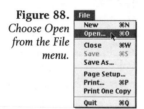

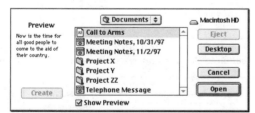

Figure 89. *Use the Open dialog box to locate and open a document.*

To save an existing document with a new name or in a new location

1. Choose Save As from the File menu (see **Figure 83**).

2. Use the Save As dialog box that appears to enter a different name or select a different location (or both) for the file (see **Figure 86**).

3. Click Save or press [Return] or [Enter].

A copy of the document is saved with the name you entered in the location you specified. The new document name appears in the document's title bar (see **Figure 87**). The original document remains untouched.

✔ Tip

■ You can use the Save As command to create a new document based on an existing document—without overwriting the original document with your changes.

To open a document

1. Choose Open from the File menu (see **Figure 88**).

   or

   Press ⌘O.

2. Use the Open dialog box that appears to locate and select the document that you want to open (see **Figure 89**).

3. Click Open or press [Return] or [Enter].

✔ Tip

■ I tell you how to use the Open dialog box earlier in this chapter.

Saving & Opening Documents

About Stationery Pads

A *stationery pad is* a document used as a form for creating similar documents. It's like a template—you open and modify it to suit your specific needs. When you're ready to save it, it automatically prompts you to give it a different name, making it very difficult to overwrite the original file.

To turn an existing document into a stationery pad

1. Select the icon for the document that you want to turn into a stationery pad (see **Figure 90**).

2. Choose Get Info from the File menu (see **Figure 91**) or press ⌘ I. The Info window for the file appears.

3. Turn on the Stationery Pad check box (see **Figure 92**).

4. Close the Info window.

✔ Tip

■ I tell you more about the Info window in **Chapter 4**.

To create a stationery pad from scratch

1. In the application of your choice, create the document that you want to turn into a stationery pad.

2. Choose Save As from the File menu.

3. In the Save As dialog box, enter a name for the file, select a disk location, and choose a file type of Stationery or Stationery Pad (see **Figures 93** and **94**).

✔ Tip

■ Not all applications let you save files as Stationery. If the application you want to use doesn't, save the file as a regular document and turn it into a stationery pad in the Finder as instructed above.

Figure 90.
Select the icon for the file that you want to turn into a stationery pad.

Figure 91.
Choose Get Info from the File menu.

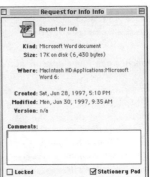

Figure 92.
Turn on the Stationery Pad check box in the Info window.

Figure 93. *SimpleText offers a radio button to choose stationery pad format.*

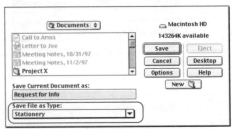

Figure 94. *Word offers a pop-up menu for file types, including stationery pad format.*

About Macintosh Drag & Drop

Macintosh drag and drop is a feature of Mac OS that is supported by many applications. It enables you to copy or move information by dragging selections from one location to another:

- Dragging a selection from one location in a document window to another moves the selection.

- Dragging a selection from one document window to another in the same application copies the selection.

- Dragging a selection from one application's document window to another application's document window copies the selection.

- Dragging a selection from a document window to the Finder creates a clipping file (see **Figure 95**) containing the selection (see **Figure 96**).

- Dragging a Finder icon into a document window copies the contents of that icon into the document.

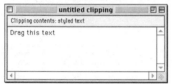

Figure 95. *Dragging a selection from a document window to the Finder creates a clipping file.* untitled clipping

✔ Tips

- Not all applications support Macintosh drag and drop. Try it in your favorite applications to see if they do.

- A selection can include text or graphics or sometimes a combination of the two.

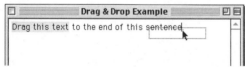

Figure 96. *Opening a clipping file displays its contents in a window.*

To use Macintosh drag & drop

1. Select the text or graphics that you want to move or copy.

2. Drag the selection to the new destination. Depending on what you're dragging, an insertion point might appear to indicate where the selection will be inserted (see **Figure 97**).

3. When the selection is in the desired position, release the mouse button. The selection moves (see **Figure 98**) or is copied.

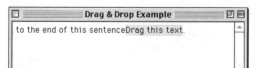

Figure 97. *Drag the selection to a new destination.*

Figure 98. *When you release the mouse button, the selection moves.*

About RAM

RAM (random access memory) is your computer's working memory. All the applications and documents you open are loaded into RAM so your computer's *CPU* (central processing unit) can access them quickly.

The amount of RAM an application needs in order to run is called its *RAM allocation* or *application heap*. Although every application's RAM allocation is preset by the programmer, you can raise it to make the application run more smoothly or lower it so the application requires less RAM to run.

✔ Tips

- Don't confuse memory or RAM with hard disk space. I tell you about hard disks in **Chapter 3**.
- The more RAM your computer has, the more applications it can run at once.
- Programs that work with large graphics files, like Photoshop and Director, need lots of RAM to work efficiently.
- Lowering an application's RAM allocation isn't recommended because it can cause the application to behave erratically and unexpectedly crash.

To change an application's RAM allocation

1. Select the icon for the application whose RAM allocation you want to change (see **Figure 99**).

2. Choose Get Info from the File menu (see **Figure 91**). The Info window for the application appears (see **Figure 100**).

3. Enter a value for the desired RAM allocation in the Preferred Size edit box (see **Figure 101**).

4. Close the Info window.

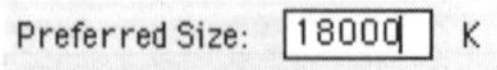

Figure 99. *Select the icon for the application whose RAM allocation you want to change.*

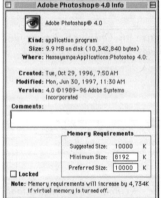

Figure 100. *Use the Info window to change an application's RAM allocation.*

Preferred Size: 18000 K

Figure 101. *Enter the desired RAM allocation value in the Preferred Size edit box.*

About OpenDoc

OpenDoc is a component software technology developed by Apple Computer, Inc. that is included with Mac OS 8. Rather than having one application with lots of features, you can use OpenDoc containers and parts to build documents with only the features you need.

For example, say you wanted to create a report that included text, graphics, and a chart. You'd start with an OpenDoc-aware application that would act as a *container*. Then you'd drag and drop mini-applications called *parts* into the container —one each for text, graphics, and chart editing. You'd create your document using the parts you added.

✔ Tips

■ Although OpenDoc technology is available now, it isn't widely used. In the spring of 1997, Apple announced that it would drop OpenDoc technology for future versions of the Mac OS.

■ To make the most of OpenDoc, you need OpenDoc containers and parts, which are available from Apple and third-party vendors.

■ You can learn more about OpenDoc by reading the documents in the Stationery folder that is automatically copied to your hard disk with OpenDoc.

About OpenDoc

USING MAC OS 8 UTILITIES

About Mac OS 8 Utilities

In addition to SimpleText, which I discuss in **Chapter 5**, Mac OS 8 includes a number of small applications and utilities that are automatically installed when you complete a basic installation:

- **Apple Menu Items**, such as Apple System Profiler, Calculator, Graphing Calculator, Find File, Jigsaw Puzzle, Key Caps, Note Pad, ScrapBook, Simple-Sound, Stickies, and recent items.

- **Player software**, including MoviePlayer, AppleCD Audio Player, and Apple Video Player.

- **Disk utilities**, such as Disk First Aid and Drive Setup.

- **AppleScript** and Automated Tasks applets.

I tell you about all these programs in this chapter.

✔ Tip

- I tell you about Mac OS 8 components in the **Introduction** and about installing Mac OS in **Chapter 1**.

About Apple Menu Items

The Apple menu (see **Figure 1**) offers easy access to whatever applications, documents, folders, or other items you want to put there. It also automatically keeps track of recently used documents, applications, and network servers.

In the following pages, I tell you:

■ How to open and use many of the items on the Apple menu.

■ How to add items to the Apple menu.

■ How to customize the appearance and functionality of the Apple menu.

✔ Tip

■ Here's some operating system trivia: Back in the days before System 7, when the average Macintosh had only 1 MB of RAM, the Apple menu offered users access to little programs called *desk accessories* that could be opened and used at any time—even when another program was running. Although it doesn't sound impressive now, back then it was a very big deal.

To open an Apple menu item

Choose the item from the Apple menu (see **Figure 2**).

or

Choose the item from a submenu under the Apple menu (see **Figure 3**).

✔ Tips

■ An item with a submenu is a folder. Mac OS automatically creates a submenu that lists the contents of the folder.

■ I tell you about using menus, including submenus, in **Chapter 2**.

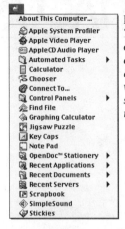

Figure 1.
The Apple menu offers quick and easy access to just about anything you want. These are the standard Apple menu items.

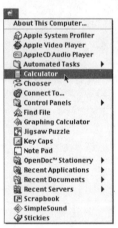

Figure 2.
Choose the item that you want.

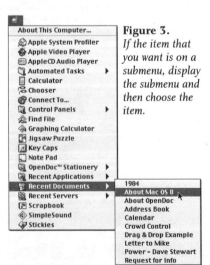

Figure 3.
If the item that you want is on a submenu, display the submenu and then choose the item.

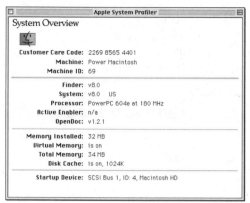

Figure 4. *The Apple System Profiler's System Overview window provides information about your computer and Mac OS version.*

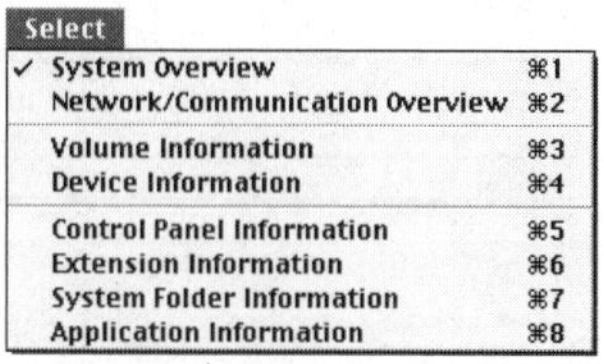

Figure 5.
To view other information about your system, choose an option from the Select menu.

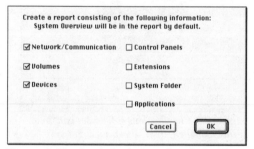

Figure 6. *Use this dialog box to select the items that you want to include in a report.*

Figure 7.
Here's the beginning of a report for my system.

To use Apple System Profiler

1. Choose Apple System Profiler from the Apple menu (see **Figure 1**). The System Overview window appears (see **Figure 4**).

2. To view other information about your system, choose an option from the Select menu (see **Figure 5**):

   ▲ **System Overview** (see **Figure 4**) provides information about your computer and Mac OS version.

   ▲ **Network/Communications Overview** provides information about network and Internet connections.

   ▲ **Volume Information** lists all accessible storage media.

   ▲ **Device Information** provides information about devices attached to your computer.

   ▲ **Control Panel Information** lists all installed control panels.

   ▲ **Extension Information** lists all installed extensions.

   ▲ **System Information** lists all System Folders on your startup disk.

   ▲ **Application Information** lists all installed applications.

3. To create a report, choose Create Report from the File menu. In the dialog box that appears (see **Figure 6**), turn on the check boxes for the information that you want, then click OK to generate the report (see **Figure 7**).

✔ Tips

■ You can use the File menu's Save As and Print commands to save and print reports you create. I tell you about saving documents in **Chapter 5** and about printing in **Chapter 8**.

■ I tell you about networking in **Chapter 9**, connecting to the Internet in **Chapter 10**, control panels and extensions in **Chapter 12**, and applications in **Chapter 5**.

107

To use the Calculator

1. Choose Calculator from the Apple menu (see **Figure 2**). The Calculator window appears (see **Figure 8**).

2. Use your mouse to click buttons for numbers and operators.

   or

   Press keyboard keys corresponding to numbers and operators.

   The numbers you enter and the results of your calculations appear at the top of the Calculator window.

✔ Tip

■ You can use the Cut, Copy, and Paste commands to copy the results of calculations into documents. I tell you about cutting and copying in **Chapter 5**.

To use the Graphing Calculator

1. Choose Graphing Calculator from the Apple menu (see **Figure 1**). The Graphing Calculator window appears (see **Figure 9**).

2. Enter the formula that you want to graph in the top of the window.

3. Click Graph to create the graph (see **Figure 10**).

✔ Tips

■ If the graph you create is three-dimensional (see **Figure 10**), it rotates.

■ You can use commands under the Demo menu (see **Figure 11**) to view Graphing Calculator demonstrations.

■ To display a clickable keypad of functions that you can include in your formulas (see **Figure 12**), choose Show Full Keypad or Show Small Keypad from the Equation menu.

■ You can use the Copy Graph command under the edit menu to copy the graph for inclusion in other documents.

Figure 8.
The Calculator desk accessory has the same functionality as a $5 pocket calculator.

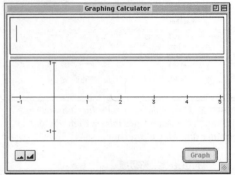

Figure 9. *The Graphing Calculator window.*

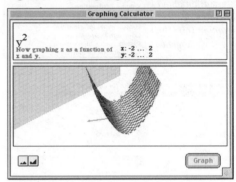

Figure 10. *The Graphing Calculator can even create animated, three-dimensional graphs.*

Figure 11.
Use the Demo menu to view a variety of Graphing Calculator demos.

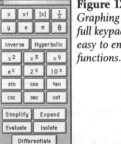

Figure 12.
Graphing Calculator's full keypad makes it easy to enter complex functions.

Figure 13.
Choose Find File from the Finder's File menu.

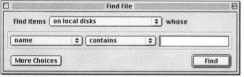

Figure 14. *The Find File window lets you set up search criteria.*

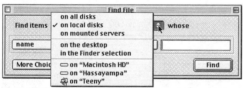

Figure 15. *Choose a location to search from the pop-up menu at the top of the Find File window.*

Figure 16.
Choose a criteria type from the first pop-up menu in the middle of the Find File window.

To use Find File

1. Choose Find File from the Apple menu (see **Figure 1**).

   or

   Choose Find from the Finder's File menu (see **Figure 13**) or press ⌘F.

   The Find File window appears (see **Figure 14**).

2. Choose a search location from the pop-up menu at the top of the window (see **Figure 15**).

3. Use the first pop-up menu in the middle of the window to choose a criteria type (see **Figure 16**). Your options are:

   ▲ **Name** is the name of the item.

   ▲ **Size** is the size of the file, in kilobytes.

   ▲ **Kind** is the type of item.

   ▲ **Label** is the Finder label assigned to the item.

   ▲ **Date created** is the date the item was created.

   ▲ **Date modified** is the date the item was changed.

   ▲ **Version** is the item's version number.

   ▲ **Comments** is the text entered into the Comments field of the item's Info window.

   ▲ **Lock attribute** is whether the item is locked or unlocked.

   ▲ **Folder attribute** is whether the item is or isn't a folder.

   ▲ **File type** is the four-character, case-sensitive type code assigned to the item.

   ▲ **Creator** is the four-character, case-sensitive creator code assigned to the item.

(continued on next page)

(continued from previous page)

4. Use the pop-up menu and edit box beside the criteria type to complete the search criteria. The options that appear in the pop-up menu vary depending on the criteria type you chose in step 3.

5. Click Find. The Items Found window, which contains the results of the search, appears (see **Figure 17**).

6. To open a found item, double-click its name in the top half of the Items Found window.

or

To view the location of a found item, click it once and look at the folder hierarchy in the bottom half of the Items Found window (see **Figure 17**).

✔ Tips

■ To narrow down your search to a specific folder, select the folder before opening the Find File window. Then choose in the Finder Selection from the top pop-up menu (see **Figure 15**).

■ I tell you about file attributes like name, size, label, and creation date in **Chapters 2** and **3**.

■ To enter a date, you must select each part of the date individually and click the up or down triangles beside it to increment or decrement the value (see **Figure 18**).

■ To include additional search criteria, click the More Choices button in the Find File window. The window expands to add an additional line of criteria (see **Figure 19**). When performing the search, Mac OS matches all criteria.

■ If you hold down Option while pulling down the criteria type pop-up menu in step 3, additional, more advanced options appear (see **Figure 20**).

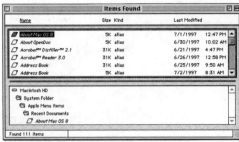

Figure 17. *The items found window lists all items that match the search criteria.*

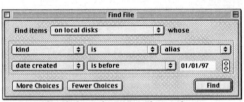

Figure 18. *Click the triangles beside the date to change digits.*

Figure 19. *Clicking the More Choices button expands the Find File window.*

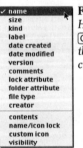

Figure 20. *Holding down* Option *expands the list of criteria types.*

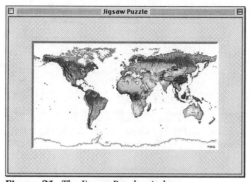

Figure 21. *The Jigsaw Puzzle window.*

Figure 22.
Choose Start New Puzzle from the Options menu.

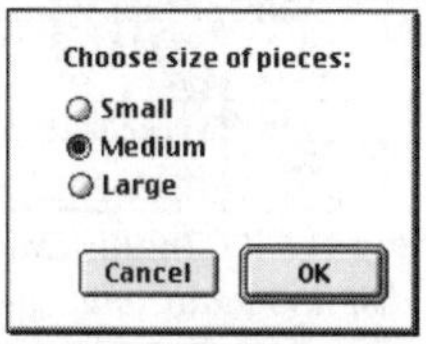

Figure 23.
Select the size that you want for the puzzle pieces.

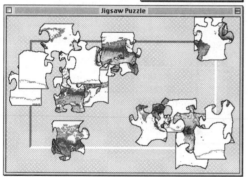

Figure 24. *The puzzle pieces are scattered in the window.*

Figure 25. *You can take your favorite picture and turn it into a puzzle by just copying it and pasting it in.*

To use the Jigsaw Puzzle

1. Choose Jigsaw Puzzle from the Apple menu (see **Figure 1**). The Jigsaw Puzzle window appears (see **Figure 21**).

2. Choose Start New Puzzle from the Options menu (see **Figure 22**).

3. In the dialog box that appears (see **Figure 23**), select the radio button for the size of the pieces you want. Then click OK. The picture breaks up into puzzle pieces that are scattered in the window (see **Figure 24**).

4. Drag the pieces into their proper position in the puzzle window. When in the correct position, they "snap" into place with a sound.

✔ Tips

■ The smaller the pieces you select in step 3, the more difficult the puzzle will be.

■ To have the puzzle solved automatically for you, choose Solve Puzzle from the Options menu.

■ To change the picture in the puzzle, use SimpleText or your favorite graphics application to open a picture that you like. Use the Edit menu's Copy command to copy the picture to the Clipboard. Then switch back to Jigsaw Puzzle and use the Edit menu's Paste command to paste the picture in (see **Figure 25**).

Using the Jigsaw Puzzle

To use Key Caps

1. Choose Key Caps from the Apple menu (see **Figure 1**). The Key Caps window appears (see **Figure 26**). It displays keyboard characters in a specific font.

2. To see what characters look like with various modifier keys pressed (like (Shift), (Option), or (Control)), press the modifier key. The characters in the Key Caps window change (see **Figure 27**).

3. To see what the characters of a different font look like, choose the font from the Key Caps menu (see **Figure 28**). The characters in the Key Caps window change (see **Figure 29**).

✔ Tips

■ You can type in the Key Caps window to see what a string of text looks like.

■ Key Caps offers a great way to learn where special characters are hidden away in a font. For example, if you hold down (Option) while looking at the Key Caps window (see **Figure 27**), you can see characters like a bullet (•), trademark symbol (™), registered trademark symbol (®), and copyright symbol (©). To type one of these characters in a document, simply hold down (Option) while pressing the appropriate keyboard key—(Option)(8) for •, (Option)(2) for ™, (Option)(R) for ®, (Option)(G) for ©, etc.

■ Some special characters, like accented characters (é, á, ü, etc.) require two keystrokes to type. First type the keystroke for the accent that you want, then type the character that you want the accent to appear over. For example, to type á, press (Option)(E) and then (A). The two-stroke characters appear in Key Caps with a gray box around them (see **Figure 27**).

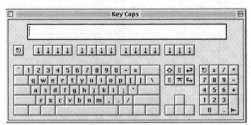

Figure 26. *The Key Caps window displaying some characters of the Charcoal font.*

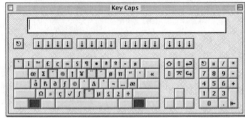

Figure 27. *In this example, holding down (Option) displays additional characters in the Charcoal font.*

Figure 28.
Choose the font whose characters you want to view from the Key Caps menu...

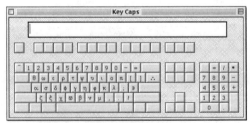

Figure 29. *...and they appear in the Key Caps window.*

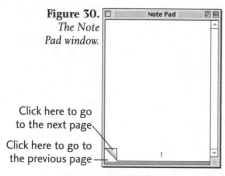

Figure 30.
The Note Pad window.

Click here to go to the next page

Click here to go to the previous page

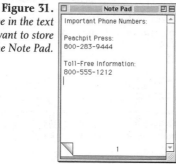

Figure 31.
Type in the text you want to store in the Note Pad.

Figure 32.
The File menu offers commands for creating, deleting, and printing notes.

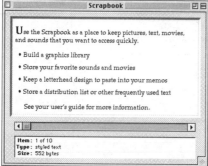

Figure 33. *The Scrapbook window.*

Figure 34.
Use the Edit menu's commands to use, add, or remove Scrapbook items.

To use the Note Pad

1. Choose Note Pad from the Apple menu (see **Figure 1**). The Note Pad window appears (see **Figure 30**).

2. Type or paste in the text you want to store in the Note Pad (see **Figure 31**).

✔ Tips

■ To turn the page, click the "folded up" corner of the page (see **Figure 30**).

■ The Note Pad starts with eight notes. You can add or remove notes using the File menu's New Note and Delete Note commands (see **Figure 32**).

■ You can print notes using the File Menu's Print Current Note or Print One commands (see **Figure 32**). I tell you more about printing in **Chapter 8**.

■ The contents of the Note Pad are automatically saved when you close it.

To use the Scrapbook

1. Choose Scrapbook from the Apple menu (see **Figure 1**). The Scrapbook window appears (see **Figure 33**).

2. Click the scroll bar arrows to view the entries in the Scrapbook file.

3. Use Edit menu commands (see **Figure 34**) to copy or cut a Scrapbook item to the Clipboard, paste a Clipboard item into the Scrapbook, or clear an item from the Scrapbook.

✔ Tips

■ You can use the scrapbook to store formatted text, graphics, movies, and sounds.

■ I tell you about the Copy, Cut, and Paste commands in **Chapter 5**.

■ The contents of the Scrapbook are automatically saved when you close it.

Using the Note Pad & Scrapbook

To use SimpleSound

1. Choose SimpleSound from the Apple menu (see **Figure 1**). The Alert Sounds window appears (see **Figure 35**).

2. To change the alert sound, click the name of the sound that you want. It plays so you can hear it.

3. To delete a sound, select it and click Remove. In the confirmation dialog box that appears (see **Figure 36**), click OK.

4. To add an alert sound, click Add.

   or

   To create a sound file, choose New from the File menu or press ⌘N.

   The Recording dialog box appears (see **Figure 37**). Follow the instructions below to record, test, and save a sound. If you added an alert sound, it appears with the others in the Alert Sounds window (see **Figure 38**). If you created a sound file, a document window with the file name appears (see **Figure 39**).

To use the Recording dialog box

1. Click Record and record a sound with your microphone.

2. When you are finished recording the sound, click Stop.

3. To play back the sound, click Play.

4. To save the sound, click Save.

   If you are recording a new alert sound, a dialog box like the one in **Figure 40a** appears. Enter a name and click OK.

   or

   If you are creating a sound file, a Save As dialog box appears (see **Figure 40b**). Enter a name and select a disk location for the file, then click Save.

✔ Tip

■ I tell you how to use the Save As dialog box in **Chapter 5**.

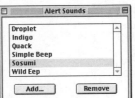

Figure 35. *The Alert Sounds window lists all installed alert sounds.*

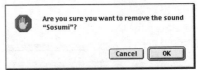

Figure 36. *This confirmation window appears when you try to delete a sound.*

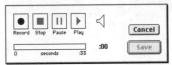

Figure 37. *Use the Recording dialog box to record, play, and save a sound.*

Figure 38. *The Alert Sounds window also lists the sounds you add.*

Figure 39. *A sound document window.*

Figure 40a. *You'll see this dialog box when you save an alert sound…*

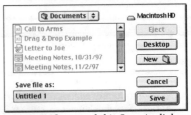

Figure 40b. *…and this Save As dialog box when you save a sound file.*

Close box   Zoom box

Figure 41.
*An empty
Stickies note.*

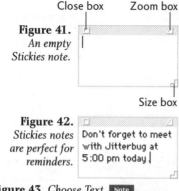

Size box

Figure 42.
*Stickies notes
are perfect for
reminders.*

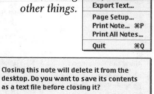

Figure 43. *Choose Text
Style from the Note menu.*

Figure 44.
*Use the Text Style
menu to format
the text in a note.*

Figure 45.
*Use the Color
menu to change
the color of a note.*

Figure 46.
*The File menu lets
you create, save, and
print notes, among
other things.*

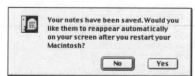

Figure 47. *This dialog box appears when
you click a note's close box.*

Figure 48. *This dialog box appears the
first time you quit Stickies.*

To use Stickies

1. Choose Stickies from the Apple menu
(see **Figure 1**). A Stickies note window
should appear (see **Figure 41**); if one
doesn't appear, choose New Note from
the File menu or press ⌘N.

2. Type the text that you want to include
in the note (see **Figure 42**).

3. To change the style of note text, choose
Text Style from the Note menu (see
Figure 43) or press ⌘T. Select font,
size, and style options in the Text Style
dialog box that appears (see **Figure
44**). Then click OK. All the text in the
note changes.

4. To change the color of the note, choose
a color from the Color menu (see
Figure 45).

✔ Tips

- You can use options under the File
menu (see **Figure 46**) to create a new
note, save all notes, or print notes.

- If you close a Stickies note, a dialog box
like the one in **Figure 47** tells you it
will be deleted from the Desktop and
offers to save its contents to a text file.
If you click Save, use a Save As dialog
box to save the note as text.

- Stickies notes remain on the Desktop
until you quit Stickies.

- When you quit Stickies, all note are
automatically saved to disk.

- The first time you quit Stickies, a dialog
box like the one in **Figure 48** lets you
specify whether you want Stickies to
automatically appear on your Desktop
when you restart your computer.

Using Stickies

To open recent items

To open a recently used application, choose its name from the Recent Applications submenu under the Apple menu (see **Figure 49**).

or

To open a recently used document, choose its name from the Recent Document submenu under the Apple menu (see **Figure 50**).

or

To open a recently used server, choose its name from the Recent Servers submenu under the Apple menu (see **Figure 51**).

✔ Tips

■ Mac OS automatically tracks the ten most recently used applications, documents, and servers. You can change the number of tracked items in the Apple Menu Options control panel, which I tell you about later in this chapter.

■ If your computer is not connected to a network, or you have never connected to a network server, there will be no Recent Servers submenu.

■ When you select a server from the Recent Servers submenu, you may be prompted to log on to the server machine.

■ I tell you about applications and documents in **Chapter 5** and about servers in **Chapter 9**.

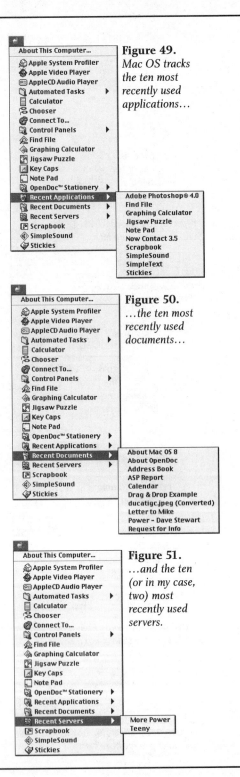

Figure 49.
Mac OS tracks the ten most recently used applications...

Figure 50.
...the ten most recently used documents...

Figure 51.
...and the ten (or in my case, two) most recently used servers.

Opening Recent Items

Figure 52. *Drag the item that you want to add to the Apple menu into the Apple Menu Items folder in your System folder.*

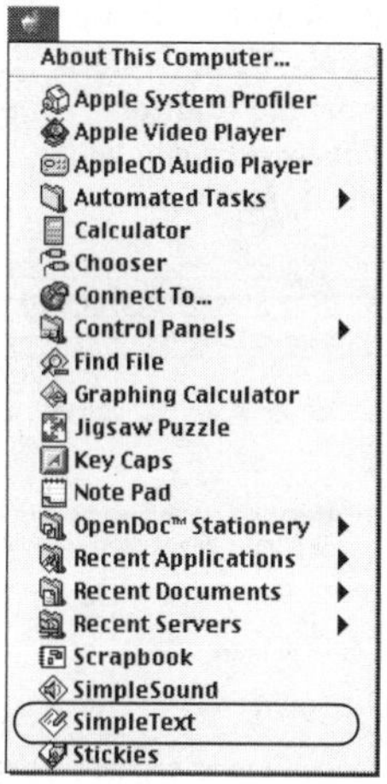

Figure 53. *The item is added to the Apple menu.*

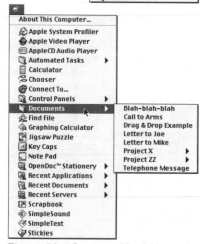

Figure 54. *When you add a folder to the Apple Menu items folder, it becomes a submenu.*

To add items to the Apple menu

1. Open the the icon for your computer's startup disk.

2. Locate and open the icon for the System Folder.

3. Drag the item that you want to add to the Apple menu into the Apple Menu Items folder in your System folder (see **Figure 52**). The item is added to the Apple menu (see **Figure 53**).

✔ Tips

■ Adding items to the Apple menu is a great way to make them quick and easy to access.

■ Your computer's startup disk is normally its internal hard disk.

■ It's a good idea to add an alias of an item to the Apple Menu Items folder rather than the original item. This makes it easy to keep applications and documents where they belong so they're easy to find and back up. I tell you about aliases in **Chapter 4**.

■ When you add a folder or an alias to a folder to the Apple Menu Items folder, a submenu with the folder's contents is automatically created (see **Figure 54**).

Adding Items to the Apple Menu

117

To set Apple Menu Options

1. Choose Apple Menu Options from the Control Panels submenu under the Apple menu (see **Figure 55**). The Apple Menu Options control panel appears (see **Figure 56**).

2. To display the contents of folders in the Apple menu as submenus, select the On radio button under Submenus.

   or

   To display the folders in the Apple menu as items without submenus, select the Off radio button under Submenus.

3. To have Mac OS automatically track recently used items, make sure the Remember recently used items check box is turned on. Then enter values in the three edit boxes to specify the number of recent items Mac OS should track.

4. Close the Apple Menu Options control panel window to save your settings.

✔ Tips

■ I tell you more about control panels in **Chapter 12**.

■ The submenus feature, which is often referred to as *hierarchical folders*, can display up to five levels of folders (see **Figure 57**).

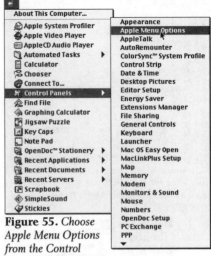

Figure 55. *Choose Apple Menu Options from the Control Panels submenu under the Apple menu.*

Figure 56.
The Apple Menu Options control panel gives you some control over the way the Apple menu works.

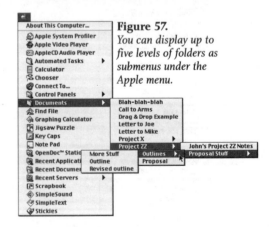

Figure 57.
You can display up to five levels of folders as submenus under the Apple menu.

About Apple Video Player

Apple Video Player enables you to view and record video on your computer. To use it:

- Your computer must have video-in ports.

- You must use appropriate cables to connect video equipment, such as a camcorder, to your computer.

✔ Tips

- Check the manuals that came with your computer to learn whether your computer has video-in ports.

- If Apple Video Player was not automatically installed as part of a basic Mac OS 8 installation, your computer probably does not support it. I tell you about Mac OS 8 components in the **Introduction** and about installing Mac OS 8 in **Chapter 1**.

Figure 58. *Apple Video Player's two main windows.*

To launch Apple Video Player

Choose Apple Video Player from the Apple menu (see **Figure 1**). Apple Video Player's two main windows—Video and Controls—appear (see **Figure 58**).

✔ Tips

- You can also launch Apple Video Player by opening its icon (see **Figure 59**), which you can find in the Applications folder on your hard disk.

- The Video window is blank when no video source is connected.

Figure 59.
Another way to launch Apple Video Player is to open its icon. Apple Video Player

To set the video source and adjust the picture

1. Click the second button on the left side of the Controls window. A number of video controls appear (see **Figure 60**).

2. In the Video Source area, click the button for the type of video connected to your computer. If everything is properly connected, a picture should appear in the Video window (see **Figure 61**).

3. Use the Brightness, Sharpness, Contrast, and Color sliders (see **Figure 60**) to adjust the picture.

To capture a picture or movie

1. Click the first button on the left side of the Controls window. Controls to capture a picture or movie appear (see **Figure 62**).

2. To capture a picture, click Freeze. The image on the screen freezes. Click Save and use the Save As dialog box (see **Figure 63**) to enter a name, select a disk location, and save the picture file.

   or

   To capture a movie, click Record. The button turns into a Stop button as the image on screen is recorded. When you're finished, click Stop. A special Save As dialog box appears (see **Figure 64**). Use it to enter a name, select a disk location, and save the movie file.

✔ Tips

■ Pictures are saved as PICT format files. Movies are saved as QuickTime movie files.

■ I tell you how to use the Save As dialog box in **Chapter 5**. I tell you more about QuickTime a little later in this chapter.

Figure 60. *Apple Video Player's video controls.*

Figure 61. *Now you know what a computer book author looks like a week before a deadline.*

Figure 62. *Apple Video Player's capture controls.*

Figure 63. *Use this Save As dialog box to save a captured picture…*

Figure 64. *…and this one to save a captured movie.*

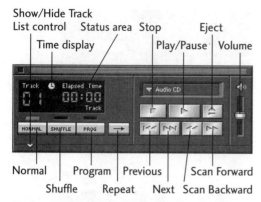

Show/Hide Track
List control   Status area   Stop   Eject
    Time display   Play/Pause   Volume

Normal   Program | Previous   Scan Forward
    Shuffle   Repeat   Next   Scan Backward

Figure 65. *The controls on AppleCD Audio Player look a lot like the ones you'd find on a regular CD player.*

Figure 66.
Another way to launch AppleCD Audio Player is to open its icon. AppleCD Audio Player

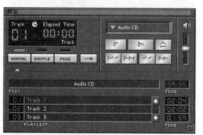

Figure 67. *AppleCD Audio Player's window expanded to show the play list.*

Figure 68. *If you enter CD and track information, it will automatically appear the next time you play the CD.*

About AppleCD Audio Player

AppleCD Audio Player enables you to play audio compact discs on your internal CD-ROM drive.

✔ Tip

■ You insert an audio CD disc just like you insert a CD-ROM disc. I tell you how in **Chapter 3**.

To launch AppleCD Audio Player

Choose AppleCD Audio Player from the Apple menu (see **Figure 1**). The AppleCD Audio Player window appears (see **Figure 65**).

✔ Tips

■ You can also launch AppleCD Audio Player by opening its icon (see **Figure 66**), which you can find in the Applications folder on your hard disk.

■ The AppleCD Audio Player window's status area is blank when no audio CD is in the CD-ROM drive.

To show the play list

Click the Show/Hide Track List control button (see **Figure 65**). The window expands to show the play list (see **Figure 67**).

✔ Tip

■ If desired, you can enter the name of the CD and each CD track in the edit boxes of AppleCD Audio Player. Click a box to select it, then type in the appropriate information. **Figure 68** shows an example. The information you enter is saved to a preferences file so it appears automatically when you play the CD.

To control audio CD play

Click the control buttons (see **Figure 65**) to control the play of an audio CD:

- **Normal** plays CD tracks in order.
- **Shuffle** plays CD tracks in random order.
- **Program** plays CD tracks in the order you specify in the Playlist (see "To program CD play" below).
- **Repeat** plays the CD until you stop it.
- **Stop** stops play.
- **Play/Pause** starts play or, if the CD is already playing, pauses play.
- **Previous** plays the previous track.
- **Next** plays the next track.
- **Scan Backward** quickly reverses the CD.
- **Scan Forward** fast forwards the CD.
- **Eject** ejects the CD.
- **Volume** control changes play volume; drag the slider up or down.

To program CD play

1. If necessary, display the play list (see **Figures 67** and **68**).

2. Click Program (see **Figure 65**). The Playlist area changes to display Tracks and Playlist (see **Figure 69**).

3. Drag a track from the Tracks side to the Playlist side (see **Figure 70**). When you release the mouse button, the track appears on the Playlist side (see **Figure 71**).

4. Repeat step 3 for each track that you want to include in the program.

To customize AppleCD Audio Player appearance & sound

Choose options under the Window Color (see **Figure 72**), Indicator Color (see **Figure 73**), and Sound (see **Figure 74**) submenus under the Options menu.

Figure 69. *Click the Program button to program CD play.*

Figure 70. *Drag a track from the list on the left to the list on the right.*

Figure 71. *When you release the mouse button, the track appears in the list on the right side.*

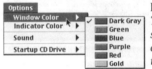

Figure 72.
The Window Color submenu lets you change the color of the window.

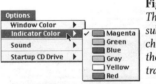

Figure 73.
The Indicator Color submenu lets you change the color of the numbers and track names.

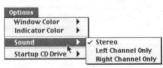

Figure 74.
The Sound submenu lets you change the way stereo sound is played.

Controlling Audio CD Play

Figure 75.
*MoviePlayer lets
you play and edit
QuickTime movies.*

Figure 76.
*Select the icon for the
QuickTime movie that
you want to open.*

Figure 77.
*Choose Open
from the File
menu.*

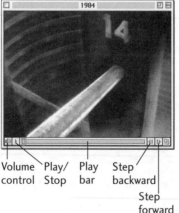

About QuickTime and MoviePlayer

QuickTime is a digital video and audio technology developed by Apple Computer, Inc. Mac OS uses the QuickTime System extension to understand files in QuickTime format.

Mac OS includes MoviePlayer (see **Figure 75**), an application designed to open, play, edit, and save QuickTime movie files.

On these two pages, I tell you enough about MoviePlayer to get you started playing and editing QuickTime movies.

✔ Tip

■ I tell you more about System extensions in **Chapter 12**.

To open a QuickTime movie

Double-click the QuickTime movie's icon.

or

1. Select the icon for the movie that you want to open (see **Figure 76**).

2. Choose Open from the File menu (see **Figure 77**) or press ⌘O.

MoviePlayer launches. The movie's first frame appears in a window (see **Figure 78**).

✔ Tip

■ If you prefer, you can launch Movie-Player, which you can find in the Movie Player folder inside the Applications folder on your hard disk, and use its Open dialog box to locate and open the QuickTime movie that you want to open. I tell you how to use the Open dialog box in **Chapter 5**.

Figure 78.
*The first
frame of the
QuickTime
movie
appears in a
MoviePlayer
window.*

Volume Play/ Play Step
control Stop bar backward
Step
forward

To control movie play

Click the control buttons (see **Figure 78**) to control the play of an audio CD:

- **Volume control** changes movie volume; click the icon to display a slider that you can drag up or down (see **Figure 79**).

- **Play/Stop** starts play or, if the movie is already playing, stops play.

- **Step Backward** moves backward through the movie, one frame at a time.

- **Step Forward** moves forward through the movie, one frame at a time.

- **Play bar** tracks movie progress. By dragging the slider, you can scroll through the movie without sound.

To specify view size

Select a size option from the Movie menu (see **Figure 80**). The size of the movie's window changes accordingly.

✔ Tip

- The larger the MoviePlayer window, the move *pixelated* (or unclear) the movie appears.

To select movie frames

1. Use the slider in the Play bar to view the first frame of the desired selection.

2. Hold down (Shift) while dragging the slider to the last frame of the desired selection. A shaded area on the Play bar indicates the selected frames (see **Figure 81**).

✔ Tip

- Once you've selected movie frames, you can copy, cut, and paste them just like any other selection. I tell you about the Copy, Cut, and Paste commands in **Chapter 5**.

Figure 79.
Click the Volume control to display a slider. Then drag the slider up or down to change the movie's volume.

Figure 80.
Options under the Movie menu let you change the viewing size of a QuickTime movie.

Figure 81. *A shaded area in the Play bar indicates selected frames.*

Figure 82.
Launch Disk First Aid by
opening its icon. 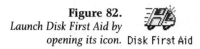 Disk First Aid

About Disk First Aid

Disk First Aid is a utility application that enables you to check your hard disk for and repair minor directory damage caused by bad media, crashes, improper shutdowns, and other problems.

✔ Tips

■ Disk First Aid is similar in function to (but not as powerful as) Norton Utilities for Macintosh, a utility by Symantec Corporation.

■ It's a good idea to use Disk First Aid to verify all your important disks on a regular basis—at least once a month.

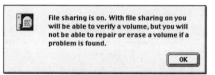

Figure 83. *A dialog box like this appears if file sharing is turned on.*

To launch Disk First Aid

1. Open the Disk First Aid icon (see **Figure 82**), which can be found in the Utilities folder on your hard disk.

2. If file sharing is turned on, a dialog box like the one in **Figure 83** appears. It explains that you cannot repair disks when file sharing is turned on. Click OK to dismiss it.

The Disk First Aid window appears (see **Figure 84**). It displays all disks mounted on the Desktop.

✔ Tips

■ If you need to repair a disk, you must turn file sharing off. I tell you about file sharing, including how to turn it on and off, in **Chapter 9**.

■ I tell you about mounting disks in **Chapter 3**.

Figure 84. *The Disk First Aid window.*

To verify or repair a disk

1. Select the disk(s) that you want to verify or repair.

2. If you select your startup disk or a disk with open files, a dialog box like the one in **Figure 85** appears, telling you that certain disks cannot be repaired. Click OK to dismiss it.

3. To verify the selected disk(s), click Verify or press [Return] or [Enter].

   or

   To Repair the selected disk(s), click Repair.

4. Wait while Disk First Aid checks and/or repairs the selected disk(s). You can monitor its progress in the bottom half of the Disk First Aid window (see **Figure 86**). When it's finished, the condition of the disk appears in bold in the window (see **Figure 87**).

✔ Tips

- To select more than one disk, hold down [Shift] while clicking each disk.

- The Repair button will be gray if file sharing is turned on or if you selected the startup disk.

- To repair the startup disk, you must start your computer from another disk, such as the Disk Tools disk that came with your computer.

- You can use the File menu's Save Results command to save a report of Disk First Aid's results.

- You can use the Option menu's Erase Disk command to erase a selected disk. Just be sure to select the correct disk!

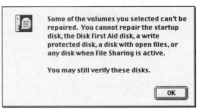

Figure 85. *A window like this appears if you select a disk that can't be repaired.*

Figure 86. *You can monitor Disk First Aid's progress in the bottom of its window.*

Figure 87. *Disk First Aid's diagnosis appears in bold in the Disk First Aid window.*

Verifying or Repairing Disks

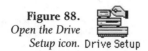

Figure 88.
*Open the Drive
Setup icon.* Drive Setup

Figure 89. *In this example, Drive
Setup has found my internal hard
disk, my internal CD-ROM drive, my
internal Zip drive, and my external
hard disk.*

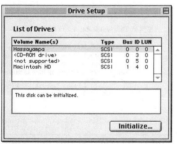

Figure 90. *When you select a disk,
a window at the bottom of the Drive
Setup window tells you whether you
can initialize it.*

Figure 91. *Click Initialize in the
Initialize window only if you're sure
you want to erase the disk.*

About Drive Setup

Drive Setup is a utility that enables you to
initialize a hard disk, install or update a
disk driver, and test a disk.

✔ Tips

- ◼ Drive Setup is not compatible with all
  hard disks. It should, however, work
  with the hard disk in your computer.

- ◼ You should use the disk utility software
  that came with your external hard disk,
  Zip disk, or other storage device to
  prepare that device's media for use.

To launch Drive Setup

Open the Drive Setup icon (see **Figure
88**), which can be found in the Utilities
folder on your hard disk. The Drive Setup
window appears. It searches for and displays all drives connected to your
computer (see **Figure 89**).

To initialize a disk

1. Select the disk that you want to initial-
    ize by clicking its name in the Drive
    Setup window (see **Figure 90**).

2. Click Initialize. The Initialize window
    appears (see **Figure 91**).

3. If you are absolutely sure you want to
    erase the disk, click Initialize.

4. Wait while Drive Setup initializes the
    disk. This can take a while, depending
    on the size of the disk.

✔ Tips

- ◼ Initializing, which is often known as
  foramatting, completely erases the disk.
  If a disk contains important files, back
  them up *before* initializing the disk!

- ◼ You cannot initialize a disk if file sharing is turned on. I tell you about file
  sharing in **Chapter 9**.

- ◼ You cannot initialize the startup disk.

To update a disk's driver

1. Select the disk whose driver you want to update by clicking its name in the Drive Setup window (see **Figure 90**).

2. Choose Update Driver from the Functions menu (see **Figure 92**).

3. Wait a moment while Drive Setup updates the driver on the disk. When it is finished, a dialog box like the one in **Figure 93** appears. Click OK.

4. Restart your computer to automatically load the updated driver.

✔ Tips

■ Every hard disk or other high-capacity magnetic storage media has a driver written to the disk. The driver tells the computer how to read the disk.

■ You should update the driver on your hard disk whenever you install a new version of Mac OS.

To test a disk

1. Select the disk that you want to test by clicking its name in the Drive Setup window (see **Figure 90**).

2. Choose Test Disk from the Functions menu (see **Figure 94**).

3. A dialog box like the one in **Figure 95** appears. It explains what the test does. Click Start to dismiss the dialog box and begin the test.

4. Wait while the test is conducted. You can monitor its progress in the Drive Setup window (see **Figure 96**). When the test is finished, its results appear in the bottom of the Drive Setup window (see **Figure 97**).

✔ Tip

■ A bad block is a portion of the disk that is badly corrupted and can no longer be used.

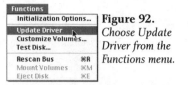

Figure 92. *Choose Update Driver from the Functions menu.*

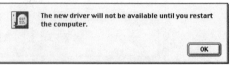

Figure 93. *This dialog box appears after the driver has been updated.*

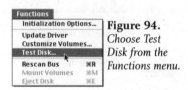

Figure 94. *Choose Test Disk from the Functions menu.*

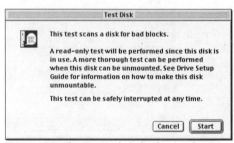

Figure 95. *The Test Disk dialog box explains what the test is for.*

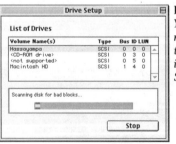

Figure 96. *You can monitor the test progress in the Drive Setup window.*

Figure 97. *Test results appear in the bottom of the Drive Setup window.*

Figure 98.
The Script Editor icon. Script Editor

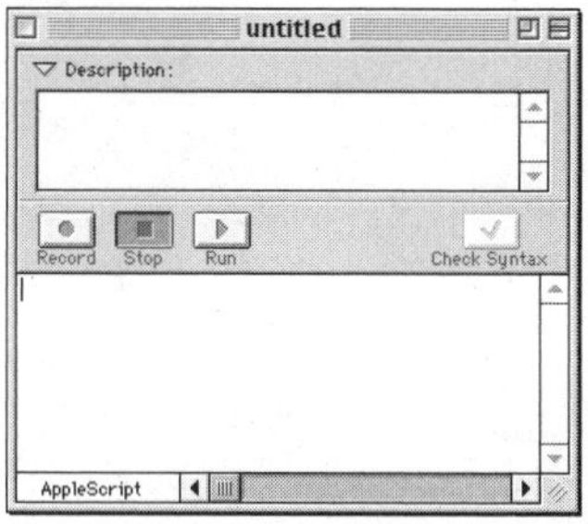

Figure 99.
A Script Editor document window.

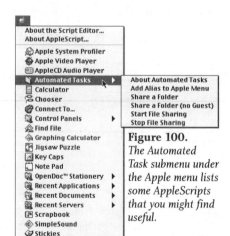

Figure 100.
The Automated Task submenu under the Apple menu lists some AppleScripts that you might find useful.

About AppleScript

AppleScript is a scripting language that's part of Mac OS. You can use it to program your computer to automatically perform a series of tasks called a *script*.

You create scripts with a program called Script Editor (see **Figure 98**), which is provided with Mac OS 8. Script Editor works with the Finder and with *scriptable applications*—applications that support AppleScript commands.

There are two ways to create a script with Script Editor:

- Use the Script Editor's recording feature to record script steps as you perform them. This is probably the best way to get started with AppleScript, although it does limit what you can do with it.

- Use the Script Editor (see **Figure 99**) to write the script. To do this, you must know the AppleScript scripting language.

As you can imagine, AppleScript is an advanced and powerful feature of Mac OS—one that is far beyond the scope of this book. But to get you started, I'll tell you how to record, run, and save a simple script.

✓ Tip

- The Automated Tasks submenu under the Apple menu (see **Figure 100**) lists a number of AppleScripts that come with Mac OS 8.

To launch Script Editor

Open the Script Editor icon (see **Figure 98**). You can find it in the AppleScript™ folder inside the Apple Extras folder on your hard disk. An untitled Script Editor window appears (see **Figure 99**).

About AppleScript, Launching Script Editor

To record a script

1. Click Record in the Script Editor window (see **Figure 99**). A recording icon blinks at the far-left end of the menu (see **Figure 101**).

2. Perform the following steps for a test script:

    1. Double-click the hard disk icon to open it.

    2. Hold down [Option] and double-click the Applications folder to open it and close the hard disk window.

    3. Hold down [Option] and double-click the SimpleText icon to open it and close the Applications window.

3. Use the Application menu at the far right end of the menu bar to activate Script Editor. The Script Editor window appears. It now has a series of script steps (see **Figure 102**).

4. Click Stop.

To run a script

Click Run in the Script Editor window (see **Figure 102**). The script should play back all the steps you just recorded.

To save a script as an application

1. Choose Save from the File menu or press ⌘⌘S. A Save As dialog box appears (see **Figure 103**).

2. Enter a name for the script and select a disk location.

3. Choose Application from the Kind pop-up menu (see **Figure 104**).

4. Click Save.

✔ Tip

■ Once a script has been saved as an application, you can simply open its icon (see **Figure 105**) to run it.

Figure 101. *An icon like this blinks over the Apple menu when Script Editor is recording.*

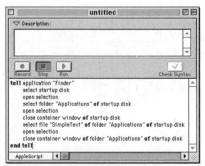

Figure 102. *Script Editor automatically writes the script steps for you.*

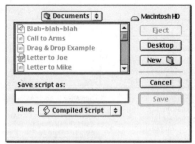

Figure 103. *Use a Save As dialog box to save your script.*

Figure 104. *Choose Application from the Kind pop-up menu.*

Figure 105. *Here's the icon for an application written in AppleScript.*

Recording, Running, & Saving Scripts

WORKING WITH PC FILES

About Working with PC Files

Documents created on a DOS- or Windows-compatible computer aren't the same as those created on a Mac OS-compatible computer. Some differences include:

- Disk formats vary based on the operating system that formatted the disk.

- Document formats vary based on characters and special codes recognized or required by each operating system.

- Document formats also vary based on application codes and formats.

Fortunately, Mac OS comes with three software tools that make working with PC documents easy:

- **PC Exchange** enables you to read PC disks on your Mac OS computer as well as map DOS extensions to Mac OS applications.

- **Mac OS Easy Open** automatically lists applications that can open the PC documents that you double-click.

- **MacLinkPlus** translates PC documents to Mac OS document formats.

I tell you about all these things in this chapter.

✔ Tip

- If you're interested in running DOS or Windows software on your computer, here are two options:

  - ▲ Apple Computer's DOS Compatibility Card is an expansion card that puts PC chips and circuitry inside your Mac OS-compatible computer.

  - ▲ Insignia Solutions' SoftWindows is software emulation that makes PC software think it's running on a PC.

About PC Exchange

PC Exchange is a control panel that enables your Mac OS computer's SuperDrive to read PC-formatted disks. It also enables you to know which Mac OS applications on your computer should open each specific type of PC file.

✔ Tip

■ A *SuperDrive* is a type of floppy drive that can read high density disks. It comes standard in every Mac OS-compatible computer made since 1989.

To read a PC-formatted disk

Insert the PC disk in your disk drive. After a moment, the disk's icon appears on your Desktop (see **Figure 1**). Work with it just like any other disk.

✔ Tips

■ If you look carefully, you can see the letters *PC* on a PC disk icon (see **Figure 1**).

■ I tell you about working with files and disks in **Chapter 3**.

To open PC Exchange

Choose PC Exchange from the Control Panels submenu under the Apple menu (see **Figure 2**). The PC Exchange control panel appears (see **Figure 3**).

To disable PC Exchange

1. Open PC Exchange.
2. Select the Off radio button in the PC Exchange control panel window (see **Figure 3**).
3. Close the PC Exchange window.

Figure 1.
When you insert a PC-formatted disk, its icon appears on the Desktop like any other disk.

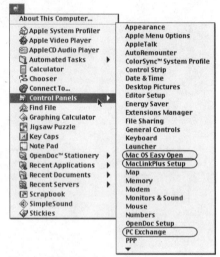

Figure 2. *PC Exchange, Mac OS Easy Open, and MacLink Plus can all be configured with control panels.*

Figure 3. *The PC Exchange control panel window.*

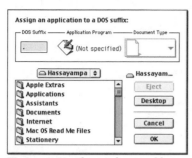

Figure 4. *Use this window to add an extension mapping.*

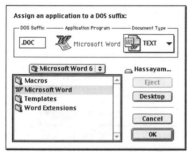

Figure 5. *Locate an application that can open the files.*

Figure 6.
The Document Type pop-up menu lists the different document types supported by the application you selected. If you can't recognize the codes, look at the icons.

Figure 7.
The completed mapping appears in the control panel window.

To map PC extensions to Mac OS applications

1. Open PC Exchange (see **Figure 3**).

2. Click Add. A dialog box like the one in **Figure 4** appears.

3. In the DOS Suffix edit box, enter the three-character extension for a type of DOS file. Be sure to include the period (or "dot") before the extension.

4. Use the directory area of the dialog box to locate and select the application with which you want to open files with the DOS extension you entered (see **Figure 5**).

5. If necessary, choose a type of document from the Document Type pop-up menu (see **Figure 6**).

6. Click OK. The mapping you created appears in the PC Exchange window (see **Figure 7**).

7. Close the PC Exchange window.

✔ Tips

■ When you map extensions to applications, you tell Mac OS which icon to place on a DOS or Windows file (see **Figure 8**). Then you can open the file in the application you selected by simply double-clicking the file's icon.

■ Mapping an extension to an application doesn't guarantee that the application can open the document. PC Exchange does not perform translations; for that, you need MacLinkPlus, which I discuss later in this chapter.

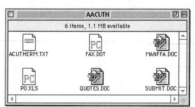

Figure 8. *Mapping extensions puts Mac OS application icons on PC files.*

Mapping Extensions to Applications

To change a PC Exchange mapping

1. Open PC Exchange (see **Figure 3**).

2. Select the mapping that you want to modify.

3. Click Change. A dialog box like the one in **Figure 5** appears.

4. Follow steps 3 through 6 on the previous page to enter revised information for the mapping. When you click OK, the changed mapping appears in the PC Exchange window.

5. Close the PC Exchange window.

To remove a PC Exchange mapping

1. Open PC Exchange (see **Figure 3**).

2. Select the mapping that you want to remove.

3. Click Remove.

4. In the confirmation dialog box that appears (see **Figure 9**), click Remove. The mapping is removed from the PC Exchange window.

5. Close the PC Exchange window.

Figure 9. *A dialog box like this appears when you try to delete a mapping from the PC Exchange window.*

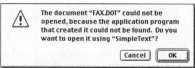

Figure 10. *With Mac OS Easy Open disabled, double-clicking an orphan's icon displays this dialog box.*

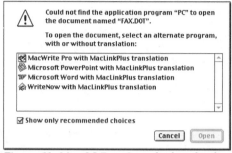

Figure 11. *Mac OS Easy Open displays this dialog box when you double-click an orphan's icon.*

Figure 12. *SimpleText is confused by text formatting in a PC file…*

Figure 13. *…but with translation, WriteNow can read it.*

About Mac OS Easy Open

Mac OS Easy Open lets you open orphan document files—including PC files that are not mapped to applications in PC Exchange—by double-clicking them. Instead of displaying the dialog box in **Figure 10**, it displays the one in **Figure 11**. The difference: you can select which application should attempt to open the file.

Unlike PC Exchange, Mac OS Easy Open does not use file extensions to identify files. Instead, it looks at the file's *header*—the invisible information at the start of the document—to figure out what kind of document file it is. That's how it knows which applications to recommend for opening the document.

✔ Tips

■ Mac OS Easy Open isn't just for PC documents. It's for any orphan document files on your computer.

■ Mac OS Easy Open takes advantage of translators installed in your computer, including MacLinkPlus translators. I tell you about MacLinkPlus later in this chapter.

■ As you can see by comparing **Figures 12** and **13**, SimpleText doesn't always do as good a job as other applications when it comes to opening orphan documents.

■ I tell you about orphan files and opening documents in **Chapter 5**.

To open a document with Mac OS Easy Open

1. Double-click the document's icon. After a moment, the Translation Choices dialog box appears (see **Figure 11**). It lists the recommended applications for opening the document.

2. If desired, turn off the Show only recommended choices check box. All the installed applications appear in the window, with the recommended ones on top of the list.

3. Select the application that you want to use to open the document.

4. Click Open.

5. If a translator is being used, a dialog box like the one in **Figure 14** appears on screen to show the progress of the translation. Then the application you selected launches and the document appears in a window (see **Figure 13**).

✔ Tips

■ The first time you use Mac OS Easy Open with a MacLinkPlus translator, a window like the one in **Figure 15** appears. Click Continue Translation to dismiss it. You may also find two alias files on your desktop: *MacLinkPlus "How To" Demo alias* and *Register MacLinkPlus*. It's safe to delete these aliases; their originals are in the MacLinkPlus 9.0 folder (see **Figure 25**). I tell you about aliases in **Chapter 4**.

■ Mac OS Easy Open remembers the choices you make. The next time you double-click the same type of file, it opens the file without displaying the Translation Choices dialog box (see **Figure 11**). On the next page, I tell you how to force it to display the dialog box every time Mac OS Easy Open goes to work.

Figure 14. *A dialog box like this appears while the file is translated.*

Figure 15. *This splash screen appears the first time you use one of the MacLinkPlus translators, even if Mac OS Easy Open uses it.*

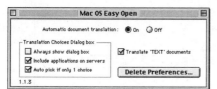

Figure 16. *Configure Mac OS Easy Open with options in its control panel window.*

Figure 17. *A confirmation dialog box like this one appears when you attempt to delete memorized translation choices.*

To configure Mac OS Easy Open

1. Choose Mac OS Easy Open from the Control Panels submenu under the Apple menu (see **Figure 2**). The Mac OS Easy Open control panel appears (see **Figure 16**).

2. To disable Mac OS Easy Open, select the Off radio button.

3. Toggle check boxes to set options for the Translation Choices dialog box (see **Figure 11**):

   ▲ **Always show dialog box** instructs Easy Open to display the dialog box any time a translation is required.

   ▲ **Include applications on servers** includes any applications it finds on mounted server volumes in the dialog box.

   ▲ **Auto pick if only 1 choice** instructs Easy Open to automatically choose a translation option if it is the only choice.

4. To always check plain documents to see if they could benefit from translation, turn on the Translate 'TEXT' documents check box.

5. To delete previously memorized translation choices, click Delete Preferences. A confirmation dialog box like the one in **Figure 17** appears. Click Delete.

6. Close the Mac OS Easy Open control panel window.

✔ Tips

■ To help your system run more quickly when opening documents, keep the Include applications on servers and Translate 'TEXT' documents check boxes turned off.

■ For complete control over translations, keep the Always show dialog box check box turned on and the Auto pick if only 1 choice check box turned off.

Configuring Mac OS Easy Open

About MacLinkPlus

MacLinkPlus is a translation package by DataViz, Inc. that is bundled with Mac OS 8. Its translators can be used two ways:

■ Mac OS Easy Open uses MacLinkPlus translators to translate the files it opens. I tell you about Mac OS Easy Open on the previous pages.

■ The MacLinkPlus Document Converter enables you to create mini applications that you can drag files onto to translate.

In this section, I explain how to configure MacLinkPlus and how to use Document Converter. I also tell you how to use Data-Viz FileView, an application that can show you the text inside almost any file—including those pesky PC files!

To configure MacLinkPlus

1. Choose MacLinkPlus Setup from the Control Panels submenu under the Apple menu (see **Figure 2**). The Mac-LinkPlus Setup control panel appears (see **Figure 18**).

2. Choose a category from the Category pop-up menu. Then select a preference from the pop-up menu beneath it. The following categories are available:

   ▲ **Languages** (see **Figure 18**) affects the way ASCII characters are translated.

   ▲ **Graphic Clipboard** (see **Figure 19**) lets you specify whether a copy of a translated graphic should be placed on the Clipboard.

   ▲ **PCX Color Output** (see **Figure 20**) lets you select a resolution for files translated to PCX format.

   ▲ **Drawing Size** (see **Figure 21**) lets you select the size of files translated to PICT format.

(continued on next page)

Figure 18.
Use the MacLinkPlus Setup control panel to configure MacLinkPlus. Configuration categories include Languages,...

Figure 19.
...Graphic Clipboard,...

Figure 20.
...PCX Color Output,...

Figure 21.
...Drawing Size,...

Figure 22.
...Bitmap Conversion,...

Figure 23.
...PC Text Translation,...

Figure 24.
...and AutoBullet, AutoNumber, & Outline.

(continued from previous page)

▲ **Bitmap Compression** (see **Figure 22**) lets you specify whether compression should be turned on or off for files translated to bitmap graphics.

▲ **PC Text Translations** (see **Figure 23**) lets you specify whether PC text documents should be treated as DOS or Windows formatted text.

▲ **AutoBullet, AutoNumber, & Outlines** (see **Figure 24**) lets you specify whether the automatic paragraph number and bullet features of a word processor should be used when translating files that include bullets, numbers, or outlines.

3. When you are finished changing settings, close the MacLinkPlus Setup control panel window.

✔ Tips

■ As you can see in **Figures 18** though **24**, the MacLinkPlus Setup control panel window includes a detailed description of a configuration category when that category is selected. This should provide enough information for you to decide which Preference option you should choose.

■ Don't be afraid to experiment with settings until you get them just the way you want them.

■ I tell you about using the Clipboard in **Chapter 5**.

To create a custom Document Converter

1. Open the MacLinkPlus 9.0 folder in the Apple Extras folder on your hard disk (see **Figure 25**).

2. Select the Document Converter icon.

3. Choose Duplicate from the File menu (see **Figure 26**) or press ⌘ D.

4. A copy of the Document Converter icon appears below it (see **Figure 27**).

5. Double-click the Document Converter copy icon.

6. In the Document Converter Setup dialog box that appears, select the type of document that you want to create with the converter. For example, if you want to convert word processing documents into Microsoft Word documents, select Microsoft Word Document with MacLinkPlus translation (see **Figure 28**).

7. Click Set.

8. The dialog box disappears and the name of the icon changes to reflect the type of document that you selected (see **Figure 29**).

✔ Tips

■ Generic icons appear in the Document Converter Setup dialog box beside file formats for applications that are not installed on your computer (see **Figure 28**).

■ If you do a lot of translations, create a folder to store all the translators you create with MacLinkPlus (see **Figure 30**).

■ MacLinkPlus translators don't just work for PC documents—they work for Mac OS documents, too. They can even change Mac OS documents into PC documents. Check the list of formats in the Document Converter Setup dialog box (see **Figure 28**) to see what formats are available.

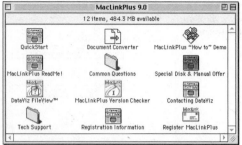

Figure 25. *The contents of the MacLinkPlus 9.0 folder inside the Apple Extras folder on your hard disk.*

Figure 26. *Choose Duplicate from the File menu.*

Figure 27. *A copy of Document Converter appears.*

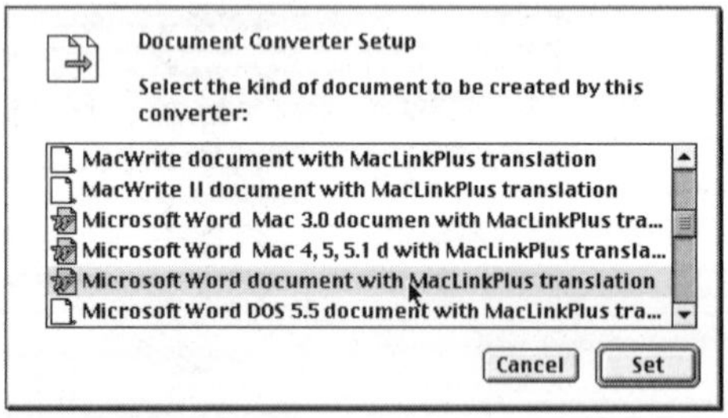

Figure 28. *Select the type of document that you want to create.*

Figure 29. *The name of the copied converter changes to reflect the document type you selected.*

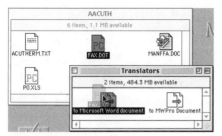

Figure 30. *Drag the file that you want to convert onto the icon for the converter that you want to use.*

Figure 31. *When the conversion finishes, an icon for the converted document appears with the converter icon. The original file remains untouched.*

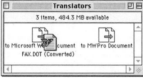

To use a custom Document Converter

Drag the icon for the document that you want to convert onto the icon for the converter (see **Figure 30**).

When you release the mouse button, a conversion dialog box like the one in **Figure 14** appears. When it disappears, a converted file icon appears with the converter icon (see **Figure 31**).

✔ Tip

■ You can convert more than one document at a time. Simply drag multiple icons onto the converter icon. I tell you how to select multiple icons in **Chapter 2**.

To use DataViz FileView

Drag the icon for the document that you want to view onto the DataViz FileView icon in the MacLinkPlus 9.0 folder.

When you release the mouse button, the DataViz FileView window appears, displaying the text contents of the document (see **Figure 32**).

✔ Tips

■ You can click buttons in the DataViz FileView window (see **Figure 32**) to open the file, get translation tips, and learn more about MacLinkPlus.

■ The DataViz FileView window (see **Figure 32**) also identifies the document's format and tells you whether MacLinkPlus can convert the file.

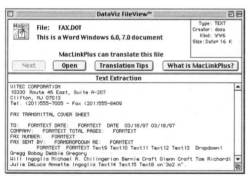

Figure 32. *FileView can display the text inside just about any file.*

PRINTING

About Printing

On a Mac OS system, printing is handled by the operating system rather than the individual applications. You choose the Print command in the application that created the document that you want to print and Mac OS steps in, displaying the Print dialog box and telling the application how to send information to the printer. There are two main benefits to this:

- If you can print documents created with one application, you can probably print documents created with any application on your computer.
- The Page Setup and Print dialog boxes, which are generated by Mac OS, look the same in every application.

This chapter covers most aspects of printing on a computer running Mac OS 8.

To print (an overview)

1. If necessary, select a printer.
2. Open the window or document that you want to print.
3. If desired, set options in the Page Setup dialog box and click OK.
4. Set options in the Print dialog box and click Print.

or

1. Drag the icon for the document that you want to print onto a desktop printer icon.
2. Set options in the Print dialog box and click Print.

✔ Tip

- I provide details on each of these steps throughout this chapter.

To print the Finder Desktop

1. If necessary, activate the Finder by choosing Finder from the Application menu.

2. Click on the Desktop to activate it rather than any open windows.

3. Choose Print Desktop from the File menu (see **Figure 1**).

4. Use the Print dialog box that appears to set print options.

5. Click Print.

Figure 1.
To print the Finder Desktop, choose Print Desktop from the File menu.

✔ Tip

■ I explain how to set options in the Print dialog box later in this chapter.

To print a Finder window

1. If necessary, activate the Finder by choosing Finder from the Application menu.

2. Activate the window that you want to print by clicking it.

3. Choose Print Window from the File menu (see **Figure 2**).

4. Use the Print dialog box that appears to set print options.

5. Click Print.

Figure 2.
To print a Finder window, choose Print Window from the File menu.

✔ Tip

■ I explain how to set options in the Print dialog box later in this chapter.

About Printer Drivers

A *printer driver*, which is a type of *Chooser extension*, is a software file that Mac OS uses to communicate with a specific kind of printer. It contains information about the printer and instructions for using it. You can't open and read a printer driver, but your computer can.

There are basically two kinds of printers:

■ A **PostScript** printer uses PostScript technology developed by Adobe Systems. Inside the printer is a *PostScript interpreter*, which can process PostScript language commands to print high-quality text and graphics. Examples of PostScript printers include most Apple LaserWriter printers and Hewlett Packard LaserJet printers.

■ A **QuickDraw** printer relies on the computer to send it all instructions for printing text and graphics. It cannot process PostScript commands. Examples of QuickDraw printers include Apple ImageWriters and StyleWriters, Hewlett-Packard DeskJet printers, and most Epson Stylus printers.

Mac OS comes with printer drivers for a variety of Apple branded PostScript and QuickDraw printers, including LaserWriters, StyleWriters, and ImageWriters. Mac OS-compatible printers by other manufacturers, such as Hewlett-Packard and Epson, come with the printer drivers you need to use them with your computer.

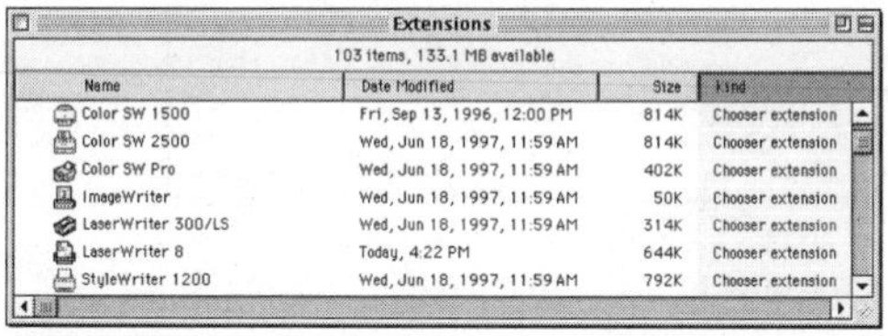

Figure 3. *The printer drivers installed as part of a Mac OS 8 basic installation.*

✔ Tips

■ If you do not have an appropriate printer driver for your printer, you may not be able to print.

■ Printer drivers are stored in the Extensions folder. **Figure 3** shows the printer drivers automatically installed as part of a basic installation of Mac OS 8.

To install a printer driver

1. Insert the disk containing the printer driver that you want to install.

2. If necessary, double-click the disk to open it and view its contents (see **Figures 4** and **5**).

3. If the disk includes an installer (see **Figure 4**), double-click it to open it. Then follow the on-screen instructions to install the printer software. You may have to restart your computer when the installation is complete.

   or

   If the disk does not include an installer application (see **Figure 5**), drag the printer driver file icon onto the System Folder icon on your hard disk (see **Figure 6**). When you release the mouse button, a dialog box like the one in **Figure 7** appears. Click OK and wait while the printer driver is properly installed in the Extensions folder.

✔ Tip

- If you need to, you can use the Mac OS 8 installer to reinstall just the printer drivers. Do a custom installation of Mac OS 8 and select just the printing software. I tell you about installing Mac OS 8 and doing custom installations in **Chapter 1**.

To uninstall a printer driver

1. Open the Extensions folder inside the System Folder on your hard disk.

2. Locate the icon for the printer driver that you want to uninstall.

3. Drag the printer driver out of the Extensions folder (see **Figure 8**). You can leave it on the Desktop or in another window if you want to keep it or you can drag it to the Trash if you want to delete it.

Figure 4. *This disk contains printer driver software and an installer…*

Figure 5. *…and this disk contains printer driver software without an installer.*

Figure 6. *Drag the printer driver icon onto the System Folder icon.*

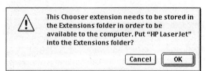

Figure 7. *When you drag a Chooser extension to the System Folder, a dialog box like this appears.*

Figure 8. *To uninstall a printer driver, simply drag it out of the Extensions folder.*

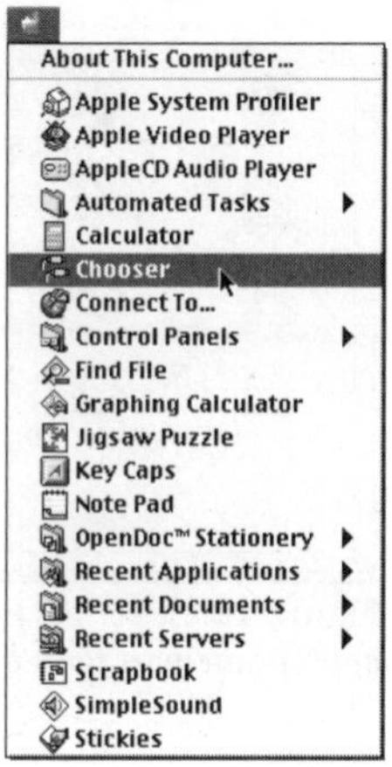

Figure 9. *Choose Chooser from the Apple menu.*

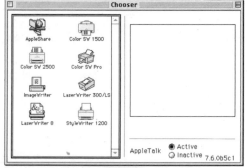

About the Chooser

The Chooser is a desk accessory that lets you select printers, file servers, and devices connected to the serial ports.

✔ Tips

■ The Mac OS Setup Assistant, which I discuss in **Chapter 1**, sets the printer in the Chooser for you.

■ I tell you about file servers in **Chapter 9**.

To open the Chooser

Choose Chooser from the Apple menu (see **Figure 9**). The Chooser window appears (see **Figure 10**). It displays icons for printer drivers and other Chooser files, such as AppleShare, in the left side of the window.

To select a network printer

1. Make sure the printer that you want to use is turned on and warmed up.

2. In the Chooser window, click once on the icon for the printer driver that you want to use (see **Figure 11**).

3. If your computer is on a network with multiple zones, click once on the name of the zone in which the printer you want to use resides.

4. In the list of printers, click once on the name of the printer that you want to use (see **Figure 11**).

Figure 10. *The Chooser window. If you're on a network with multiple zones, the Chooser window will look a little different on your computer.*

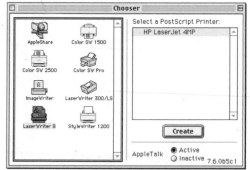

Figure 11. *Select the printer driver, the zone (if applicable; not shown here), and the printer.*

✔ Tips

■ If you have a laser printer but don't have its manufacturer's printer driver installed, try the LaserWriter 8 printer driver. It works for most laser printers.

■ If you're not sure which zone to select in a multiple-zone network, ask your System Administrator.

■ When selecting a network printer, make sure the Active radio button beside AppleTalk is selected (see **Figure 11**).

Opeing the Chooser, Selecting a Printer

To select a directly connected printer

1. Make sure the printer that you want to use is turned on and warmed up.

2. In the Chooser window, click once on the icon for the printer driver that you want to use (see **Figure 12**).

3. In the Connect to list, click once on the name or icon for the port to which the printer is connected (see **Figure 12**).

✔ Tips

■ If you're not sure which port the printer is connected to, check to see where the printer cable is connected to the back of your computer.

■ If a printer is directly connected to the printer port, you'll have to turn Apple-Talk off by selecting the Inactive button in the AppleTalk area of the Chooser (see **Figure 12**).

To set background printing options

After selecting a printer in the Chooser window, select the Background Printing area's On or Off radio button (see **Figure 12**) to set your preference.

✔ Tips

■ Background printing, when turned on, enables your computer to print while you continue working on other things.

■ The Background Printing option is not available for all printer drivers or printers. Consult the documentation that came with your printer for more information about this option.

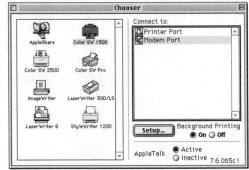

Figure 12. *Select the printer driver and the appropriate port for a directly-connected printer.*

Figure 13. *Click the Auto Setup button in this dialog box to have Mac OS automatically set up your printer.*

Figure 14. *When this dialog box appears, wait while Mac OS gets setup information from your printer.*

Figure 15. *Choose a PPD file for your printer or click the Generic button.*

To create or set up a PostScript printer

1. After selecting a printer in the Chooser window, click Create (see **Figure 11**) or Setup.

2. If you clicked a Setup button in step 1, a Setup dialog box like the one in **Figure 13** appears. Click Auto Setup. Then continue following the steps below.

   or

   If you clicked a Create button in step 1, a dialog box like the one in **Figure 14** appears. After a moment, a dialog box like the one in **Figure 15** appears. Use it to locate and select a PPD file for your printer. If there's no PPD file listed for your specific printer, click Generic.

3. If you clicked a Create button in step 1, wait while your computer creates a desktop printer.

   or

   If you clicked a Setup button in step 1, the Setup dialog box (see **Figure 14**) reappears. Click OK to dismiss it.

✔ Tips

- The name of the button in step 1 depends on which printer driver is selected and whether the printer has been used before.

- PPD (or *PostScript printer description files*) files, which usually come with printer drivers, should be installed in the Printer Descriptions folder inside the Extensions folder inside the System Folder on your hard disk.

- I tell you about desktop printers later in this chapter.

Creating/Setting Up PostScript Printers

To set sharing setup options for a directly connected printer

1. After selecting a printer in the Chooser window, click Setup (see **Figure 12**). A Sharing Setup dialog box appears (see **Figure 16**).

2. To share the printer with other network users, turn on the Share this Printer check box. Then enter a printer name and, if desired, password (see **Figure 17**).

3. To automatically create a log of printer use, turn on the Keep Log of Printer Usage check box.

4. Click OK to save your settings.

✔ Tips

- Not all directly connected printers can be shared.

- When you name a directly connected printer, its name appears in the Chooser window (see **Figure 18**).

To close the Chooser

1. Click the Chooser's close box (see **Figure 18**).

   or

   Choose Close from the Chooser's File menu (see **Figure 19**) or press ⌘W.

2. If you selected a different printer than what was originally selected, a dialog box like the one in **Figure 20** appears, telling you to check the options in the Page Setup dialog box of open applications. Click OK to dismiss it.

✔ Tips

- I tell you about the Page Setup dialog box next.

- If a desktop printer does not already exist for the printer you selected, one is created. I tell you about desktop printers later in this chapter.

Figure 16. *The Sharing Seup dialog box lets you share a directly connected printer with other users on your network.*

Figure 17. *Once you turn on the Share this Printer check box, you can enter a name and password for the printer.*

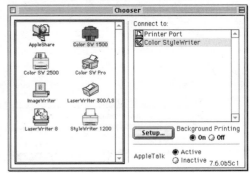

Figure 18. *The name of a shared printer appears in the Chooser window.*

Figure 19. *Choose Close from the Chooser's File menu.*

Figure 20. *When you change your printer, a dialog box like this appears.*

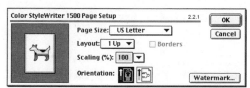

Figure 21. *A Color StyleWriter 1500 offers only a few Page Setup options.*

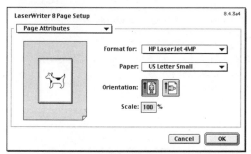

Figure 22. *A LaserWriter offers two categories of Page Setup options: Page Attributes…*

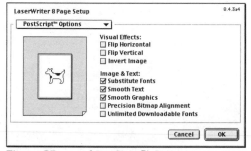

Figure 23. *…and PostScript™ Options.*

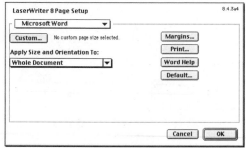

Figure 24. *Some applications offer more Page Setup options. These are options for Microsoft Word …*

About the Page Setup dialog box

The Page Setup dialog box lets you set page options prior to printing. Although it is a standard dialog box, two things can cause its appearance and options to vary:

■ Page Setup options vary depending on the selected printer driver (see **Figures 21**, **22**, and **23**).

■ Additional options may be offered by specific applications (see **Figures 24** and **25**).

In this section, I tell you how to set the basic options—those options available for most printers and most applications—in the Page Setup dialog box.

✔ Tips

■ For information about using Page Setup options specific to an application, consult the documentation that came with the application.

■ Because Page Setup options can change when you change printers, it's a good idea to check Page Setup options after changing your printer. That's what the dialog box in **Figure 20** is all about.

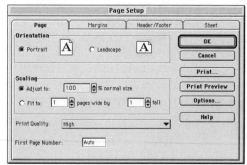

Figure 25. *…and these are options for Microsoft Excel.*

About the Page Setup Dialog Box

To open the Page Setup dialog box

Choose Page Setup from the File menu (see **Figures 26a**, **26b**, and **26c**).

To set Page Attributes

1. Open the Page Setup dialog box (see **Figures 21** and **22**).

2. In the Page Setup dialog box for a Post-Script printer, select Page Attributes from the top pop-up menu (see **Figure 27**).

3. If necessary, select the correct printer from the Format for pop-up menu (see **Figure 22**).

4. Select the correct paper size from the Paper or Page Size pop-up menu (see **Figures 21** and **22**).

5. To print more than one document page on each sheet of paper, choose a Layout option (see **Figure 21**). If you select an option other than 1 Up, you can also turn on the Borders check box to put a border around each document page (see **Figure 28**).

6. Enter a scaling percentage in the Scaling (%) or Scale edit box (see **Figures 21** and **22**). You may also be able to select a percentage from a pop-up menu beside the Scaling (%) edit box (see **Figure 29**).

7. Select an Orientation option by clicking it (see **Figures 21** and **22**).

8. Click OK to save your settings and dismiss the Page Setup dialog box.

✔ Tip

■ Options in each of the above steps vary depending on the printer driver selected for the printer.

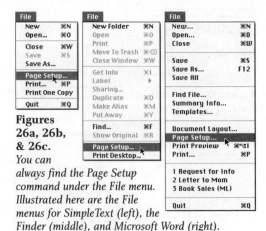

Figures 26a, 26b, & 26c. *You can always find the Page Setup command under the File menu. Illustrated here are the File menus for SimpleText (left), the Finder (middle), and Microsoft Word (right).*

Figure 27. *In the Page Setup dialog box for a PostScript printer, select Page Attributes.*

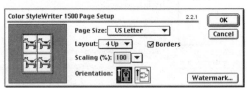

Figure 28. *Layout options enable you to print more than one document page on each sheet of paper.*

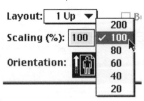

Figure 29. *Some Page Setup dialog boxes let you select a scaling percentage from a pop-up menu like this one.*

Figure 30. *Choose PostScript™ Options from the pop-up menu at the top of the Page Setup dialog box for a PostScript printer.*

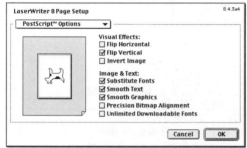

Figure 31. *Changing check box settings changes the dogcow in the sample image.*

To set PostScript options

1. Open the Page Setup dialog box for your PostScript printer (see **Figure 22**).

2. Select PostScript™ Options from the top pop-up menu (see **Figure 30**).

3. Click check boxes (see **Figure 23**) to turn the following PostScript features on or off:

   ▲ **Flip Horizontal** makes a mirror image of the page.

   ▲ **Flip Vertical** turns the page upside down.

   ▲ **Invert Image** turns black to white and white to black.

   ▲ **Substitute Fonts** uses Times, Helvetica, and Courier PostScript fonts instead of New York, Geneva, and Monaco TrueType fonts.

   ▲ **Smooth Text** prints bitmapped fonts more clearly.

   ▲ **Smooth Graphics** prints graphics more clearly by smoothing jagged edges.

   ▲ **Precision Bitmap Alignment** reduces the document to correct for possible distortions in bitmap graphic images.

   ▲ **Unlimited Downloadable Fonts** lets you use as many fonts as you like in a document. This could, however, slow printing.

4. Click OK to save your settings and dismiss the Page Setup dialog box.

✔ Tips

■ Many of the changes you make in the check boxes are reflected in the sample image to the left of the check boxes in the Page Setup dialog box (see **Figure 31**).

■ Another piece of Mac OS trivia: the animal that appears in the Page Setup dialog box is called a *dogcow*.

Setting PostScript Options

To set application-specific options

1. Open the Page Setup dialog box (see **Figures 22** and **32**).

2. In the Page Setup dialog box for a PostScript printer, select the name of the application from the top pop-up menu (see **Figure 33**). That application's additional options appear (see **Figure 24**).

3. Set options as desired.

4. Click OK to save your settings and dismiss the Page Setup dialog box.

✔ Tips

■ Some applications automatically display their own custom Page Setup dialog boxes when you choose Page Setup from their File menus. Microsoft Excel (see **Figure 25**) is an example.

■ To learn more about the Page Setup options available in your favorite application, check the documentation that came with the application.

■ If the name of the application does not appear in the pop-up menu at the top of a PostScript printer's Page Setup dialog box (see **Figures 27** and **30**), there are no application-specific options to set.

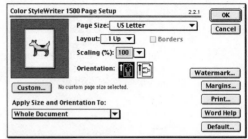

Figure 32. *The Page Setup dialog box for a non-PostScript printer displays all options—including application-specific options like these for Microsoft Word.*

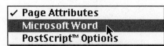

Figure 33. *For a PostScript printer, choose the name of the application from the pop-up menu at the top of the Page Setup dialog box.*

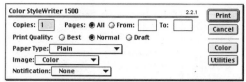

Figure 34. *The Print options for a Color Style-Writer 1500.*

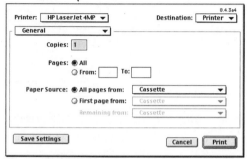

Figure 35. *The General options of the Print dialog box for a LaserWriter printer.*

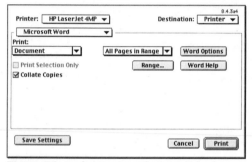

Figure 36. *Application-specific Print dialog box options for Microsoft Word…*

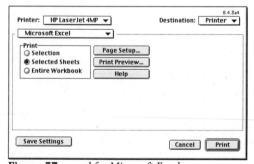

Figure 37. *…and for Microsoft Excel.*

About the Print Dialog Box

The Print dialog box lets you set printing options and send the print job to the printer. Like the Page Setup dialog box, the Print dialog box is a standard dialog box, but two things can cause its appearance and options to vary:

■ Print options vary depending on the selected printer driver (see **Figures 34** and **35**).

■ Additional options may be offered by specific applications (see **Figures 36** and **37**).

In this section, I tell you how to set the basic options—those options available for most printers and most applications—in the Print dialog box.

✔ Tip

■ For information about using Print options specific to an application, consult the documentation that came with the application.

About the Print Dialog Box

To open the Print dialog box

Choose Print from the File menu (see **Figures 38a**, **38b**, and **38c**).

or

Press ⌃⌘P.

✔ Tip

■ To use the Finder's Print command, you must first select the icon for the document that you want to print.

To set QuickDraw printer Print options

1. Open the Print dialog box (see **Figures 34** and **39**).

2. Enter the number of copies of the document that you want to print in the Copies edit box.

3. In the Page Range area, select either the All radio button to print all pages or enter values in the From and To edit boxes (see **Figure 40**) to print specific pages.

4. Select a Quality radio button. Some of the options you might see include:

   ▲ **Best** is the best quality. It takes longer to print and uses more ink.

   ▲ **Normal** or **Faster** is standard quality; you'll use it most often.

   ▲ **Draft** prints only the text of the document, in one font and size. It's the quickest print option, but what you get on paper may not match what you see on screen.

5. Select other options specific to your printer, including Paper Type (see **Figure 34**), Paper Feed (see **Figure 39**), Image (see **Figure 34**), and Notification (see **Figure 34**). These options are self-explanatory; if you need more information, consult the documentation that came with your printer.

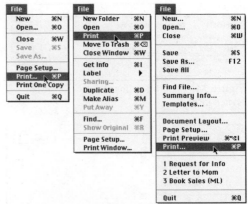

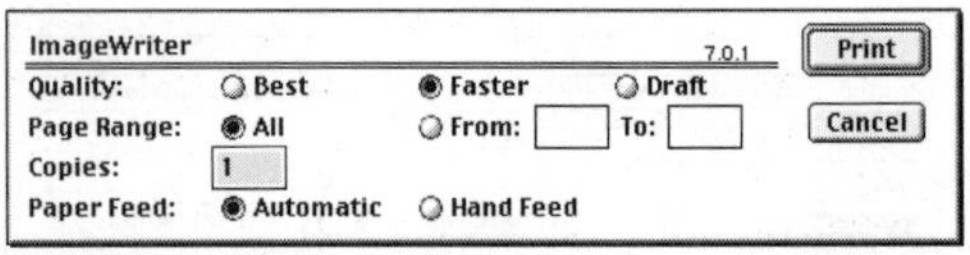

Figure 38a, 38b, & 38c. *You can always find the Print command under the File menu. Here are the File menus for SimpleText (left), the Finder (middle), and Microsoft Word (right).*

Figure 39. *The Print dialog box for an ImageWriter printer.*

Figure 40. *When you enter values in the From and To edit boxes the From radio button is automatically selected.*

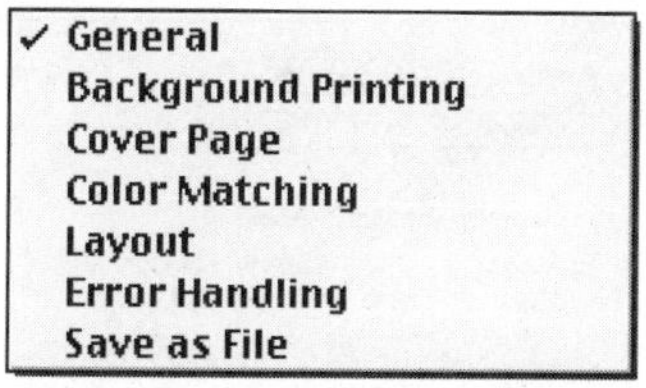

✓ General
Background Printing
Cover Page
Color Matching
Layout
Error Handling
Save as File

Figure 42. *Use the pop-up menu beneath the Printer pop-up menu to select a category of printing options.*

Paper Source: ○ All pages from: [Cassette ▼]
      ● First page from: [Manual Feed ▼]
      Remaining from: [Cassette ▼]

Figure 43. *The Paper Source options make it possible to print the first page of a document on letterhead you manually feed and the rest of the pages on plain paper from the paper cassette.*

Figure 44. *The Background Printing options in the Print dialog box for a PostScript printer.*

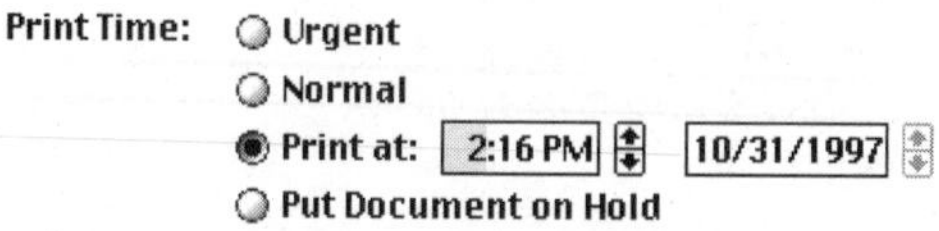

Print Time: ○ Urgent
      ○ Normal
      ● Print at: [2:16 PM] [10/31/1997]
      ○ Put Document on Hold

Figure 45. *When you select the Print at radio button, you can enter a date and time to print the document.*

To set PostScript printer General options

1. Open the Print dialog box (see **Figure 35**).

2. If necessary, choose General from the pop-up menu beneath the Printer pop-up menu (see **Figure 42**).

3. Enter the number of copies of the document that you want to print in the Copies edit box.

4. In the Page Range area, select either the All radio button to print all pages or enter values in the From and To edit boxes to print specific pages.

5. Select a Paper Source radio button. If you select the First page from radio button, you can specify different paper sources for the first page and remaining pages (see **Figure 43**).

To set PostScript printer Background Printing options

1. Open the Print dialog box (see **Figure 35**).

2. Choose Background Printing from the pop-up menu beneath the Printer pop-up menu (see **Figure 42**) to display Background Printing options (see **Figure 44**).

3. To print while you wait, turn on the Foreground (no spool file) radio button.
   or
   To print while you continue to work with your computer, turn on the Background radio button.

4. Select a Print Time radio button:
   ▲ **Urgent** puts the job in the print queue before jobs marked Normal.
   ▲ **Normal** puts the job in the print queue in the order it was received.
   ▲ **Print at** lets you specify a date and time to print the job (see **Figure 45**).
   ▲ **Put Document on Hold** puts the job in the print queue but does not schedule it for printing.

To set PostScript printer Cover Page options

1. Open the Print dialog box (see **Figure 35**).

2. Choose Cover Page from the pop-up menu beneath the Printer pop-up menu (see **Figure 42**) to display Cover Page options (see **Figure 46**).

3. To print a cover page before or after the document, select either the Before Document or After Document radio button. You can then use the Cover Page Paper Source pop-up menu to specify whether the cover page should be from the paper cassette or manually fed (see **Figure 47**).

✔ Tips

- A cover page is a sheet of paper that identifies the source of the print job.

- Cover pages waste paper. Unless you're on a network and need to separate your print job from others, don't print a cover page.

To set PostScript printer Color Matching options

1. Open the Print dialog box (see **Figure 35**).

2. Choose Color Matching from the pop-up menu beneath the Printer pop-up menu (see **Figure 42**) to display Color Matching options (see **Figure 48**).

3. Choose an option from the Print Color pop-up menu (see **Figure 49**):

   ▲ **Black and White** prints in black and white.

   ▲ **Color/Grayscale** prints in color on a color printer or in shades of gray on a monochrome printer.

   ▲ **ColorSync Color Matching** and **PostScript Color Matching** prints in color using characteristics of a specific printer. You must select the printer's profile from the Printer Profile pop-up menu.

Figure 46. *The Cover Page options in the Print dialog box for a PostScript printer.*

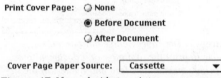

Figure 47. *If you decide to print a cover page, you can select a paper source for it.*

Figure 48. *The Color Matching options in the Print dialog box for a PostScript printer.*

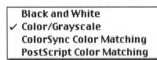

Figure 49. *There are four options under the Print Color pop-up menu.*

✔ Tip

- Color matching technology is beyond the scope of this book. If you have a color PostScript printer (lucky you!), consult the documentation that came with it for more information.

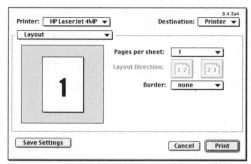

Figure 50. *The Layout options in the Print dialog box for a PostScript printer.*

Figure 51.
Choose the number of document pages that you want to appear on each printed page.

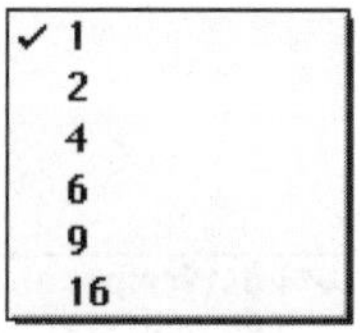

| ✓ 1 |
| 2 |
| 4 |
| 6 |
| 9 |
| 16 |

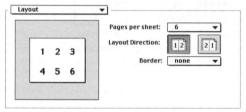

Figure 52. *The Print dialog box displays a sample layout for the number of pages you selected.*

Figure 53.
Choose an option from the Border pop-up menu to remove or add a border around document pages.

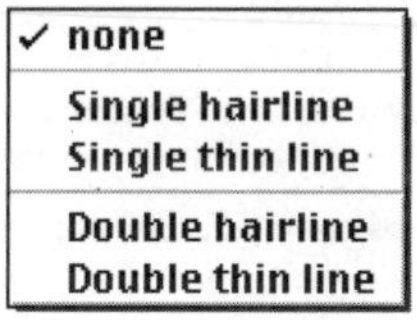

| ✓ none |
| **Single hairline** |
| **Single thin line** |
| **Double hairline** |
| **Double thin line** |

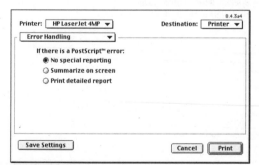

Figure 54. *The Error Handling options in the Print dialog box for a PostScript printer.*

To set PostScript printer Layout options

1. Open the Print dialog box (see **Figure 35**).

2. Choose Layout from the pop-up menu beneath the Printer pop-up menu (see **Figure 42**) to display Layout options (see **Figure 50**).

3. Choose the number of document pages that you want to print on each sheet of paper from the Pages per Sheet pop-up menu (see **Figure 51**).

4. If you select a value higher than 1 in step 3, click a Layout Direction button (see **Figure 52**) to specify the order in which document pages should appear on the printed pages.

5. To add a border around each document page, choose an option from the Border pop-up menu (see **Figure 53**).

✔ Tip

- Select 2 or 4 from the Pages per Sheet pop-up menu (see **Figure 51**) to print legible page proofs with less paper.

To set PostScript printer Error Handling options

1. Open the Print dialog box (see **Figure 35**).

2. Choose Error Handling from the pop-up menu beneath the Printer pop-up menu (see **Figure 42**) to display Error Handling options (see **Figure 54**).

3. Select the option that you want to report PostScript Errors:

   ▲ **No special reporting** does not report PostScript errors.

   ▲ **Summarize on screen** displays PostScript errors on screen as they occur.

   ▲ **Print detailed report** prints a report of PostScript errors after they occur.

Setting PostScript Printer Options

To set PostScript printer Save as File options

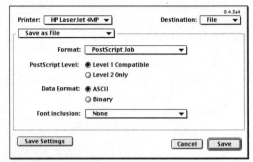

1. Open the Print dialog box (see **Figure** 35).

2. Choose Save as File from the pop-up menu beneath the Printer pop-up menu (see **Figure 42**) to display Save as File options (see **Figure 55**).

3. Choose File from the Destination pop-up menu (see **Figure 55**).

Figure 55. *The Save as File options in the Print dialog box for a PostScript printer.*

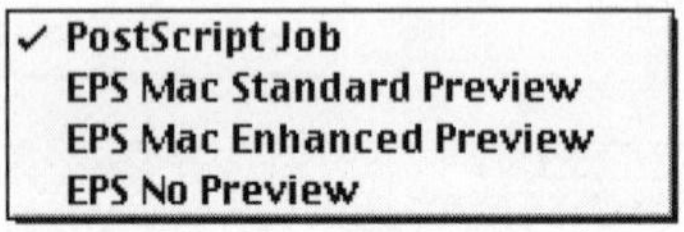

4. Choose an option from from the Format pop-up menu (see **Figure 56**):

   ▲ **PostScript Job** saves the document as a standard PostScript file.

   ▲ **EPS Mac Standard Preview** saves the document as an encapsulated PostScript file with a bitmap preview.

   ▲ **EPS Mac Enhanced Preview** saves the document as an encapsulated PostScript file with a QuickDraw PICT preview.

   ▲ **EPS No Preview** saves the document as an encapsulated PostScript file without a preview.

Figure 56. *Choose an option from the Format pop-up menu to specify a PostScript file format.*

5. Select a PostScript Level radio button.

6. Select a Data Format radio button.

7. Choose an option from the Font Inclusion pop-up menu (see **Figure 57**):

   ▲ **None** does not save the fonts with the file.

   ▲ **All** saves all the fonts with the file.

   ▲ **All But Standard 13** saves all the fonts with the file except the 13 fonts found on most PostScript printers.

   ▲ **All But Fonts in PPD file** saves all the fonts with the file except the fonts listed in the PPD file selected for the printer.

Figure 57. *Choose an option from the Font Inclusion pop-up menu to specify which fonts should be included with the file.*

✔ Tip

■ Details about PostScript options are beyond the scope of this book.

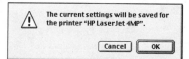

Figure 58. *The dialog box confirms that you really do want to save settings for your printer.*

To save PostScript printer Print options

1. Click the Save Settings button at the bottom of the Print dialog box (see **Figures 35**, **44**, **46**, **48**, **50**, **54**, and **55**).

2. A dialog box like the one in **Figure 58** appears. Click OK to save the current settings for the printer.

✔ Tip

■ Saving the settings for your printer displays the options you selected as the default options for the printer each time you use the Print dialog box.

To process the print job

1. Click the Print button in the Print dialog box (see **Figures 35**, **44**, **46**, **48**, **50**, and **54**).

   or

   Click the Save button in the Print dialog box (see **Figure 55**).

2. If background printing is turned on, the print job is sent to the print queue, where it waits for its turn to be printed. You can continue working as soon as the spooling window disappears.

   or

   If background printing is turned off, the print job is sent to the printer and printed. You'll have to wait until it's completely spooled to the printer before you can continue working with your computer.

   or

   If you saved the document as a Post-Script file, a Save As dialog box appears (see **Figure 59**). Use it to enter a name, select a disk location, and save the file.

Figure 59. *Use this Save As dialog box to enter a name, select a location, and Save a document as a PostScript file.*

✔ Tips

■ You can normally cancel a print job as it is spooled to the print queue or printer by pressing ⌘. . Any pages spooled *before* you press ⌘. , however, may be printed anyway.

■ I tell you how to cancel a print job that has already been spooled to a print queue later in this chapter.

■ I tell you how to use the Save As dialog box in **Chapter 5**.

About the Print One Command

Some applications include a Print One or Print One Copy command under the File menu (see **Figure 60**). This command sends a single copy of the active document to the printer using the current Page Setup and Print options. The print dialog box does not appear.

Figure 60.
The Print One Copy command does just that—it prints one copy of the active document without displaying the Print dialog box.

✔ Tip

■ The Print One command is a quick way to print one copy of a document, avoiding the Print dialog box.

About Desktop Printers

When you use the Chooser to select and set up a printer, Mac OS automatically creates a desktop printer for it. As the name suggests, it appears on the desktop as a printer driver icon (see **Figure 61**).

Desktop printers can be used for a number of things:

■ Identify and change the default printer.

■ Print documents using drag and drop.

■ Check or change items in a print queue.

■ Stop or start a print queue.

I tell you about these things on the following pages.

Figure 61. *Desktop printer icons. The one on the right is the default printer.*

To identify the default printer

If you only have one desktop printer icon, it represents the default printer.

or

If you have multiple desktop printer icons, the one with the dark border around it represents the default printer (see **Figure 61**).

✔ Tip

■ The default printer is the currently selected printer.

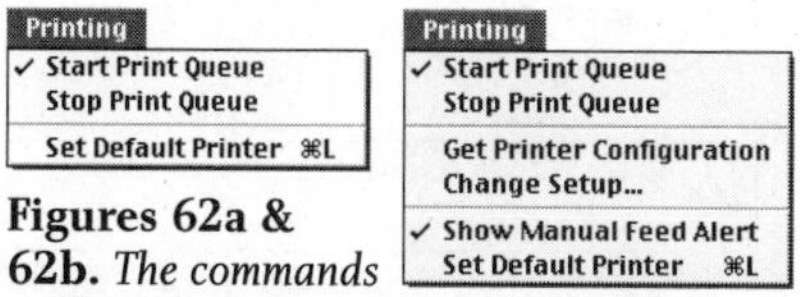

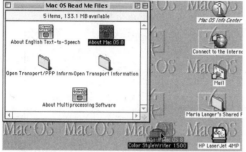

Figures 62a & 62b. *The commands on the Printing menu vary depending on what desktop printer icon is selected. These Printing menus are for a Color StyleWriter 1500 (left) and a LaserWriter (right).*

Figure 63. *Drag the icon for the document that you want to print onto the desktop printer icon for the printer on which you want to print it.*

Figure 64. *A page icon appears on a desktop printer that has at least one print job queued.*

Figure 65. *Choose Open from the File menu.*

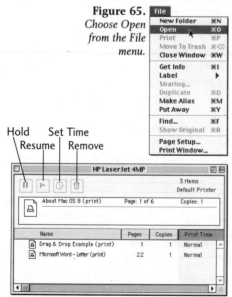

Hold Set Time
Resume Remove

Figure 66. *Opening a desktop printer displays its print queue.*

To change the default printer

1. Select the desktop printer icon for the printer that you want to set as the default printer.

2. Choose Set Default Printer from the Printing menu (see **Figures 62a** and **62b**).

   or

   Press ⌘L.

To print a document with drag & drop

1. Drag the icon for the document that you want to print onto the desktop printer icon for the printer on which you want to print it (see **Figure 63**). If the application that created the document is not already running, Mac OS launches it.

2. Set options in the Print dialog box that appears.

3. ClickPrint.

✔ Tips

■ Drag and drop printing is a great way to print documents on any printer—without changing the default printer.

■ When a desktop printer contains one or more documents to be printed, a page icon appears on it (see **Figure 64**).

■ I tell you about the Print dialog box earlier in this chapter.

To open a desktop printer

Double-click the desktop printer icon.

or

Select the desktop printer icon and choose Open from the File menu (see **Figure 65**) or press ⌘O.

The desktop printer's window opens. If any print jobs are waiting to be printed, they appear in a list (see **Figure 66**).

Changing Printers, Drag & Drop Printing

To change the order of items in a print queue

1. Open the desktop printer for the print queue that you want to change (see **Figure 66**).

2. Drag the item that you want to move into a higher (see **Figure 67**) or lower position on the list of files to be printed. When you release the mouse button, the item moves (see **Figure 68**).

To set print time for a job

1. Open the desktop printer for the print queue that you want to change (see **Figure 66**).

2. Select the icon for the print job that you want to schedule (see **Figure 68**).

3. Click the Set Time (clock) button. The Set Print time dialog box appears (see **Figure 69**).

4. Select the radio button for the time option that you want:
   ▲ **Urgent** puts the job in the print queue before jobs marked Normal.
   ▲ **Normal** puts the job in the print queue in the order it was received.
   ▲ **At Time** lets you specify a date and time to print the job (see **Figure 70**).

5. Click OK. The date and time you set appears in the Print Time column of the desktop printer window (see **Figure 71**).

To remove a job from a print queue

1. Open the desktop printer for the print queue that you want to change (see **Figure 66**).

2. Select the icon for the print job that you want to cancel (see **Figure 71**).

3. Click the Remove (trash can) button. The selected print job disappears.

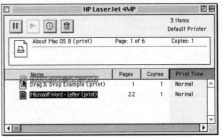

Figure 67. *Drag the item that you want to move into a new position in the print queue.*

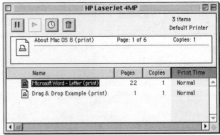

Figure 68. *When you release the mouse button, the job moves.*

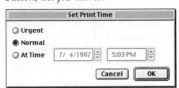

Figure 69. *The Set Print Time dialog box lets you specify when a job should print.*

Figure 70. *When you select the At Time radio button, you can enter the date and time for a job to print.*

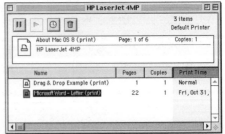

Figure 71. *The print time column of the desktop printer window displays the date and time a job is scheduled to print.*

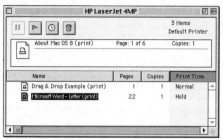

Figure 72. *When you put a print job on hold, the word* Hold *appears in the Print Time column.*

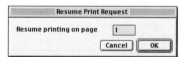

Figure 73. *The Resume Print Request dialog box lets you specify the page from which to resume printing.*

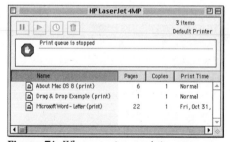

Figure 74. *When you stop a print queue, a stop sign appears in the print queue window...*

Figure 75.
...and on the desktop printer icon.

To put a print job on hold

1. Open the desktop printer for the print queue that you want to change (see **Figure 66**).
2. Select the icon for the print job that you want to put on hold (see **Figure 71**).
3. Click the Hold (double red bar) button. The word *Hold* appears in the Print Time column of the window (see **Figure 72**).

✔ Tip

■ A print job on hold will remain on hold until you resume it.

To resume a job

1. Open the desktop printer for the print queue that you want to change (see **Figure 66**).
2. Select the icon for a print job on hold that you want to resume (see **Figure 71**).
3. Click the Resume (green triangle) button.
4. The Resume Print Request dialog box appears (see **Figure 73**). Enter the number of the page on which you want to resume printing and click OK. The word *Normal* appears in the Print Time column of the window (see **Figure 66**).

To stop a print queue

Choose Stop Print Queue from the Printing menu (see **Figures 62a** and **62b**). A stop sign icon appears in the print queue window (see **Figure 74**) and on the desktop printer icon (see **Figure 75**).

✔ Tip

■ A stopped print queue will remain stopped until you restart it.

To restart a print queue

Choose Start Print Queue from the Printing menu (see **Figures 62a** and **62b**). The stop sign icons disappear.

Holding Print Jobs, Stopping Print Queues

About Troubleshooting Printing Problems

When a printing problem occurs, Mac OS can often give you hints to help you figure out why. Here are some examples:

- A dialog box like the one in **Figure 76** appears when your computer can't find the selected printer. Check to make sure the printer is properly connected and turned on.

- A dialog box like the one in **Figure 77** appears when your printer is out of paper. Add paper!

- The desktop printer's print queue window can often provide information about the printer's status. In **Figure 78**, the printer is off line; touching a button on the printer solves the problem.

✔ Tip

- If you have printing problems that Mac OS can't help you identify, check the troubleshooting section of the documentation that came with your printer.

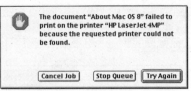

Figure 76. *This dialog box appeared when my printer wasn't turned on.*

Figure 77. *This dialog box appeared when my printer ran out of paper.*

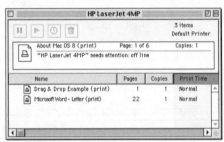

Figure 78. *This desktop printer window notes that my printer is off line.*

NETWORKING & TELECOMMUNICATIONS

About Networking & Telecommunications

Mac OS-compatible computers offer two ways to connect to other computers:

- **Networking** uses direct connections and network protocols to connect your computer to others on a network. Once connected, you can share files, access e-mail, and run special network applications on server computers.

- **Telecommunications** uses a modem, telephone line, and communications software to connect your computer to another computer. Once connected, you can exchange files, access e-mail, and work with other features offered by the host computer.

✔ Tips

- If you use your computer at work, you may be connected to a companywide network; if so, you'll find the networking part of this chapter very helpful. But if you use your computer at home and have only one computer, you won't have much need for the networking information here.

- Online services, such as America Online and CompuServe, are huge computer systems offering a wealth of information and entertainment for a fee. You can access these systems via modem or Internet connection.

- You can access the Internet either through a network or modem connection. I tell you about connecting to the Internet in **Chapter 10**.

About Open Transport & Network Connections

Mac OS 8 includes *Open Transport*, System software that enables a Mac OS computer to connect to virtually any kind of network.

Most networks use one of the following two types of cables and connectors:

- **LocalTalk** connectors and standard telephone cables connect to the serial ports of computers and network printers. Devices are *daisy-chained*—linked one after another in a chain. LocalTalk is cheap and easy networking that is available on every Mac OS computer, but it is very slow.

- **Ethernet** cables connect to the Ethernet ports or Ethernet network interface cards of computers and network printers. Depending on the type of port and size of the network, additional hardware such as *transceivers* and *hubs* may be needed. Ethernet is faster than LocalTalk, and is widely used for company and corporate networks.

✔ Tips

- Open Transport software replaces *AppleTalk* software, which is now called *Classic Networking*. Just to confuse you, however, the term AppleTalk is still often used to refer to networking.

- Details on network configurations are far beyond the scope of this book. The information here is provided primarily to give you an idea of how network connections work and introduce some of the network terms you might encounter when working with your computer and other documentation.

- If your computer is on a large network, consult the System Administrator before changing any network configuration options.

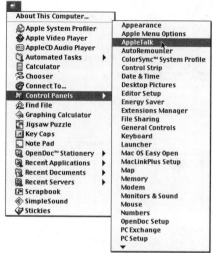

Figure 1. *Choose AppleTalk from the Control Panels sub-menu under the Apple menu.*

Figure 2. *The AppleTalk control panel lets you select the network connection port.*

Figure 3.
Choose a port from the Connect via pop-up menu.

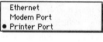

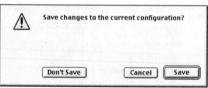

Figure 4. *Click Save in this dialog box if you're sure that you've selected the correct port.*

To select the network connection port

1. Choose AppleTalk from the Control Panels submenu under the Apple menu (see **Figure 1**).

2. In the AppleTalk control panel that appears (see **Figure 2**), use the Connect via pop-up menu (see **Figure 3**) to select the port to which the network is connected to your computer.

3. Close the AppleTalk control panel.

4. If you changed the configuration, a dialog box like the one in **Figure 4** appears. Click Save.

✔ Tips

■ The Mac OS Setup Assistant should automatically configure the network connection for you—if you are connected to the network when you run it. I tell you about the Mac OS Setup Assistant in **Chapter 1**.

■ If you select the wrong port in step 2, your network connection will not work.

■ I tell you more about control panels in **Chapter 12**.

Selecting the Network Connection Port

To turn on AppleTalk

1. Choose Chooser from the Apple menu (see **Figure 5**).

2. Select the AppleShare icon on the left side of the Chooser window (see **Figure 6**).

3. If necessary, select the Active radio button at the bottom of the Chooser window. A dialog box like the one in **Figure 7** appears. Click OK.

4. Close the Chooser to save your settings.

✔ Tip

■ As the dialog box in **Figure 7** reminds you, you must be connected to an AppleTalk network to activate AppleTalk.

To connect to another computer

1. Choose Chooser from the Apple menu (see **Figure 5**).

2. Select the AppleShare icon on the left side of the Chooser window (see **Figure 6**).

3. If you're on a multiple-zone network, select the name of the zone in which the computer to which you want to connect is listed.

4. Select the name of the computer to which you want to connect (see **Figure 8**).

5. Click OK.

6. A connection dialog box appears (see **Figure 9**). Enter your name and password in the Name and Password edit boxes.

7. Click OK.

8. In the list of folders or volumes that appears (see **Figure 10**), select the one that you want to open.

9. Click OK. The icon for the item appears on your desktop (see **Figure 11**).

10. Close the Chooser window.

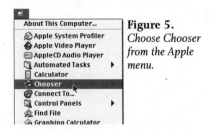

Figure 5.
Choose Chooser from the Apple menu.

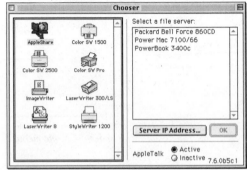

Figure 6. *Click the AppleShare icon on the left side of the Chooser window. The Chooser window may look different if you're on a multiple-zone network.*

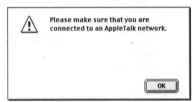

Figure 7. *If you have to turn AppleTalk on, a dialog box like this reminds you to make sure you're connected to a network.*

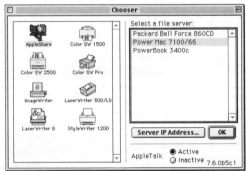

Figure 8. *Select the computer to which you want to connect.*

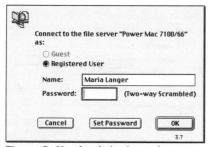

Figure 9. *Use this dialog box to log onto the computer.*

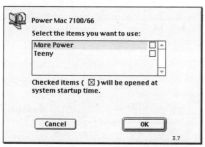

Figure 10. *Select the volume or folder to which you want to connect.*

Figure 11.
The icon for the item to which you are connected appears on the Desktop.

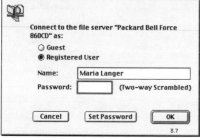

Figure 12. *Some computers allow guest connections. If so, the Guest radio button will be available in the connection dialog box.*

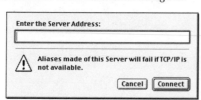

Figure 13. *Enter a server's IP address in this dialog box.*

✔ Tips

- If you're not sure which zone to select in step 3, ask your System Administrator.

- You can only connect to computers that recognize you as a user or allow guest connections (see **Figure 12**).

- Although computers are referred to as "file servers" in the Chooser (see **Figures 6** and **8** and connection dialog box (see **Figures 9** and **12**), you can connect to any computer on the network that allows connections— not just dedicated file servers.

- To select more than one server item in step 8, hold down (Shift) while clicking each item.

- To automatically connect to a server item every time you start your computer, turn on the check box beside the item name (see **Figure 10**).

- To connect to a server using its IP address, click the Server IP Address button in the Chooser window (see **Figures 6** and **8**). Then enter the server's IP address in the dialog box that appears (see **Figure 13**) and click Connect. TCP/IP must be installed for this to work. I tell you about TCP/IP in **Chapter 10**.

To disconnect from a computer

Drag the icons for the items to which you are connected to the Trash.

✔ Tip

- Dragging a server item to the trash does not delete the contents of that item.

About Sharing Files

You can share files on your computer with other network users. To do this, you must do three things:

1. Use the File Sharing control panel to set a network identity and turn on file sharing.

2. Create user and group accounts for the individuals who you want to access your computer.

3. Set privileges for the items that you want to share.

About the File Sharing Control Panel

The File Sharing control panel (see **Figures 14** and **22**) enables you to do the following:

■ Set the network identity for your computer, including the owner name, owner password, and computer name.

■ Turn file sharing and program linking on or off.

■ See who is connected to your computer and what items are being shared.

To open the File Sharing control panel

Choose File Sharing from the Control Panels submenu under the Apple menu (see **Figure 15**).

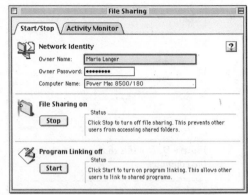

Figure 14. *The Start/Stop options for the File Sharing control panel.*

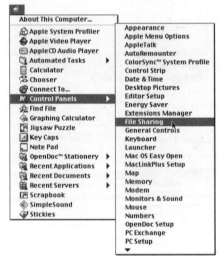

Figure 15. *Choose File Sharing from the Control Panels submenu under the Apple menu.*

To set or change your computer's network identity

1. Open the File Sharing control panel.

2. If necessary, click the Start/Stop tab to display its options (see **Figure 14**).

3. Enter your name in the Owner Name edit box.

4. Enter a password to protect your computer in the Owner Password edit box. The characters you type turn to bullet characters when you advance to another edit box.

5. Enter a name for your computer in the Computer Name edit box.

6. Close the File Sharing control panel to save your settings.

✔ Tips

- If you used the Mac OS Setup Assistant to configure your computer after installing Mac OS 8, your computer's network identity will already be set. I tell you about the Mac OS Setup Assistant in **Chapter 1**.

- You can name your computer anything you like. I use model names on my network, but you may want to name your computer after yourself so that other network users know it's yours.

- The Computer Name is what identifies your computer in the Chooser window of other computers on the network.

- Although you can leave the Owner Password edit box blank, doing so enables other users to connect to your computer without a password.

Setting the Network Identity

To turn file sharing on

1. Open the File Sharing control panel.

2. If necessary, click the Start/Stop tab to display its options (see **Figure 14**).

3. Click the Start button in the File Sharing area (see **Figure 16**). The status area indicates that sharing is starting up (see **Figure 17**). After a moment, it indicates that file sharing is on (see **Figure 14**).

4. Close the File Sharing control panel.

✔ Tips

■ File sharing enables other users to access files and folders on your hard disk as specified by users and groups settings and access privileges.

■ If there is no Start button in the File Sharing area of the File Sharing control panel, file sharing is already turned on.

■ If AppleTalk is not turned on when you attempt to start file sharing, a dialog box like the one in **Figure 18** appears. Click OK to dismiss the dialog box and turn AppleTalk on. I tell you about turning AppleTalk on earlier in this chapter.

To turn program linking on

1. Open the File Sharing control panel.

2. If necessary, click the Start/Stop tab to display its options (see **Figure 14**).

3. Click the Start button in the Program Linking area (see **Figure 14**). After a moment, the status area indicates that program linking is on.

4. Close the File Sharing control panel.

✔ Tip

■ Program linking enables other users to link to shared programs on your computer. If you're not sure if an application can be linked, check its documentation.

Figure 16. *Click the Start button to turn file sharing on.*

Figure 17. *The status area tells you that file sharing is starting up.*

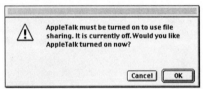

Figure 18. *As this dialog box points out, AppleTalk must be turned on before you turn on file sharing.*

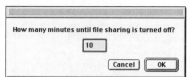

Figure 19. *Enter the number of minutes before users are disconnected.*

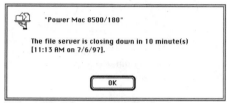

Figure 20. *When you stop file sharing, connected users see one or more warning messages like this one...*

Figure 21. *...before they're disconnected and see a message like this one.*

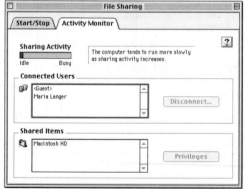

Figure 22. *The Activity Monitor tab of the File Sharing control panels lets you see who's connected.*

To turn file sharing or program linking off

1. Open the File Sharing control panel.
2. If necessary, click the Start/Stop tab to display its options (see **Figure 14**).
3. Click the Stop button in the File Sharing area (see **Figure 14**) or Program Linking area.
4. If you turned off file sharing, a dialog box like the one in **Figure 19** appears. Enter the number of minutes before users are disconnected and click OK.
5. Close the File Sharing control panel.

✔ Tips

■ When you turn off file sharing, connected users see dialog boxes like the ones in **Figures 20** and **21**.

■ When file sharing is turned off, all users are automatically disconnected.

To monitor file sharing activity

1. Open the File Sharing control panel.
2. If necessary, click the Activity Monitor tab. It displays connected users and shared items, as well as an activity meter (see **Figure 22**).

✔ Tips

■ You can disconnect a specific user by selecting his name in the Connected Users list and clicking the Disconnect button. A dialog box like the one in **Figure 19** lets you enter the number of minutes before the user is disconnected.

■ You can check privileges for shared items by selecting the item name in the Shared Items list and clicking the Privileges button. I tell you more about privileges later in this chapter.

Turning File Sharing Off, Monitoring Activity

About Users & Groups

File sharing is allowed on an individual or group basis set by users and groups:

■ A **user** is an individual account consisting of a user name and password.

■ A **group** is a number of users with the same privileges.

Users and groups are set up and modified with the Users & Groups control panel (see **Figure 23**).

✔ Tip

■ You should set up a user account for each network user with which you expect to share files.

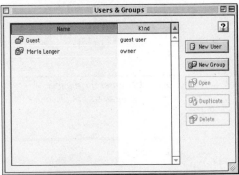

Figure 23. *The Users & Groups control panel enables you to maintain accounts for the people who access files on your computer.*

To open the Users & Groups control panel

Choose Users & Groups from the Control Panels submenu under the Apple menu (see **Figure 24**). The Users & Groups control panel appears (see **Figure 23**). It lists all the users and groups set up for your computer.

✔ Tip

■ By default, your computer is set up with two users: the owner (you) and a guest user (Guest).

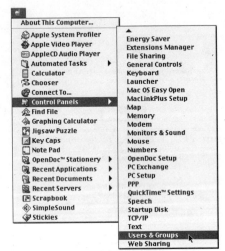

Figure 24. *Choose Users & Groups from the Control Panels submenu under the Apple menu.*

Figure 25. *You create users with the New User window.*

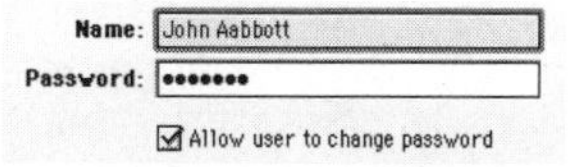

Figure 26.
Enter a user's name and password.

Figure 27. *Choose Sharing from the pop-up menu at the top of the window.*

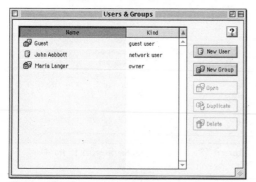

Figure 28. *Choose Sharing from the pop-up menu to set sharing options.*

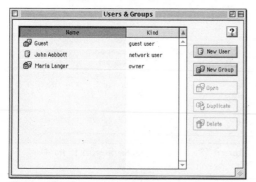

Figure 29. *The new user appears in the Users & Groups control panel window.*

To create a new user

1. Open the Users & Groups control panel (see **Figure 23**).

2. Click the New User button. A New User window appears (see **Figure 25**).

3. Enter the user's name in the Name edit box. The name appears in the title bar for the window when you advance to the next edit box.

4. Enter the user's password in the Password edit box. The characters you type change to bullets when you advance to another edit box (see **Figure 26**).

5. To allow the user to change his password, make sure the Allow user to change password check box is turned on.

6. Select Sharing from the Show pop-up menu near the top of the window (see **Figure 27**). The sharing options appear (see **Figure 28**).

7. To enable file sharing for the user, make sure the Allow user to connect to this computer check box is turned on.

8. To enable program linking for the user, make sure the Allow user to link to programs on this computer check box is turned on.

9. Click the window's close box. The user's name appears in the list of users and groups (see **Figure 29**).

✔ Tip

■ I explain file sharing and program linking earlier in this chapter.

To create a group

1. Open the Users & Groups control panel (see **Figure 23**).

2. Click the New Group button. A New Group window appears (see **Figure 30**).

3. Enter the group's name in the Name edit box. The name appears in the title bar for the window when you click outside the edit box.

4. Drag the icons for a user that you want to include in the group from the Users & Groups control panel window to the group window (see **Figure 31**). When you release the mouse button, the user appears in the window (see **Figure 32**).

5. Repeat step 4 for each user that you want to include in the group.

6. Click the group window's close box to close it. The group name appears in the Users & Groups control panel window (see **Figure 33**).

✔ Tips

■ You must create a user before you can add it to a group. I tell you how to create users on the previous page.

■ You can add each user to as many groups as you like.

Figure 30.
Use the New Group window to name a group and add users to it.

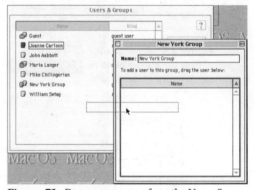

Figure 31. *Drag a user name from the Users & Groups control panel to the group window.*

Figure 32. *When you release the mouse button, the user's name appears in the group window.*

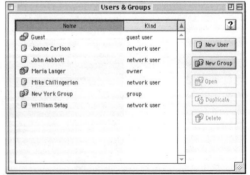

Figure 33. *The group name appears in the Users & Groups control panel window.*

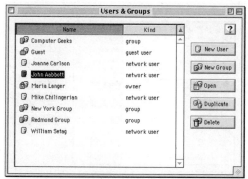

Figure 34. *Select the name of the user or group that you want to modify.*

To modify a user or group

1. Open the Users & Groups control panel.
2. Select the name of the user or group that you want to modify (see **Figure 34**),and click Open.

   or

   Double-click the name of the user or group that you want to modify.
3. Make changes in the user or group window (see **Figures 25**, **28**, and **32**) as desired.
4. Click the window's close box to save your changes.

To remove a user from a group

1. Open the Users & Groups control panel.
2. Double-click the name of the user that you want to remove from a group.
3. Choose Sharing from the pop-up menu at the top of the user window (see **Figure 35**).
4. Click the name of the group from which you want to remove the user.
5. Press (Delete).
6. In the confirmation dialog box that appears (see **Figure 36**), click Remove. The user's name disappears from the list.
7. Click the window's close box to save your changes.

   or

1. Open the Users & Groups control panel.
2. Double-click the name of the group from which you want to remove a user.
3. Click the name of the user that you want to remove from the group.
4. Press (Delete).
5. In the confirmation dialog box that appears (see **Figure 36**), click Remove.
6. Click the window's close box to save your changes.

Figure 35. *The sharing settings in the user window list the groups to which the user belongs.*

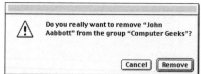

Figure 36. *A confirmation dialog box like this appears when you try to remove a user from a group.*

To duplicate a user or group

1. Open the Users & Groups control panel.
2. Select the name of the user or group that you want to duplicate (see **Figure 34**).
3. Click Duplicate. A copy of the item appears beneath the original (see **Figure 37**).

✔ Tips

- Duplicating a user or group is a quick way to create a new user or group with most of the same settings as an existing user or group.
- Once you duplicate a user or group, you can open its window to modify it. I tell you about modifying users and groups on the previous page.

To delete a user or group

1. Open the Users & Groups control panel.
2. Select the name of the user or group that you want to delete (see **Figure 34**).
3. Click Delete.
4. A confirmation dialog box like the one in **Figure 38** appears. Click Delete.

✔ Tip

- If you delete a user of group that owns items on your computer, those items are automatically reassigned to the computer's owner (you).

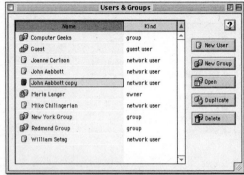

Figure 37. *When you duplicate a user or group, the copy appears beneath the original in the list.*

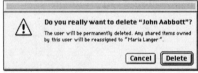

Figure 38. *A confirmation dialog box like this one appears when you try to delete a user or group.*

Duplicating & Deleting Users & Groups

Figure 39. *The sharing window for a folder...*

Figure 40. *...and for a disk.*

About Setting Privileges

The final step to sharing items is to specify which items will be shared and how users can access them. A user's access to an item is referred to as his *privileges*.

There are four types of privileges:

- **Read & write** privileges allow the user to open and save files.

- **Read only** privileges allow the user to open files, but not save files.

- **Write only** privileges allow the user to save files, but not open them.

- **None** means the user can neither open nor save files.

Privileges can be set for three categories of users:

- **Owner** is the user or group who can set access privileges for the item. You will probably be the owner for most, if not all, of the folders on your computer.

- **User/Group** is the user or group which has access of the item. This can be set to None if only the owner should have access.

- **Everyone** is everyone else on the network.

You set privileges in the sharing window for a specific folder (see **Figure 39**) or disk (see **Figure 40**).

✔ Tips

- A disk or folder with write only privileges is sometimes referred to as a *drop box* because users can drag and drop files into it but cannot see its contents.

- It's vital that you set privileges correctly if there are confidential files on your computer. Otherwise those files could be accessible by other users on your network.

About Setting Privileges

To open the sharing window

1. Select the folder or disk for which you want to open the sharing window.

2. Choose Sharing from the File menu (see **Figure 41**). The sharing window appears (see **Figures 39** and **40**).

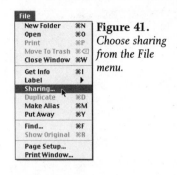

Figure 41.
Choose sharing from the File menu.

✔ Tip

■ You cannot open a sharing window for an individual file.

To turn on sharing

1. Open the sharing window for the folder or disk (see **Figures 39** and **40**).

2. Turn on the Share this item and its contents check box.

3. Close the sharing window.

✔ Tip

■ If the folder is inside another folder or disk that is shared, the sharing window will look like the one in **Figure 42**. If desired, you can turn on the Use enclosing folder's privileges check box to automatically assume the privileges of the folder or disk in which this folder resides—even if it is moved.

To prevent a shared folder from being moved, renamed, or deleted

1. Open the sharing window for the folder (see **Figures 39** and **42**).

2. Turn on the Can't move, rename, or delete this item check box.

3. Close the sharing window.

✔ Tip

■ It's a good idea to enable this option if you're concerned about users modifying folders on your hard disk.

Figure 42. *If a folder resides inside a shared folder or disk, there will be no Share this item and its contents check box.*

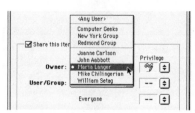

Figure 43. *Choose an owner from the Owner pop-up menu.*

Figure 44.
The Privileges pop-up menus list all four types of privileges.

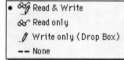

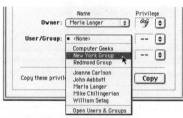

Figure 45. *Choose the primary user from the User/Group pop-up menu.*

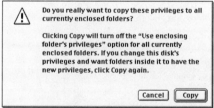

Figure 46. *When you click the Copy button, a confirmation dialog box like this one appears.*

Figures 47a & 47b.
Two examples of how privileges can be set.

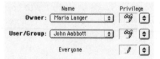

To set privileges

1. Open the sharing window for the folder or disk (see **Figures 39**, **40**, and **42**).

2. Choose a user or group name from the Owner pop-up menu (see **Figure 43**). Then choose a privilege from the Privilege pop-up menu on the same line (see **Figure 44**).

3. If desired, choose a user or group name from the User/Group pop-up menu (see **Figure 45**). Then choose a privilege from the Privilege pop-up menu on the same line (see **Figure 44**).

4. If desired, choose a privilege from the Privilege pop-up menu on the Everyone line (see **Figure 44**).

5. To assign the same privileges to every folder within the folder or disk, click the Copy button. A confirmation dialog box like the one in **Figure 46** appears. Click Copy to copy the privileges.

6. Close the sharing window.

✔ Tips

■ The Owner and User/Group pop-up menus include all users and groups in the Users & Groups control panel. I tell you about users and groups earlier in this chapter.

■ Confused? These two examples may help you understand how users and groups work.

▲ In **Figure 47a**, the item is owned by Maria Langer, who can open and save files. The primary group is New York Group, whose members can only save files. No one else can access the item.

▲ In **Figure 47b**, the item is owned by Maria Langer, who can open and save files. The primary user is John Aabbott, who can also open and save files. Everyone else can only save files.

Setting Privileges

About Icons & Windows of Shared Items

The appearance of a shared item provides visual clues to its privilege settings.

■ Folders that cannot be opened have buckles around them (see **Figure 48**). If you try to open of these folders, a dialog box like the one in **Figure 49** tells you why you can't.

■ A drop-box folder has a down-pointing arrow above it (see **Figure 48**). When you drop an item into one of these folders, a dialog box like the one in **Figure 50** reminds you that you won't be able to see it once it's gone.

■ The window for a read-only folder displays a tiny pencil with a slash icon on the left side of the header (see **Figure 51**). When you try to drag an item into it, a dialog box like the one in **Figure 52** tells you why you can't.

Figure 48. *Folders that can't be opened have buckles around them; a drop box folder has an arrow above it.*

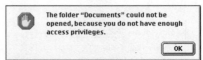

Figure 49. *When you try to open a folder you're not allowed to open, a dialog box like this appears.*

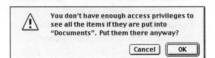

Figure 50. *When you use a drop box, a dialog box like this appears.*

Figure 51. *A tiny icon on the left side of the header indicates that this is a read-only folder.*

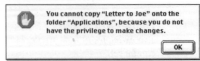

Figure 52. *When you try to copy a file to a folder with read-only privileges, a dialog box like this appears.*

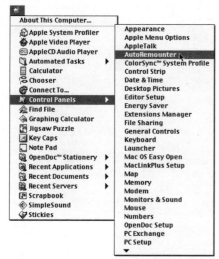

Figure 53. *Choose AutoRemounter from the Control Panels submenu under the File menu.*

Figure 54.
Set options in the AutoRemounter control panel.

About AutoRemounter

When your computer goes to sleep, network connections are lost. You can use AutoRemounter to instruct your computer to automatically reconnect to a shared disk after sleep.

✔ Tips

■ Not all computers are compatible with the sleep feature. I tell you about sleep in **Chapter 2**.

■ AutoRemounter is especially useful for PowerBooks since sleep mode is commonly used to save power. I tell you about PowerBooks in **Chapter 11**.

To use AutoRemounter

1. Choose AutoRemounter from the Control Panels submenu under the Apple menu (see **Figure 53**). The AutoRemounter control panel appears (see **Figure 54**).

2. To automatically remount shared disks after sleep, select the After Sleep radio button. Then select one of the Connect To Disks By radio buttons to either connect without a password or with a password.

   or

   To disable AutoRemounter, select the Off Radio button.

3. Close AutoRemounter to save your settings.

✔ Tip

■ If you're concerned about security, be sure to select the Always Requiring Passwords radio button in step 2. Otherwise someone could wake your computer while you're away from your desk and automatically have access to the network—logged on as you!

About Modem Connections

You can also use a modem and a standard telephone line to connect to other computers. A *modem* is a hardware device that is either inside your computer (an *internal* modem) or connected to one of your computer's serial ports (an *external* modem). You configure a modem connection with the Modem control panel.

Having a modem isn't enough to connect to another computer. You also need telecommunications software. The software you use depends on the type of system you are connecting to. For example, to connect to a friend's computer, you could use a general purpose program like ZTerm; to connect to an online service like America Online, you would use the freely distributable America Online client software. Modems usually come with one or more kinds of telecommunications software.

✔ Tips

- Although Mac OS 8 does not include any general purpose telecommunications software, it does include Apple Remote Access (ARA) Client, which I discuss at the end of this chapter.

- Most of today's modems can also send and receive faxes. Software to utilize this modem feature normally comes with the modem.

- There are many modem makes and models that will work with Mac OS-compatible computers—far too many to discuss in detail here. Read the documentation that came with your modem to learn more about using it and its features.

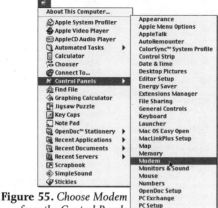

Figure 55. *Choose Modem from the Control Panels submenu under the Apple menu.*

Figure 56. *The Modem control panel.*

Figures 57 & 58. *Use pop-up menus like these to select a connection port (above) and a modem make and model (right).*

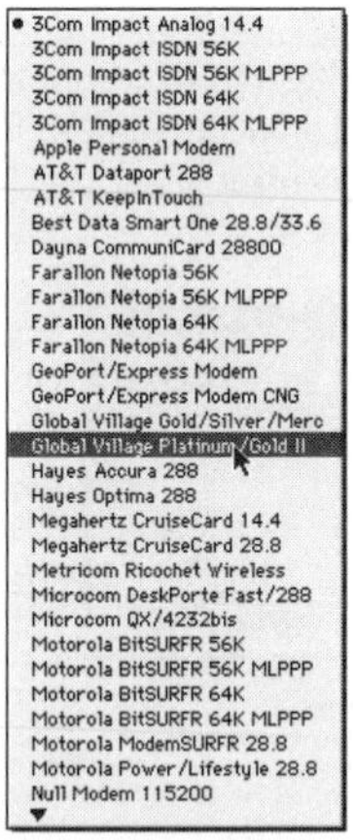

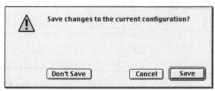

Figure 59. *Click Save to save your settings.*

To set modem options with the Modem control panel

1. Choose Modem from the Control Panels submenu under the Apple menu (see **Figure 55**). The Modem control panel appears (see **Figure 56**).

2. Choose an option from the Connect Via pop-up menu (see **Figure 57**). The options offered in the menu will vary depending on your computer model.

3. Select a modem make and model from the Modem pop-up menu (see **Figure 58**).

4. Select one of the Sound radio buttons to turn the modem speaker On or Off.

5. Select one of the Dialing radio buttons to specify whether you have Tone or Pulse dialing.

6. To instruct the modem dial no matter what the dialog tone sounds like, turn on the Ignore dial tone check box.

7. Click the Modem control panel's close box.

8. In the confirmation dialog box that appears (see **Figure 59**), click Save.

✔ Tips

■ If you cannot find your modem make and model in the Modem pop-up menu (see **Figure 58**), try another modem with the same brand name or one of the Hayes modems.

■ Turn on the Ignore dial tone check box in step 6 if you have a telephone answering system that changes the sound of a dial tone when messages are waiting.

■ The telecommunications software you use with your modem may have other settings. Check the documentation that came with the software for configuration information.

Using the Modem Control Panel

About Remote Access Client

Apple Remote Access (ARA) Client is tele-communications software that's part of Mac OS 8. It enables you to connect to Remote Access Server, which can give you access to one or more computers on a network.

✔ Tips

■ To use Remote Access Client, Remote Access Server software must be installed on the computer or network to which you want to connect. Remote Access Server does not come with Mac OS 8 so its installation and configuration is not discussed in this book.

■ Remote Access Client is not installed as part of a basic installation of Mac OS 8; you must select it in the installer's main installation window. I tell you about installing Mac OS 8 in **Chapter 1**.

To set up Remote Access

1. Choose Remote Access Setup from the Control Panels submenu under the Apple menu (see **Figure 60**). The Remote Access Setup control panel window appears (see **Figure 61**).

2. Choose your modem make and model from the Modem pop-up menu (see **Figure 58**).

3. Select the port to which the modem is connected from the Port pop-up menu (see **Figure 62**).

4. Select a Modem Speaker radio button to turn the speaker On or Off.

5. Select one of the Dialing radio buttons to specify whether you have Tone or Pulse dialing.

6. To instruct the modem dial no matter what the dial tone sounds like, turn on the Ignore dial tone check box.

7. Close the Remote Access Setup control panel window.

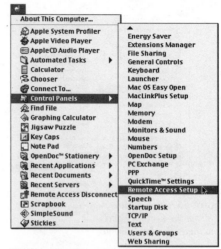

Figure 60. *Choose Remote Access Setup from the Control Panels submenu under the Apple menu*

Figure 61. *Configure your modem for a connection in the Remote Access Setup control panel.*

Figure 62. *Choose a port from the Port pop-up menu.*

✔ Tip

■ If you used the Modem control panel to configure your modem, the settings in the Remote Access Setup control panel should already be correct. I tell you about the Modem control panel on the previous page.

Figure 64.
The Remote Access Client Folder window.

Figure 65.
Use this window to create a settings file for the network to which you want to connect.

Figure 66.
Choose Save from the File menu.

Figure 67. *Use a standard Save As dialog box to save the settings file.*

Figure 68.
A completed settings file might look something like this.

To create a Remote Access Client settings file

1. Open the Remote Access Client Folder in the Applications folder on your hard disk (see **Figure 64**).

2. Double-click the Remote Access Client icon. A untitled settings file window like the one in **Figure 65** appears.

3. Enter your network connection information in the Connect As section of the dialog box. To have Remote Access Client save your password, turn on the Save my password check box.

4. Enter the phone number for the modem connected to the Remote Access Server in the Number edit box.

5. Choose Save from the File menu (see **Figure 66**) or press ⌃⌘⑤.

6. Use the Save As dialog box that appears (see **Figure 67**) to enter a name, select a location, and save the settings file. The file name appears in the window's title bar (see **Figure 68**).

7. To connect, follow the instructions on the next page.

   or

   To quit, choose Quit from the File menu.

✔ Tips

■ You can create a separate settings file for each network to which you connect.

■ The Options button in the settings file window (see **Figure 68**) lets you set preferences for redialing and for dialing an alternate phone number.

To connect to a Remote Access Server

1. If the settings file you want to use is not already open, double-click its icon to open it (see **Figure 68**).

2. Click Connect. The Remote Access Status window appears (see **Figure 69**) while Remote Access Client attempts to connect. When a connection is established, information about it appears in the window (see **Figure 70**).

3. Follow the instructions in the section titled "To connect to another computer" near the beginning of this chapter to connect to a computer on the network.

✔ Tips

■ The Chooser looks and works the same when connecting via Remote Access (see **Figure 71**) as it does when connecting from a computer on the network (see **Figure 6**).

■ Once connected, you can share files and applications and even print just as you would if you were on the network. Access speed, however, will be quite a bit slower.

To disconnect from a Remote Access Server

1. Drag the icons for shared disks to the trash.

2. Click Disconnect in the Remote Access Status window (see **Figure 70**).

   or

   Choose Remote Access Disconnect from the Apple menu (see **Figure 72**).

3. A confirmation dialog box like the one in **Figure 73** appears. Click Yes.

4. Wait while Remote Access Client disconnects.

Figure 69.
The Remote Access Status window tells you the status of the connection...

Figure 70.
...even after a connection has been established.

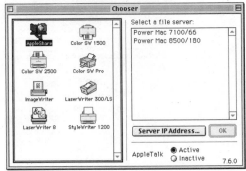

Figure 71. *Use the Chooser to connect to a computer.*

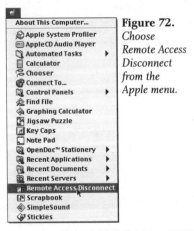

Figure 72.
Choose Remote Access Disconnect from the Apple menu.

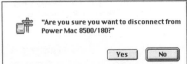

Figure 73. *Click Yes in this dialog box to confirm that you want to disconnect.*

CONNECTING TO THE INTERNET

About Connecting to the Internet

The *Internet* is a vast, worldwide network of computers that offers information, communication, online shopping, and entertainment for the whole family.

There are two ways to connect to the Internet:

- In a *direct* or *LAN connection*, your computer has a live network connection to the Internet all the time. This is costly for individuals, but if your computer is on a companywide network, you may have access through the network.

- In a *modem* or *dial-up connection*, your computer uses its modem to dial in to a server which gives it access to the Internet. This is a cheaper way to connect, but your access speed is limited by the speed of your modem.

No matter how you connect, you need special software to access Internet features. Mac OS includes the Apple Internet Connection Kit, a collection of software that makes it easy to connect to the Internet.

In this chapter, I tell you how to configure your system for an Internet connection, connect to the Internet, and use the Internet applications and utilities included with Mac OS 8.

✔ Tips

- The *World Wide Web* is part of the Internet. I tell you about the Web and the *Web browser* software you use to access it later in this chapter.

- I tell you more about modems in **Chapter 9**.

- The Apple Internet Connection Kit is automatically installed as part of a basic installation of Mac OS 8. I tell you about installing Mac OS 8 in **Chapter 1**.

About the Internet Setup Assistant

The Internet Setup Assistant is an application that steps you through the process of configuring your computer to connect to the Internet. It has two parts that are launched automatically as you need them:

■ **ISP Registration Assistant** helps you open an account with an Internet Service Provider (ISP). This is the part you'll use if you don't have an account with an ISP and want to open one.

■ **Internet Editor Assistant** helps you add or modify existing Internet configuration settings. This is the part you'll use if you already have an account with an ISP or a direct connection to the Internet.

✔ Tip

■ An *Internet Service Provider* or *ISP* is an organization that provides access to the Internet for a fee.

To launch the Internet Setup Assistant

Double-click the Internet Setup Assistant icon in the Assistants folder on your hard disk (see **Figure 1**). The Internet Setup Assistant's main window appears (see **Figure 2**).

✔ Tip

■ The Internet Setup Assistant is automatically launched when you click the Continue button at the end of a Mac OS 8 installation. I tell you about installing Mac OS 8 in **Chapter 1**.

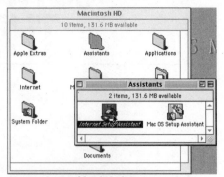

Figure 1. *Double-click the Internet Setup Assistant icon in the Assistants folder.*

Figure 2. *The main window of the Internet Setup Assistant.*

Figure 3. *The Introduction window tells you what the assistant does.*

Figure 4. *The Personal Information window is for entering your name and phone number.*

Figure 5. *The Modem Settings window lets you configure your modem.*

Figure 6.
The Port pop-up menu

To register with an ISP

1. Click Register in the Internet Setup Assistant's main window (see **Figure 2**).

2. Read the information in the Introduction window that appears (see **Figure 3**). Then click the right arrow at the bottom of the window.

3. The Personal Information window appears next (see **Figure 4**). Enter your first name, last name, and phone number in the appropriate edit boxes. Then click the right arrow.

4. The Modem Settings window appears (see **Figure 5**). Select the make and model of your modem from the scrolling list near the top of the window. Use the Port pop-up menu (see **Figure 6**) to select the port to which your modem is connected. Select the radio button for either Tone or Pulse dialing. Then click the right arrow.

5. Read the information in the Conclusion window (see **Figure 7**). If you need to dial additional digits before the toll-free number listed, enter them in the edit box. Then click Go Ahead.

6. A connection status window appears while your modem dials a toll-free number (see **Figure 8**). When you

(continued on next page)

Figure 7. *The Conclusion window offers tips for choosing an ISP.*

(continued from previous page)

successfully connect, Netscape Navigator launches. A dialog box like the one in **Figure 9** may appear; if so, click OK.

7. Wait while the Internet Account Server Web page loads. When it's finished, it'll look something like **Figure 10**.

8. Click each of the ISP buttons (Sprint, Concentric, and Netcom in **Figure 10**) to compare Internet deals. You can click the Back button on any page (see **Figure 11**) to go back to a previous page.

9. When you've decided on an ISP, click the Next button on its page (see **Figure 11**).

10. Follow the instructions that appear on screen to fill out forms. The information you'll have to provide includes:

   ▲ Your service preferences (if the ISP offers multiple levels of service)

   ▲ Your user ID and password

   ▲ Credit card information for payment

   ▲ Your billing address

   During this process, you'll also select the phone number that your modem will dial to connect to the Internet.

11. Wait while the information you entered is processed.

12. A page like the one in **Figure 12** appears. Read it carefully and write down the important support and log on information. Although this information will be automatically entered in your system, it's a good idea to have it written down somewhere in case you ever need to enter it manually.

13. Click Configure.

14. Wait while the Internet Setup Assistant completes the configuration process. When it's finished, it quits and displays the Internet Dialer window (see **Figure 13**).

Figure 8. *The Connection Status window tracks your connection progress.*

Figure 9. *A dialog box like this may appear just after Netscape launches.*

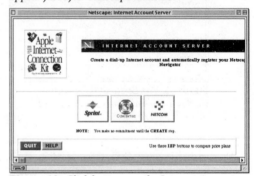

Figure 10. *Click buttons on the Internet Account Server page to learn more about ISP deals.*

Figure 11. *Once you've decided on an ISP, click the Next button on its page.*

Figure 12. *When your account has been processed, a page like this appears. Write down the information inside it and click the Configure button.*

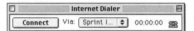

Figure 13. *After configuring your computer the Internet Setup Assistant launches Internet Dialer and quits.*

✔ Tips

■ If your modem's make and model are not listed in the scrolling list in step 4, try a similar model from the same manufacturer or one of the Hayes models. I tell you more about modems in **Chapter 9**.

■ The options that appear on the Port pop-up menu (see **Figure 6**) vary depending on your computer model.

■ If you click the Show Details button in step 5, you'll see a summary of the information you entered in step 3.

■ While comparing Internet deals in step 8, note the toll-free numbers for the ISPs. You can call these organizations directly if you have more questions.

■ If you live an an out-of-the-way place (like Wickenburg, AZ), you may want to see which ISP has an access number that is local to you. (None of them had local numbers for Wickenburg.) If you can't find a local provider using the Internet Setup Assistant, do some research with the phone book to find the best ISP for you. (I called a local computer consultant; she gave me the name and number of the only local ISP.) Then use the Update button in the Internet Assistant's main window (see **Figure 2**) to enter that ISP's information. I tell you how to add a configuration next.

Registering with an ISP

To add a dialup configuration

1. Click Update in the Internet Setup Assistant's main window (see **Figure 2**).

2. Read the information in the Introduction window that appears (see **Figure 14**). Then click the right arrow at the bottom of the window.

3. In the Internet Configuration window that appears (see **Figure 15**) select the Add Internet Configuration radio button. Then click the right arrow.

4. The Configuration name and connection type window appears next (see **Figure 16**). Enter a name for the configuration in the edit box. Then select the Modem radio button and click the right arrow button.

5. The Modem Settings window appears (see **Figure 5**). Select the make and model of your modem from the scrolling list near the top of the window. Use the Port pop-up menu (see **Figure 6**) to select the port to which your modem is connected. Select the radio button for either Tone or Pulse dialing. Then click the right arrow.

Figure 14. *The Introduction window explains what the Internet Setup Assistant does.*

Figure 15. *Use the Internet Configuration window to specify whether you want to add, modify, or remove a configuration.*

(continued on next page)

Figure 16. *Enter a name and select a connection type in the Configuration name and connection type window.*

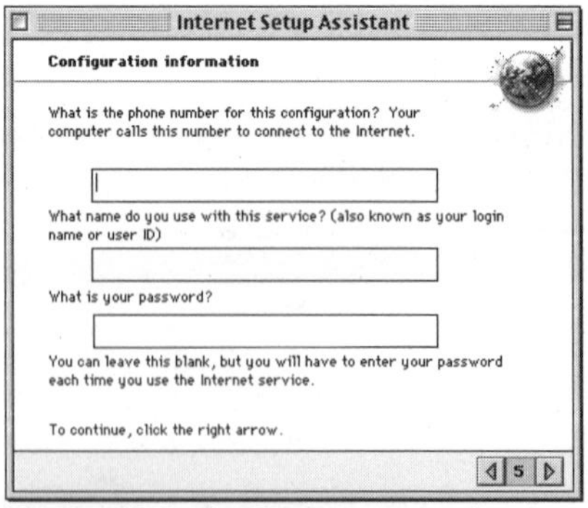

Figure 17. *In the Configuration information window, enter the local access number and log on information for your ISP.*

Figure 18. *Use this IP Address window to specify whether you have your own IP address.*

Figure 19. *Use this IP Address window to enter your IP address if you selected Yes in the previous window.*

Figure 20. *Use the Domain Name Servers window to enter the DNS address(es) and domain name for your ISP.*

(continued from previous page)

6. In the Configuration information window that appears next (see **Figure 17**), enter the local access number for your ISP in the top edit box, your user ID in the middle edit box, and your password in the bottom edit box. Then click the right arrow.

7. The IP Address window appears next (see **Figure 18**). If you have been assigned your own IP address, select the Yes radio button. If not, select the No radio button. Click the right arrow.

8. If you selected Yes in step 7, another IP Address window appears (see **Figure 19**). Enter the IP address in the edit box and click the right arrow.

9. The Domain Name Servers window appears next (see **Figure 20**). Enter the DNS address(es) in the top edit box. If there is more than one, make sure you press [Return] between each one. Then enter the domain name in the bottom edit box. Click the right arrow.

10. In the E-mail address and password window (see **Figure 21**), enter your e-mail address in the top edit box and your e-mail password in the bottom edit box. Then click the right arrow.

(continued on next page)

Figure 21. *Enter your e-mail address and e-mail password in this window.*

Adding a Dialup Configuration

(continued from previous page)

11. In the E-mail account and host computer window (see **Figure 22**), enter the pop account in the top edit box and the SMTP host in the bottom edit box. Click the right triangle.

12. In the Newsgroup Host Computer window (see **Figure 23**), enter the NNTP host. Then click the right triangle.

13. The Conclusion window finally appears (see **Figure 24**). To connect to the ISP when the settings have been entered, make sure the Connect when finished check box is turned on. To complete the configuration, click Go Ahead.

14. The Internet Setup Assistant window indicates the progress of your configuration. Once completed, if you turned on the Connect when finished check box in step 13, the software attempts to connect to the ISP. Otherwise, it quits.

✔ Tips

■ If your modem's make and model are not listed in the scrolling list in step 4, try a similar model from the same manufacturer or one of the Hayes models. I tell you more about modems in **Chapter 9**.

■ The options that appear on the Port pop-up menu (see **Figure 6**) vary depending on your computer model.

■ You can get most of the configuration information you need from your ISP.

■ It is not necessary to enter your password in steps 6 and 10. If you omit it, you'll have to enter it when connecting to your ISP or checking your e-mail.

■ If you click the Show Details button in step 14, you'll see a summary of all the information you entered.

Figure 22. *In the E-mail account and host computer window, enter the pop account and SMTP host provided by your ISP.*

Figure 23. *Enter the NNTP host provided by your ISP in the Newsgroup Host Computer window.*

Figure 24. *The Conclusion window lets you know you're done entering information.*

Figure 25. *Use the Subnet mask and router address window to enter additional information if you have your own IP address on the LAN.*

Figure 26. *Use the Dynamic Configuration window to specify the protocol for the dynamic configuration.*

To add a LAN configuration

1. Click Update in the Internet Setup Assistant's main window (see **Figure 2**).

2. Read the information in the Introduction window that appears (see **Figure 14**). Then click the right arrow at the bottom of the window.

3. In the Internet Configuration window that appears (see **Figure 15**) select the Add Internet Configuration radio button. Then click the right arrow.

4. The Configuration name and connection type window appears next (see **Figure 16**). Enter a name for the configuration in the edit box. Then select the LAN radio button and click the right arrow button.

5. The IP Address window appears next (see **Figure 18**). If you have been assigned your own IP address, select the Yes radio button. If not, select the No radio button. Click the right arrow.

6. If you selected Yes in step 5, another IP Address window appears (see **Figure 19**). Enter the IP address in the edit box and click the right arrow. Then, in the Subnet mask and router address window (see **Figure 25**), enter the subnet mask in the top edit box and the router address in the bottom edit box. Click the right arrow.

    or

    If you selected No in step 5, the Dynamic Configuration window appears (see **Figure 26**). Select the radio button for the protocol for the dynamic configuration. Click the right arrow. If you selected MacIP, select the correct zone in the Mac IP Zone window that appears. Click the right arrow.

(continued on next page)

Adding a LAN Configuration

Adding a LAN Configuration

(continued from previous page)

7. The Domain Name Servers window appears next (see **Figure 20**). Enter the DNS address(es) in the top edit box. If there is more than one, make sure you press (Return) between each one. Then enter the domain name in the bottom edit box. Click the right arrow.

8. In the E-mail address and password window (see **Figure 21**), enter your e-mail address in the top edit box and your e-mail password in the bottom edit box. Then click the right arrow.

9. In the E-mail account and host computer window (see **Figure 22**), enter the pop account in the top edit box and the SMTP host in the bottom edit box. Click the right triangle.

10. In the Newsgroup Host Computer window (see **Figure 23**), enter the NNTP host. Then click the right triangle.

11. The Conclusion window appears (see **Figure 24**). To complete the configuration, click Go Ahead.

12. The Internet Setup Assistant window indicates the progress of your configuration. Once completed, it quits.

✔ Tips

- You can get most of the configuration information you need from your LAN Aministrator.

- It is not necessary to enter your password in step 8. If you omit it, you'll have to enter it when checking your e-mail.

- If you click the Show Details button in step 11, you'll see a summary of all the information you entered.

Figure 27. *Use this Internet Configurations window to select the configuration that you want to modify.*

Figure 28. *Use this Internet Configurations window to select the configuration that you want to delete. The active configuration does not appear in this list.*

To modify a configuration

1. Click Update in the Internet Setup Assistant's main window (see **Figure 2**).

2. Read the information in the Introduction window that appears (see **Figure 14**). Then click the right arrow at the bottom of the window.

3. In the Internet Configuration window that appears (see **Figure 15**) select the Modify Internet configuration radio button. Then click the right arrow.

4. If you have more than one Internet configuration, an Internet Configurations window appears (see **Figure 27**). Select the configuration that you want to modify. Then click the right arrow.

5. If you are modifying a modem configuration, follow the steps in the "To add a modem configuration" section to modify the contents of the windows that appear.

   or

   If you are modifying a LAN configuration, follow the steps in the "To add a LAN configuration" section to modify the contents of the windows that appear.

To remove a configuration

1. Click Update in the Internet Setup Assistant's main window (see **Figure 2**).

2. Read the information in the Introduction window that appears (see **Figure 14**). Then click the right arrow at the bottom of the window.

3. In the Internet Configuration window that appears (see **Figure 15**) select the Remove Internet configuration radio button. Then click the right arrow.

4. If you have more than one Internet configuration, an Internet Configurations window appears (see **Figure 28**). Select the configuration that you want to remove. Then click the right arrow.

5. In the Conclusion window that appears, click the Go Ahead button to remove the configuration. The Internet Setup Assistant quits when it's finished.

Modifying & Removing Configurations

About TCP/IP & PPP

Your computer accesses the Internet through via a TCP/IP network connection. *TCP/IP* is a standard Internet protocol or set of rules for exchanging information.

A TCP/IP connection works a lot like a pipeline. Once established, Internet applications—like your Web browser and e-mail program—reach through the TCP/IP pipeline to get the information they need. When the information has been sent or received, it stops flowing through the pipeline. But the pipeline is not disconnected.

If you have a direct or network connection to the Internet, the Internet is accessible all the time. But if you have to connect via modem, you need to use Open Transport/PPP. This software, which comes with Mac OS, uses PPP to connect to TCP/IP networks via modem. *PPP* is a standard protocol for connecting to networks.

When you connect via modem using PPP, you set up a temporary TCP/IP pipeline. Internet applications are smart enough to automatically use PPP to connect to the Internet when necessary. When you're finished accessing Internet services you should tell PPP to disconnect.

TCP/IP and PPP can be configured using the TCP/IP and PPP control panels. Fortunately, the Internet Setup Assistant does all the configuration for you, so you shouldn't have to use them. In this section, however, I show you both control panels in case you ever want to modify settings without using the Internet Setup Assistant.

✔ Tip

- If your Internet configuration is working fine, don't use the TCP/IP or PPP control panels to change it! Internet connections follow one of the golden rules of computing: If it ain't broke, don't fix it.

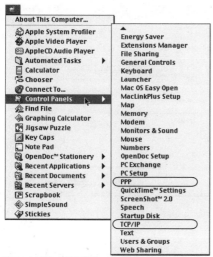

Figure 29. *TCP/IP and PPP can be found under the Control Panels submenu under the Apple menu.*

Figure 30. *The TCP/IP control panel.*

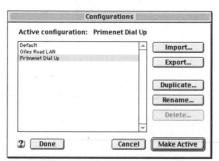

Figure 31. *Select the configuration that you want and click Make Active. This dialog box looks the same for TCP/IP and PPP except the PPP version does not include LAN configurations*

To use the TCP/IP control panel

1. Choose TCP/IP from the Control Panels submenu under the Apple menu (see **Figure 29**). The TCP/IP control panel appears (see **Figure 30**). It includes the name of the active configuration file in the title bar.

2. To select a different configuration, choose Configurations from the File menu. In the Configurations window that appears (see **Figure 31**), select the configuration that you want to use and click Make Active.

3. If desired, make changes in the TCP/IP control panel window (see **Figure 30**).

4. Close the TCP/IP control panel window.

5. If you made changes to the configuration, a dialog box like the one in **Figure 32** appears. Click Save.

✔ Tips

■ Do not change settings in the TCP/IP control panel unless you have to. Changes that are incorrect could prevent your Internet connection from functioning properly.

■ If you're not sure what to select or enter in the TCP/IP control panel, use the Internet Setup Assistant to modify settings. Although it may take longer to work with its interface, it's a lot easier to use and understand.

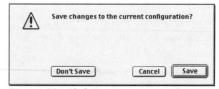

Figure 32. *Click Save to save your changes.*

Using the TCP/IP Control Panel

To use the PPP control panel

1. Choose PPP from the Control Panels submenu under the Apple menu (see **Figure 29**). The PPP control panel appears (see **Figure 33**). It includes the name of the active configuration file in the title bar.

2. To select a different configuration, choose Configurations from the File menu. In the Configurations window that appears (see **Figure 31**), select the configuration that you want to use and click Make Active.

3. If desired, make changes in the PPP control panel window (see **Figure 33**).

4. If desired, click Options to display the Options dialog box (see **Figure 34**). Click tabs to display and change redialing, connection, and protocol options. When you are finished, click OK.

5. Close the PPP control panel window.

6. If you made changes to the configuration, a dialog box like the one in **Figure 32** appears. Click Save.

✔ Tips

- If you have a direct or LAN connection to the Internet, you do not need to set up or modify PPP configurations.

- You can also use the PPP control panel to establish a connection to the Internet. I tell you more about connecting to the Internet later in this chapter.

- Do not change settings in the PPP control panel unless you have to. Changes that are incorrect could prevent you from successfully connecting to your ISP.

- If you're not sure what to select or enter in the PPP control panel, use the Internet Setup Assistant to modify settings. Although it may take longer to work with its interface, it's a lot easier to use and understand.

Figure 33. *The PPP control panel.*

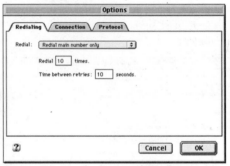

Figure 34. *Use the Options dialog box to change redialing, connection, and protocol options.*

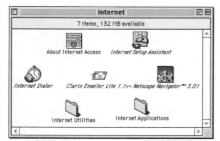

Figure 35. *The Internet folder contains a number of useful Internet applications and utilities.*

About Apple Internet Connection Kit Applications

The Apple Internet Connection Kit (AICK) comes with a number of Internet applications and utilities:

■ **Internet Dialer** enables you to connect via modem to an ISP using PPP.

■ **Claris Emailer Lite** enables you to exchange Internet e-mail with others.

■ **Netscape Navigator** enables you to browse the World Wide Web.

■ **Internet Setup Utility** lets you specify which applications or documents should automatically be launched when you use Internet Dialer to connect to the Internet.

■ **StuffIt Expander** automatically decodes and decompresses files downloaded from the Internet or attached to e-mail messages.

■ **Internet Config** enables you to enter your Internet preferences once and have them recognized by all your Internet applications.

You can find all these applications in the Internet folder (see **Figure 35**) on your hard disk.

Because of space constraints, I can't provide details on all components of AICK. Instead, I concentrate on the ones you'll use most—Internet Dialer, Claris Emailer Lite, and Netscape Navigator—and let you explore the others on your own.

About Establishing a PPP Connection

There are two ways to establish a PPP connection:

- Use Internet Dialer or the PPP control panel to dial in whenever you want.

- Launch an application that requires an Internet connection (like Netscape Navigator); a PPP connection is automatically established.

✔ Tip

- If you have a direct or LAN connection to the Internet, you don't have to worry about establishing a connection—it's always there.

To connect to an ISP with Internet Dialer

1. Double-click the Internet Dialer icon in the Internet folder on your hard disk (see **Figure 35**). Internet Dialer's main window appears (see **Figure 36**).

2. If necessary, select an Internet configuration from the Via pop-up menu (see **Figure 37**).

3. Click Connect. Internet Dialer initializes your modem and dials.

   When Internet Dialer has successfully connected, the Connect button turns into a Disconnect button, red lines appear above the telephone icon in the window, and the timer starts. You can see all this in **Figure 38**.

✔ Tip

- Internet Dialer does not have to be running while you are connected to the Internet. To quit Internet Dialer, choose Quit from its File menu (see **Figure 39**), press ⌘Q, or close its window.

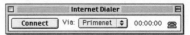

Figure 36. *Internet Dialer's main window.*

Figure 37. *The Via pop-up menu lists all configurations.*

Figure 38. *The clock starts when Internet Dialer connects.*

Figure 39. *Either of these File menu commands will quit Internet Dialer.*

Figure 40. *The PPP control panel's Status area keeps you informed about a connection as you connect...*

Figure 41. *...and while you're connected.*

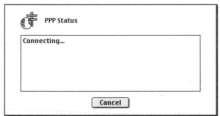

Figure 42. *The PPP status dialog box appears when you launch a program that requires an Internet connection but you are not connected to the Internet.*

Figure 43. *An icon like this blinks over the Apple menu while you are connected to the Internet—no matter how you connected.*

To connect to an ISP with the PPP control panel

1. Choose PPP from the Control Panels submenu under the Apple menu (see **Figure 29**).

2. Click Connect in the PPP control panel window that appears (see **Figure 31**). PPP initializes your modem and dials. It displays the connection status in its status area (see **Figure 40**).

   When PPP has successfully connected, the Connect button turns into a Disconnect button and the Status area fills with connection information. You can see all this in **Figure 41**.

✔ Tip

- The PPP control panel does not have to be open while you are connected to the Internet.

To automatically connect to an ISP

Launch any program that requires an internet connection. After the program's splash screen appears, a dialog box like the one in **Figure 42** appears to show connection status. When the PPP connection is established, the dialog box disappears.

To disconnect from an ISP

1. Open or activate Internet Dialer or the PPP control panel (see **Figures 38** and **41**).

2. Click Disconnect. The connection is terminated.

✔ Tip

- You can always tell if you're connected to the Internet by looking at the Apple menu icon. If it blinks with an icon like the one in **Figure 43**, you are connected to the Internet.

Disconnecting from an ISP

About Claris Emailer Lite

Claris Emailer Lite is a limited-feature version of Emailer, a popular e-mail application from Claris Corporation. It enables you to send and receive e-mail messages using your Internet account.

To launch Emailer

Double-click the Claris Emailer Lite icon in the Internet folder on your hard disk (see **Figure 35**).

or

Double-click the Mail icon on your Desktop (see **Figure 44**).

To configure Emailer

1. The first time you launch Emailer, a registration screen like the one in **Figure 45** appears. Enter your name and, if desired, your organization. Then click OK.

2. The first time you launch Emailer, the Internet Service Entry dialog box (see **Figure 46**) appears. You can display it by choosing Internet Setup from the Setup menu (see **Figure 47**). Enter a name for the e-mail account in the Account name edit box. The other fields should already include information from the Internet Setup Assistant.

4. Click Save.

5. The first time you run Emailer, a dialog box like the one in **Figure 48** appears next. Click No.

✔ Tip

■ If the information in the Internet Service Entry dialog box is not filled in, quit Emailer and follow the instructions earlier in this chapter to run the Internet Setup Assistant.

Figure 44.
One way to launch Emailer is to double-click the Mail icon on your Desktop.

Figure 45. *The first time you run Emailer, you must enter your name in the registration screen.*

Figure 46.
Most of the information in the Internet Service Entry dialog box is automatically entered by the Internet Setup Assistant.

Figure 47. *If the Internet Service Entry window does not automatically appear, select Internet Setup from the Setup menu to display it.*

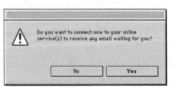

Figure 48. *This dialog box asks if you want to check for mail.*

Figure 49.
*Choose New
from the
Mail menu.*

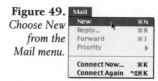

To create an e-mail message

1. Choose New from Emailer's Mail menu (see **Figure 49**) or press ⌘N. An Out Box Item window appears (see **Figure 50**).

2. Enter a subject for the message in the Subject edit box.

3. Press Tab three times to activate the address field.

4. Enter the e-mail address for the intended recipient in the address field.

5. Press Tab three times to activate the large message field.

6. Type in your message.

7. When you are finished, it might look something like the one in **Figure 51**. Click Save to put it in the Out Box.

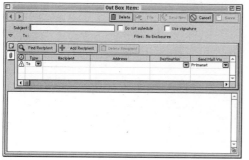

Figure 50. *An Out Box item is an empty message window.*

✔ Tips

- When you enter an address, Emailer automatically fills in the Destination and Send Mail Via fields.

- You can use Emailer's address book feature to maintain a directory of names and e-mail addresses for the people to whom you write.

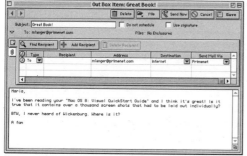

Figure 51. *When you're finished, your message might look like this one.*

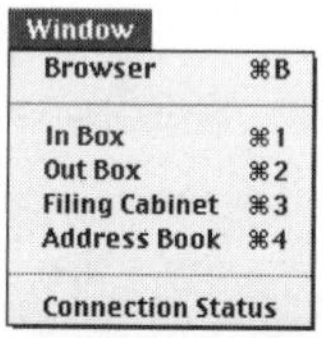

To view the Out Box

If the Browser window is not already showing, choose Out Box from the Window menu (see **Figure 52**).

or

If the Browser window is showing, click its Out Box tab.

The Out Box appears in the Browser window (see **Figure 53**).

Figure 52.
*Use commands
under the Window
menu to display
the Browser.*

✔ Tips

- Items remain in the Out Box until you send them.

- To open an item in the Out Box, double-click it.

Figure 53. *The Out Box lists all outgoing messages.*

To send & get e-mail messages

1. Choose Connect Now from the Mail menu (see **Figure 53**) or press ⌘K.

2. In the Connect Now Setup dialog box that appears (see **Figure 54**), make sure the Get and Send check boxes are turned on.

3. Click Connect.

4. A connection window like the one in **Figure 55** appears. It reports the status of your session. When it's finished retrieving and sending e-mail, the word *Idle* appears its title bar (see **Figure 56**).

✔ Tip

- Turning on the Get and Send check boxes in step 2 (see **Figure 55**) tells Emailer to retrieve all e-mail items waiting on the mail server and send all items in the Out Box.

To view the In Box

If the Browser window is not already showing, choose In Box from the Window menu (see **Figure 52**).

or

If the Browser window is already showing, click its In Box tab.

The In Box appears in the Browser window (see **Figure 57**).

✔ Tips

- Incoming mail appears in the In Box.
- To open an item in the In Box double-click it.

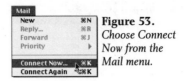

Figure 53. *Choose Connect Now from the Mail menu.*

Figure 54. *Use the Connect Now Setup dialog box to specify what you want to do when you connect.*

Figure 55. *The Connection window shows the connection status.*

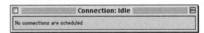

Figure 56. *When a connection is complete, the Connection window's title bar displays the word* Idle.

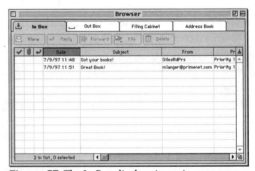

Figure 57. *The In Box displays incoming messages.*

Figure 58. *Double-clicking an In Box item displays it in a window.*

Figure 59. *When you click Reply, a preaddressed Out Box item message window appears.*

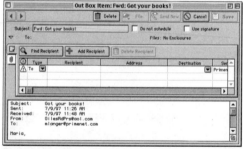

Figure 60. *When you click Forward, the message is copied into a new Out Box item message window.*

Figure 61. *Selecting message text before clicking Reply turns the text into a quote.*

To read incoming e-mail messages

1. In the In Box (see **Figure 57**), double-click the message that you want to read.

2. Read the message in the window that appears (see **Figure 58**).

3. To reply to the message, click Reply or press ⌘R. A preaddressed message window appears (see **Figure 59**). Type your reply and click Save.

4. To forward the message to another e-mail address, click Forward or press ⌘J. A message window containing a copy of the message appears (see **Figure 60**). Enter the e-mail address for the recipient in the Address field near the top of the message form and click Save.

5. To close the message, click its close box.

✔ Tips

- Selecting text in the incoming message window before clicking the Reply button window turns the selected text into a quoted reply (see **Figure 61**).

- Clicking the Save button in any outgoing message window saves the message to the Out Box, where it remains until the next time e-mail is sent.

- You can take advantage of Emailer's filing cabinet feature to sort and store the e-mail messages you have sent and received.

Reading Incoming E-Mail Messages

About Netscape Navigator

Netscape Navigator is a popular Web browser application from Netscape Corporation. It enables you to view or *browse* pages on the World Wide Web.

A Web *page* is a window full of formatted text and graphics (see **Figures 62**). You move from page to page by clicking text or graphic links or by opening *URLs* (*uniform resource locators*) for specific Web pages. These two methods of navigating the World Wide Web can open a whole world of useful or interesting information.

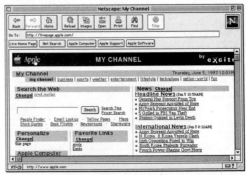

Figure 62. *When you launch Navigator, it connects to the Internet and displays the default home page—in this case the Live Page page on Apple's Web site.*

✔ Tips

■ The version of Netscape Navigator included with Mac OS has been customized to start with a specific home page and offer directory buttons with links to Apple pages.

■ You can easily identify a link by pointing to it; the mouse pointer turns into a pointing finger (see **Figure 62**).

■ If you're interested in learning more about Navigator than what's on these two pages, check out *Netscape 3 for Macintosh: Visual QuickStart Guide.*

Figure 63.
One way to launch Navigator is to double-click the Browse the Internet icon on your Desktop.

To launch Navigator

Double-click the Netscape Navigator icon in the Internet folder on your hard disk (see **Figure 35**).

or

Double-click the Browse the Internet icon on your desktop (see **Figure 63**).

Netscape starts up. After a moment, it displays the Live Page home page (see **Figure 62**).

✔ Tip

■ If you are not connected to the Internet when you launch Navigator, Mac OS attempts to connect automatically.

Figure 64. *Clicking the link in* **Figure 62,** *displays this page.*

Figure 65.
*Choose Open
Location from the
File menu…*

Figure 66. …*then enter the URL in the
Open Location dialog box.*

Figure 67.
*Choose Connect
To from the
Apple menu…*

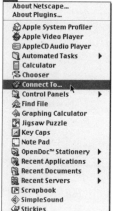

Figure 68. …*then enter the URL in the
dialog box that appears.*

Figure 69. *Or enter the URL in the edit box at the
top of the Navigator window and press* Enter.

To follow a link

1. Position the mouse pointer on a text or
   graphic link. The mouse pointer turns
   into a pointing finger (see **Figure 62**).

2. Click. After a moment, the page or
   other location for the link you clicked
   will appear (see **Figure 64**).

To view a specific URL

1. Choose Open Location from the File
   menu (see **Figure 65**) or press ⌃⌘L.

2. Enter the URL in the Open Location
   dialog box (see **Figure 66**) and click
   Open.

or

1. Choose Connect To from the Apple
   menu (see **Figure 67**).

2. Enter the URL in the dialog box that
   appears (see **Figure 68**) and click
   Connect.

or

Enter the URL in the edit box near the top
of the Navigator window (see **Figure 69**)
and press Return or Enter.

To return to the home page

Click the Home button at the top of the
Navigator window (see **Figure 69**).

✔ Tip

■ You can use the General Preferences
   dialog box to change the default home
   page. The page you specify will load
   each time you launch Navigator.

Following Links, Viewing Specific URLs

About Personal Web Sharing

Personal Web Sharing is a feature of Mac OS that enables you to create your own Web server. With it, you can use Web pages to share information with others on your network.

Here's how it works. First create one or more Web pages with the information that you want to share. Place them in a folder on your hard disk. Then use the Web Sharing control panel (see **Figure 70**) to specify the Web folder and home page, set privileges, and enable Web sharing. When another network user uses his Web browser to open your IP address, the home page you specified appears.

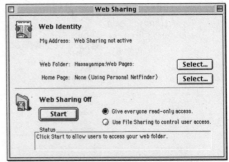

Figure 70. *Use the Web Sharing control panel to configure and enable Personal Web Sharing.*

✔ Tips

■ To use Personal Web Sharing, you must be connected to a TCP/IP network and have an IP address. I tell you about TCP/IP earlier in this chapter.

■ Personal Web Sharing is installed automatically as part of a basic Mac OS 8 installation. I tell you about installing Mac OS 8 in **Chapter 1**.

■ Instructions for creating Web pages are far beyond the scope of this book. If you're looking for a program that makes creating Web pages easy and a book to make the program easy, try Adobe PageMill and *PageMill 2 for Macintosh: Visual QuickStart Guide*.

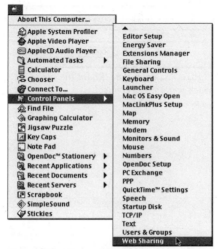

Figure 71. *Choose Web Sharing from the control panels submenu under the Apple menu.*

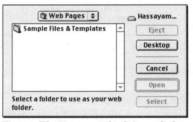

Figure 72. *Use a standard Open dialog box to locate and select the Web folder.*

Figure 73.
Use a dialog box like this one to select a home page for your Web site.

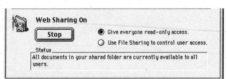

Figure 74. *The words* Web Sharing On *appear in the bottom part of the Web Sharing control panel.*

To configure & enable Personal Web Sharing

1. Choose Web Sharing from the Control Panels submenu under the Apple menu (see **Figure 71**). The Web Sharing control panel appears (see **Figure 70**).

2. To specify the the location of the folder containing your Web pages, click the Select button beside Web Folder. Then use an Open dialog box (see **Figure 72**) to locate and select the folder.

3. To specify the home page for your Web site, click the Select button beside Home Page. Then use the dialog box that appears (see **Figure 73**) to select the document for your home page.

4. Select a radio button to either give everyone who accesses your Web site read-only access or use file sharing privileges to control access.

5. Click Start. After a moment, the words Web Sharing On appear in the bottom half of the Web Sharing control panel (see **Figure 74**).

✔ Tips

- Mac OS includes a folder on your hard disk called Web Sharing. Inside it, you'll find sample Web pages to get you started.

- I tell you how to use an Open dialog box in **Chapter 5**.

To connect to a personal Web site

1. Choose Connect To from the Apple menu (see **Figure 67**).

2. In the dialog box that appears, enter the URL for the site to which you want to connect (see **Figure 75**) and click Connect. After a moment, the page appears in your Web browser (see **Figure 76**).

✔ Tip

■ The URL for a personal Web site consists of the characters *http://* followed by the IP address for the computer (see **Figure 75**).

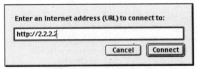

Figure 75. *Enter the URL for the site to which you want to connect.*

Figure 76. *A page published with Personal Web Sharing can look like any other Web page.*

POWERBOOK CONSIDERATIONS

About PowerBook Considerations

Mac OS 8 offers a few additional controls and features for PowerBook users:

- The **PowerBook** control panel enables you to set energy conservation options.
- The **PowerBook Setup** control panel enables you to set the SCSI disk mode and automatic wake up time.
- The **Trackpad** control panel lets you set the way the trackpad works.
- The **Infrared** control panel lets you specify the type of infrared connection you want to establish.
- **Apple IR File Exchange** enables you to exchange files with other users using IRTalk.
- The **Location Manager** control panel lets you set up and switch between multiple system configurations.
- **File Assistant** helps you keep the most up-to-date files on both your Power-Book and a desktop computer.

In this chapter, I tell you about all these things.

✔ Tip

- Most PowerBook models also display a control strip across the bottom of the screen. Since many desktop models also support the control strip feature, I tell you about it in **Chapter 12**.

About the PowerBook Control Panel

The PowerBook control panel (see **Figures 2** and **3**) enables you to set power conservation options for your PowerBook. How you set options affects both the performance of the computer and the life of the battery.

✔ Tip

- The PowerBook control panel maintains two settings: one for when the PowerBook is plugged in and one for when it isn't. These are referred to as the Power Adapter and Battery settings.

To open the PowerBook control panel

Choose PowerBook from the Control Panels submenu under the Apple menu (see **Figure 1**).

✔ Tip

- How the PowerBook control panel appears depends on whether the Easy (see **Figure 2**) or Custom (see **Figure 3**) window is displayed. You can switch from one to the other by clicking the button between Easy and Custom.

To set easy options

1. Open the PowerBook control panel.

2. Make sure the Easy/Custom selection switch is set to Easy. The PowerBook control panel window should look like the one in **Figure 2**.

3. Drag the slider between Better Conservation and Better Performance. If the PowerBook is plugged in, your change will affect the Power Adapter settings; if it is not plugged in, your change will affect the Battery settings.

4. Close the PowerBook control panel.

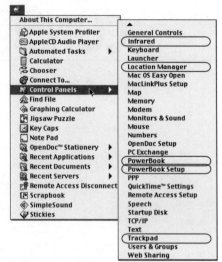

Figure 1. *Many of the PowerBook's additional controls can be set with control panels listed on the Control Panels submenu under the Apple menu.*

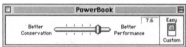

Figure 2. *The Easy window of the PowerBook control panel.*

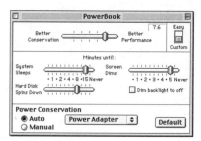

Figure 4. *Choose a conservation setting from the pop-up menu at the bottom of the window.*

Battery
✓ Power Adapter

To set custom options

1. Open the PowerBook control panel.

2. Make sure the Easy/Custom selection switch is set to Custom. The PowerBook control panel window should look like the one in **Figure 3**.

3. Select the conservation setting that you want to change by choosing an option from the pop-up menu at the bottom of the window (see **Figure 4**).

4. Drag the three sliders in the Minutes until area to set your preferences:

   ▲ **System Sleeps** is the number of minutes of idle time before the computer goes into sleep mode.

   ▲ **Hard Disk Spins Down** is the number of minutes of idle time before the hard disk stops spinning.

   ▲ **Screen Dims** is the number of minutes of idle time before the screen's brightness fades.

5. To shut off the computer's backlight (if available) when the screen dims, turn on the Dim backlight to off check box.

6. To change the other conservation setting, choose it from the pop-up menu at the bottom of the window. Then follow steps 4 and 5 above to modify settings.

7. Close the PowerBook control panel.

✔ Tips

- As you make changes to the three sliders in the Minutes until area, the top slider changes to indicate the overall effect of the change.

- If you use your PowerBook for presentations, set the System Sleeps and Screen Dims sliders to Never. Otherwise, your presentation could go blank while you're giving a lengthy explanation of a slide.

- To return the dialog box to its default settings, click Default.

- If you select the Manual radio button at the bottom of the window, the settings in the rest of the window will affect the computer whether it's plugged in or running on battery power.

Setting PowerBook Options

219

About the PowerBook Setup Control Panel

The PowerBook Setup control panel (see **Figure 5**) enables you to adjust two settings:

Figure 5. *The PowerBook Setup control panel.*

■ **SCSI Disk Mode** is the SCSI ID number assigned to the PowerBook when it is attached to another computer via a SCSI cable.

■ **Automatic Wake-Up** instructs the PowerBook to wake up at the time and date you specify.

To set PowerBook Setup options

1. Choose PowerBook Setup from the Control Panels submenu under the Apple menu (see **Figure 1**). The Power-Book Setup control panel appears (see **Figure 5**).

2. To change the SCSI ID for your Power-Book, select the radio button for the ID number that you want.

Figure 6. *Turn on the Automatic Wake-Up check box, then change the numbers in the time and/or date.*

3. To set an automatic wake up time, turn on the Wake-Up at check box. Select and change numbers in the time and/ or date to set the wake up time and date (see **Figure 6**).

4. Close the PowerBook Setup control panel.

✔ Tip

■ When attaching your PowerBook to another computer via SCSI cable, it's vital that the PowerBook's ID number be different than all other connected SCSI devices.

Setting PowerBook Setup Options

Figure 7.
*The Trackpad
control panel.*

About the Trackpad Control Panel

The Trackpad control panel (see **Figure 7**) lets you change the way the trackpad works:

■ **Tracking Speed** is the speed at which the mouse pointer moves.

■ **Double-Click Speed** is the time between the two clicks of a double-click.

■ **Use Trackpad for** options enable you to use the trackpad for clicking and dragging—without touching the trackpad's button. (This feature may not be supported by all PowerBook models.)

To set Trackpad options

1. Choose Trackpad from the Control Panels submenu under the Apple menu (see **Figure 1**). The Trackpad contrl panel appears (see **Figure 7**).

2. To change the tracking speed, select a Tracking Speed radio button.

3. To change time between double-click clicks, select a Double-Click Speed radio button—the one on the left is for more time between double-clicks and the one on the right is for less time..

4. To use the trackpad for clicking, dragging, and drag lock, turn on the appropriate check boxes in the Use Trackpad for area.

5. Close the Trackpad control panel.

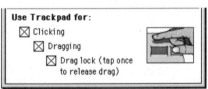

Figure 8. *To turn on the Dragging and Drag lock check boxes, you must turn on the check boxes above them.*

✔ Tips

■ To turn on the Dragging or Drag lock check box, you must turn on the check box(es) above it (see F**igure 8**).

■ To use the trackpad dragging feature, tap the item you want to drag, then tap and move your finger on the trackpad to drag it. When Drag lock is enabled, you must tap again to release the item.

Setting Trackpad Options

About Infrared Communication

Recent PowerBook models have infrared communication capabilities. If you have one of these PowerBooks, you can use one of two methods of infrared communication:

■ IRTalk enables you to exchange files with another computer that has infrared capabilities.

■ IrDA enables you to connect to a network using infrared communication.

In this section, I briefly discuss what you need to do to use each of these methods of infrared communication.

To set up IRTalk

1. Choose Infrared from the Control Panels submenu under the Apple menu (see **Figure 1**). The Infrared control panel appears (see **Figure 9**).

2. If IRTalk does not appear at the top left corner of the window, click Options. Then select the IRTalk radio button in the Options dialog box (see **Figure 10**) and click OK.

3. Close the Infrared control panel. Click Save or OK in any confirmation or warning dialog boxes that appear.

4. Choose AppleTalk from the Control Panels submenu under the Apple menu. The AppleTalk control panel appears (see **Figure 11**).

5. Select Infrared Port (IRTalk) from the Connect via pop-up menu (see **Figure 12**).

6. Close the AppleTalk control panel. Click Save or OK in any confirmation or warning dialog boxes that appear.

7. Open the Apple IR File Exchange folder in the Apple Extras folder on your hard disk (see **Figure 13**).

8. Double-click the Apple IR File Exchange application icon. You are now ready to send and receive files via IRTalk.

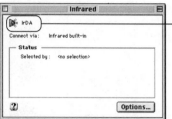

The type of connection appears here.

Figure 9. *The Infrared control panel.*

Figure 10. *Select the IRTalk radio button in the Options dialog box.*

Figure 11. *The AppleTalk control panel.*

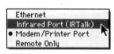

Figure 12. *Select Infrared Port (IRTalk) from the Connect Via pop-up menu.*

Figure 13. *The contents of the Apple IR File Exchange folder.*

Figure 14. *Select the IrDA radio button in the Options dialog box.*

Figure 15. *Select Infrared Port (IrDA) from the Connect Via pop-up menu.*

Figure 16. *The Infrared control panel shows the connection status.*

To set up IrDA

1. Choose Infrared from the Control Panels submenu under the Apple menu (see **Figure 1**). The Infrared control panel appears (see **Figure 9**).

2. If IrDA does not appear at the top left corner of the window, click Options. Then select the IrDA radio button in the Options dialog box (see **Figure 14**) and click OK.

3. Close the Infrared control panel. Click Save or OK in any confirmation or warning dialog boxes that appear.

4. Choose AppleTalk from the Control Panels submenu under the Apple menu. The AppleTalk control panel appears (see **Figure 11**).

5. Select Infrared Port (IrDA) from the Connect via pop-up menu (see **Figure 15**).

6. Close the AppleTalk control panel. Click Save or OK in any confirmation or warning dialog boxes that appear.

7. Position the infrared port on your PowerBook within 3 feet of the LAN access device. You can now utilize network services.

✔ Tip

■ If you open the Infrared control panel while your computer is set up for IrDA communication, you can see the status of the connection (see **Figure 16**).

Setting Up IrDA

About Location Manager

Location Manager (see **Figure 17**) is a control panel that enables you create locations. A *location* is a group of computer settings for a specific place or purpose.

The settings you can include in a location depend on Location Manager modules installed in your computer. The modules that come with Mac OS 8 let you include the following settings:

■ **Auto-Open Item** is an application or other file that opens automatically when you switch to the location. (I tell you about launching applications in **Chapter 5**.)

■ **Default Printer** is the preferred printer for the location. (I tell you about setting the default printer in **Chapter 5**.)

■ **Extensions Manager** is the settings in the Extensions Manager control panel. (I tell you about the Extensions Manager control panel in **Chapter 12**.)

■ **File Sharing** is the setting (On or Off) in the File Sharing control panel. (I tell you about file sharing in **Chapter 9**.)

■ **Networking** is the setting in the Apple-Talk or TCP/IP control panel. (I tell you about networking in **Chapter 9**.)

■ **Sound** is the Sound setting in the Monitors and Sounds control panel. (I tell you about setting speaker volume in **Chapter 12**.)

■ **Time Zone** is the time zone or location set in the Date & Time or Map control panel. (I tell you about setting the time zone or location in **Chapter 12**.)

In this section, I tell you how to use Location Manager to create and switch to locations.

Figure 17. *The Location Manager control panel.*

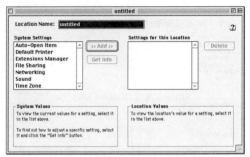

Figure 18. *An untitled location settings window.*

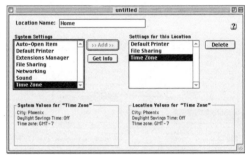

Figure 19. *After adding settings to the location, the window might look something like this.*

Figure 20.
*Choose Save
Location from the
File menu.*

Figure 21. *The setting you create is added to the Location Manager control panel window.*

To create a location

1. Configure your computer with the settings that you want the location to include.

2. Choose Location Manager from the Control Panels submenu under the Apple menu (see **Figure 1**). The Location Manager control panel appears (see **Figure 17**).

3. Click New. An untitled window like the one in **Figure 18** appears.

4. Enter a name for the location in the Location Name edit box.

5. In the System Settings list, select a setting that you want to include in the location.

6. Click Add. The setting is copied to the Settings for this Location list.

7. Repeat steps 5 and 6 for each setting that you want to include in the location. When you're finished, the window might look like the one in Figure 19.

8. Choose Save Location from the File menu (see **Figure 20**) or press ⌘S. The location's name appears in the title bar.

9. Close the settings window. The location appears in the Location manager control panel window (see **Figure 21**).

10. Close the Location Manager window.

✔ Tips

■ Consult the chapters referenced on the previous page for specific instructions on setting configuration options.

■ You can learn more about a setting in the System Settings list (see **Figures 18** and **19**) by selecting it and clicking Get Info. Click OK to dismiss the Info window when you're finished with it.

■ If you add a setting in error in step 6, you can remove it. Just select the setting and click Delete.

Creating Locations

To modify a location

1. Configure your computer with the settings that you want the location to include.

2. Choose Location Manager from the Control Panels submenu under the Apple menu (see **Figure 1**). The Location Manager appears (see **Figure 21**).

3. In the Location Editing list, select the location that you want to modify.

4. Click Open. The settings window for the location appears (see **Figure 22**). Settings that you have changed since you created the location are marked with a bullet.

5. To update a location setting to match the current setting, select the setting in the System Settings list (see **Figure 23**) and click Update.

6. Repeat step 5 for each setting that you want to update.

7. Choose Save Location from the File menu (see **Figure 20**) or press ⌃⌘S.

8. Close the settings window.

9. Close the Location Manager window.

To duplicate a location

1. Choose Location Manager from the Control Panels submenu under the Apple menu (see **Figure 1**). The Location Manager appears (see **Figure 21**).

2. In the Location Editing list, select the location that you want to duplicate.

3. Click Duplicate. A copy of the location appears in the Location Manager window (see **Figure 24**).

✔ Tip

■ Duplicating a location is a quick way to create a new location with similar settings.

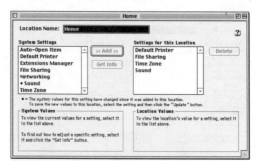

Figure 22. *Changed settings are marked with a bullet.*

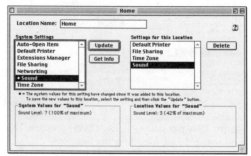

Figure 23. *Select the setting that you want to change and click Update.*

Figure 24. *When you duplicate a location, the copy appears in the Location Manager window beneath the original.*

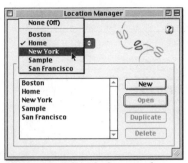

Figure 25. *Select the location that you want from the Current Location pop-up menu.*

Figure 26. *This dialog box appears to show switching progress…*

Figure 27. *…and to summarize the changes made when the switch is complete.*

To delete a location

1. Choose Location Manager from the Control Panels submenu under the Apple menu (see **Figure 1**). The Location Manager appears (see **Figure 24**).

2. In the Location Editing list, select the location that you want to delete.

3. Click Delete. The location disappears.

4. Close the Location Manager control panel window.

To switch to a location

1. Choose Location Manager from the Control Panels submenu under the Apple menu (see **Figure 1**). The Location Manager appears.

2. Choose a location from the Current Location pop-up menu (see **Figure 25**).

   A dialog box like the one in **Figure 26** appears while Location Manager switches to the chosen location's settings. When it's finished, the dialog box displays a summary of the changes made (see **Figure 27**).

3. Close the Location Manager control panel window.

About File Assistant

File Assistant is an application that enables PowerBook users to synchronize specific documents that exist on both a desktop computer and a PowerBook. This helps ensure that you are always working with the most current version of the file.

Figure 28. *The contents of the PowerBook File Assistant folder.*

✔ Tips

■ File Assistant is automatically installed on a PowerBook as part of a basic installation of Mac OS 8. I tell you about installing Mac OS 8 in **Chapter 1**.

■ File Assistant requires that you have a network connection between your PowerBook and desktop computer. I tell you about networks in **Chapter 9**.

■ To make the most of File Assistant, you should use it every time you return from a trip with your PowerBook and every time you prepare to leave for a trip with your PowerBook.

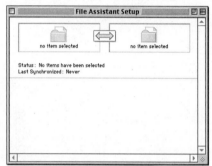

Figure 29. *The File Assistant Setup window.*

To open File Assistant

1. Open the PowerBook File Assistant folder inside the Portables folder inside the Apple Extras folder on your hard disk (see **Figure 28**).

2. Double-click File Assistant. The File Assistant Setup window should appear (see **Figure 29**); if it does not, choose Show Setup Window from the Window menu (see **Figure 30**) or press ⌃⌘H.

Figure 30. *If the File Assistant Setup window isn't displayed, choose Show Setup Window from the Window menu.*

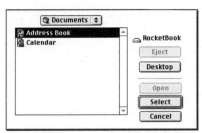

Figure 31. *Use a standard Open dialog box to locate and select the file that you want to synchronize.*

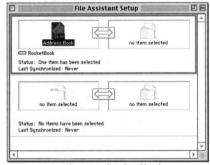

Figure 32. *The icon for the file that you selected appears in the File Assistant Setup window.*

Figure 33. *The icon for the second file that you selected appears beside the first.*

Figure 34.
Use the Synchronize menu to select a synchronization direction and choose other synchronization options.

To set up a synchronization

1. Open File Assistant. If necessary, display the Setup window (see **Figure 29**).

2. Double-click the no item selected icon on the left side of the window.

3. A standard Open dialog box appears (see **Figure 31**). Use it to locate and select a file or folder on your Power-Book that you want to synchronize. When you click Select, the dialog box disappears and the icon for the file appears in the File Assistant Setup window, along with a new line for another entry (see **Figure 32**).

4. Double-click the no item selected icon on the right side of the window.

5. Use the standard Open dialog box appears (see **Figure 31**) to locate and select the same file or folder on your desktop computer. When you click Select, the dialog box disappears and the icon for the file appears in the File Assistant Setup window (see **Figure 33**).

6. Choose a synchronization direction for the file from the Synchronize menu (see **Figure 34**):

   ▲ **Two Way** (the default selection) updates either file in the pair when the other file changes.

   ▲ **Left To Right** only updates the file on the right when the file on the left changes.

   ▲ **Right To Left** only updates the file on the left when the file on the right changes.

7. Repeat steps 2 through 6 for each file that you want to synchronize.

✔ Tip

■ With Two Way synchronization selected, if both files change, File Assistant cannot synchronize them.

To synchronize files

1. Open File Assistant. If necessary, display the Setup window (see **Figure 33**).

2. Choose Synchronize Now from the Synchronize menu (see **Figure 34**) or press ⌘G.

3. The files are synchronized. The synchronization date and time appear in the File Assistant Setup window (see **Figure 35**).

✔ Tips

■ If you move or delete either file in a pair, a dialog box like the one in **Figure 36** appears. Click OK to dismiss it and either change the File Assistant Setup or put the file back where it was.

■ To automatically synchronize files every time your PowerBook connects to the desktop computer while File Assistant is running, choose Automatic from the Synchronize menu (see **Figure 34**) or press ⌘T. This turns on automatic synchronization.

Figure 35. *The date and time of the last synchronization appears in the File Assistant Setup window for each pair of files.*

Figure 36. *If you move or delete one of the files in a pair, File Assistant can't synchronize.*

CUSTOMIZING MAC OS 8

About Customizing Mac OS 8

One of the great things about Mac OS is the way it can be customized to look and work the way you want.

Throughout this book, I show you ways to change System settings so things work the way you need them to. In this chapter, I provide a closer look at the System software that extends or customizes the system—extensions, control panels, and fonts—and show you some other ways to customize Mac OS 8.

✔ Tip

■ Some customization options explored elsewhere in this book that are not repeated here include:

▲ Window views, in **Chapter 3**.

▲ Finder preferences and the Info window, in **Chapter 4**.

▲ The Apple Menu Items control panel, Note Pad, Scrapbook, and SimpleSound, in **Chapter 6**.

▲ PC Exchange, Mac OS Easy Open, and MacLinkPlus Setup, in **Chapter 7**.

▲ Chooser and desktop printers, in **Chapter 8**.

▲ AppleTalk, File Sharing, Users & Groups, AutoRemounter, Modem, and Remote Access Setup control panels, in **Chapter 9**.

▲ TCP/IP and PPP control panels, in **Chapter 10**.

▲ PowerBook, PowerBook Setup, Trackpad, Infrared, and Location Manager control panels, in **Chapter 11**.

▲ Balloon Help, in **Chapter 13**.

About the System Folder

The software that makes up Mac OS 8 resides in the System Folder on your hard disk (see **Figure 1**). The System software consists primarily of the System file, Finder file, and the following types of items:

- **Extensions** are files that add features or extend the functionality of the system. Their features are preset and cannot be modified—just install them and they work. You can find them in the Extensions folder.

- **Drivers** are files that enable your computer to use hardware devices such as printers and CD-ROM drives. Like extensions, their features are preset and cannot be modified—install them and the devices they control become available for use. You can find them in the Extensions folder.

- **Control panels** are files that either add features to the system or enable you to set system options. They offer an interface you can use to modify their settings. You can find them in the Control Panels folder.

- **Fonts** are typefaces that are used to display text on screen and in printed documents. When you install them properly, they're available for use in every application that can access fonts. You can find them in the Fonts folder.

- **Startup Items** are items that open when you start your computer. You can find them in the Startup Items folder, which is empty by default.

- **Shutdown Items** are items that open when you shut down your computer. You can find them in the Shutdown Items folder, which is empty by default.

Figure 1.
The contents of a Mac OS 8 System folder.

✔ Tips

- As shown in **Figure 1**, there are more items in the System folder than what I've listed here. The ones I discuss in this chapter are the ones you can use to customize your system.

- Do not remove any item from your System folder or a folder within it unless you know what you are doing or are instructed by someone who knows what he or she is doing. Removing a required item in error could prevent your computer from starting!

- To prevent all extensions, control panels, and startup items from loading, hold down (Shift) while the computer is starting up.

About the System Folder

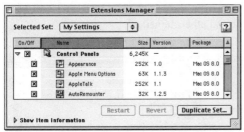

Figure 2. *The Extensions Manager control panel.*

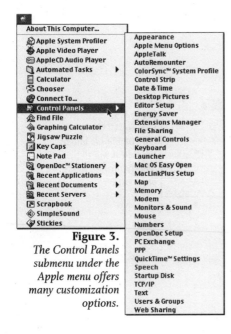

Figure 3.
*The Control Panels
submenu under the
Apple menu offers
many customization
options.*

About Extensions Manager

Extensions Manager (see **Figure 2**) is a control panel that enables you turn individual extensions, drivers, control panels, startup items, and shutdown items on or off. A item that is turned off does not load at startup so it is disabled.

Extensions Manager also lets you create sets of item settings. By creating a variety of sets for different purposes, changing settings is as quick and easy as selecting a menu item.

✔ Tip

- After making changes in the Extensions Manager control panel, you must restart your computer for the changes to take affect.

To open Extensions Manager

Choose Extensions Manager from the Control Panel submenu under the Apple menu (see **Figure 3**).

To open Extensions Manager during startup

Hold down Spacebar while the computer is starting up. Do not release Spacebar until the Extensions Manager window appears (see **Figure 2**).

✔ Tip

- If you open Extensions Manager during startup and make changes, it is not necessary to restart your computer for the changes to take affect. The change takes effect as the startup process finishes after you close Extensions Manager.

To toggle item settings

1. Open the Extensions Manager control panel (see **Figure 2**).
2. Click the check box to the left of an item name to turn it on or off (see **Figure 4**).
3. Repeat step 2 for each item whose setting you want to toggle.

✔ Tip

■ If you want to start over with the settings that were in the Extensions Manager window when you first opened it, click Revert.

To turn all items on or off

1. Open the Extensions Manager control panel (see **Figure 4**).
2. To turn all items on, choose All On from the Edit menu (see **Figure 5**).

   or

   To turn all items off, choose All Off from the Edit menu (see **Figure 5**).

To save settings

To save the settings and immediately restart your computer, click Restart.

or

To save your settings without restarting your computer, close the Extensions Manager window.

✔ Tips

■ If you opened Extensions Manager while the computer was starting up, click Continue; there is no Restart button.

■ You can also save settings to the current set by switching to another set. I tell you about sets next.

Folder with some items turned on and others turned off.

Item turned off

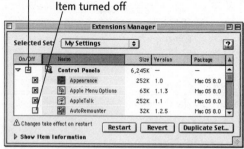

Figure 4. *Click a check box to toggle its setting.*

Figure 5.
Use the All On or All Off commands under the Edit menu to quickly turn all items on or off.

Toggling Item Settings

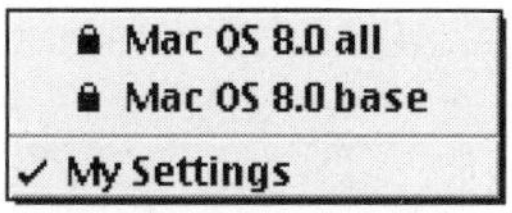

Figure 6. *The Selected Set pop-up menu lists all settings.*

Figure 7. *The File menu includes commands to create, duplicate, rename, and delete sets.*

Figure 8. *Enter a name for the set in the New Set dialog box.*

To choose a set

In the Extensions Manager control panel (see **Figure 4)**, choose the set that you want from the Selected Set pop-up menu (see **Figure 6)**. The settings for the set are applied.

✔ Tips

■ Extensions Manager comes configured with three sets:

▲ **Mac OS 8.0 all** consists of all the Mac OS 8 items that are installed.

▲ **Mac OS 8.0 base** consists of the items that make up a basic Mac OS 8 system.

▲ **My Settings** starts with all items turned on but can be changed.

■ You cannot change the settings in or delete the Mac OS 8.0 all or Mac OS base sets.

To create a set

1. Open the Extensions Manager control panel (see **Figure 2)**.
2. Choose New Set from the File menu (see **Figure 7)**.
3. Enter a name for the set in the New Set dialog box that appears (see **Figure 8)** and click OK. The name of the set appears in the Select Set pop-up window.
4. Toggle item check boxes as desired for the set.

✔ Tip

■ Other commands under the File menu (see **Figure 7)** let you delete, rename, and duplicate the currently selected set.

Working with Sets

To show information about items

Click the Show Item Information triangle in the Extensions Manager window (see **Figure 4**). The window expands. When you select an item, its description appears in the expanded area (see **Figure 9**).

To sort items

In the Extensions Manager window (see **Figure 4**), click the heading at the top of the column by which you want to sort. The item order changes (see **Figure 10**).

✔ Tip

■ Items are sorted within the folders that they reside.

To hide the items in a folder

In the Extensions Manager window (see **Figure 4**), click the triangle to the left of the folder whose items you want to hide. The items disappear (see **Figure 11**).

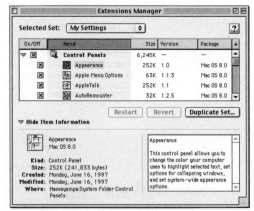

Figure 9. *When you expand the Extensions Manager window, information about a selected item is displayed in the expanded area.*

Figure 10. *Click a heading to sort by its contents.*

Figure 11. *Click the triangle to the left of a folder to hide its items.*

About Appearance & Sound Options

The overall appearance of your Mac OS work environment can be changed with a number of control panels:

- **Appearance** lets you change color, system font, and collapsing windows options.

- **Desktop Pictures** lets you select a pattern or picture to display on the Desktop.

- **Monitors & Sound** lets you change the color depth and resolution of your monitor, speaker volume, and alert sounds.

- **Speech** lets you select a default voice and instruct your computer to speak alerts.

In this section, I tell you about all of these control panels.

To set system accent and highlight color

1. Choose Appearance from the Control Panels submenu under the Apple menu (see **Figure 3**).

2. If necessary, click the Color button in the Appearance window that appears (see **Figure 12**).

3. Use the horizontal scroll bar in the Accent Color area to view all the color combinations. Click the one that you want to select.

4. Choose a color from the Highlight Color pop-up menu (see **Figure 13**).

5. Close the Appearance window.

✔ Tip

- If you choose Other from the Highlight Color pop-up menu (see **Figure 13**), you can use a color picker to select a custom color.

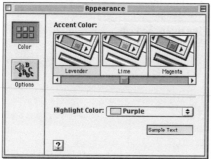

Figure 12. *Use the Color options in the Appearance control panel to set the system accent and highlight color.*

Figure 13. *Choose a color from the Highlight Color pop-up menu.*

To set collapsing window options

1. Choose Appearance from the Control Panels submenu under the Apple menu (see **Figure 3**).

2. If necessary, click the Options button in the Appearance window that appears (see **Figure 14**).

3. To collapse a window by double-clicking its title bar, turn on the Double-click title bar to collapse check box.

4. To play a *swoosh* sound when collapsing and expanding windows, turn on the Play sound when collapsing windows check box.

5. Close the Appearance window.

To set system appearance options

1. Choose Appearance from the Control Panels submenu under the Apple menu (see **Figure 3**).

2. If necessary, click the Options button in the Appearance window that appears (see **Figure 14**).

3. Choose a font from the System Font pop-up menu (see **Figure 15**).

4. To apply the platinum appearance to the dialog boxes, menus, and windows of other applications, turn on the System-wide platinum appearance check box.

5. Close the Appearance window.

✔ Tip

■ Chicago is the traditional system font of Mac OS. Charcoal is a new font introduced with Mac OS 8.

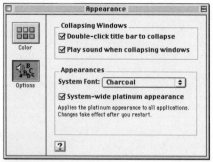

Figure 14. *You can also use the Appearance window to set the way collapsing windows work and sound, and set the system appearance.*

Figure 15. *You can choose from two system fonts.*

Figure 16. *The Patterns options of the Desktop Pictures window with a pattern applied.*

Figure 17. *Select the picture that you want to use. You can find some samples in the Apple Extras folder on your hard disk.*

Figure 18.
Choose a position option from this pop-up menu.

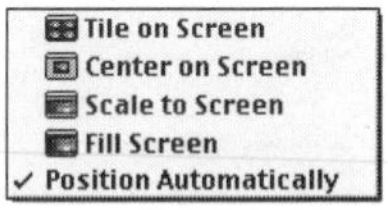

Tile on Screen
Center on Screen
Scale to Screen
Fill Screen
✓ Position Automatically

Figure 19. *The Picture options of the Desktop Pictures window with a picture applied.*

To set the Desktop pattern

1. Choose Desktop Pictures from the Control Panels submenu under the Apple menu (see **Figure 3**).
2. If necessary, click the Pattern button in the Desktop Pictures window that appears.
3. Use the horizontal scroll bar beneath the sample image to view the available desktop patterns.
4. When you see a pattern that you like, click Set Desktop. The pattern is applied to the Desktop (see **Figure 16**).
5. Close the Desktop Pictures window.

To set the Desktop picture

1. Choose Desktop Pictures from the Control Panels submenu under the Apple menu (see **Figure 3**).
2. If necessary, click the Pictures button in the Desktop Pictures window that appears.
3. Click Select Picture.
4. Use the Open dialog box that appears to locate, select, and open the picture that you want (see **Figure 17**). When you click Open, it appears in the Desktop Pictures window.
5. Choose a position option from the pop-up menu near the bottom of the Desktop Pictures window (see **Figure 18**).
6. Click Set Desktop. The picture appears on your Desktop (see **Figure 19**).
7. Close the Desktop Pictures window.

✔ Tip

■ To remove a Desktop picture, click Remove Picture in the Pictures options of the Desktop Pictures window (see **Figure 19**).

Setting Desktop Patterns & Pictures

To set monitor options

1. Choose Monitors & Sounds from the Control Panels submenu under the Apple menu (see **Figure 3**).

2. If necessary, click the Monitor button in the Monitors & Sounds window that appears (see **Figure 20**).

3. Select a color depth from the list in the Color Depth area. If you choose 256, you can select the Grays radio button to switch to grayscale display.

4. Select a resolution from the list in the Resolution area.

5. To adjust the contrast and brightness of the display, drag the two sliders at the bottom of the Monitors & Sounds window until the display is set the way that you want it.

6. Close the Monitors & Sounds window.

✔ Tips

- The options that appear in **Figure 20** vary depending on the type of monitor and amount of VRAM (video RAM) installed in your computer.

- Some computer models do not support the Monitors & Sounds control panel. If your computer doesn't, choose Monitors from the Control Panels submenu under the Apple menu (see **Figure 3**). You can set the color depth in the Monitors window that appears (see **Figure 21**) and the resolution in the dialog box that appears (see **Figure 22**) when you click the Options button in the Monitors window.

- If the options in the Monitors & Sounds or Monitors window look very different from what you see here, check the documentation that came with your monitor.

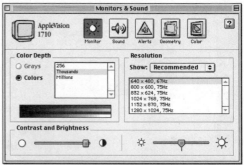

Figure 20. *Use the Monitors options part of the Monitors & Sounds window to set up your monitor.*

Figure 21.
If your computer has a Monitors control panel, use it to set color depth. Then click its Options button...

Figure 22. *...to set resolution in this dialog box.*

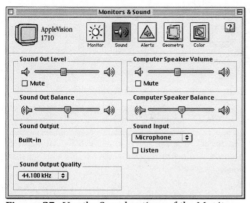

Figure 23. *Use the Sound options of the Monitors & Sounds window to change volume and balance levels and select input and output devices.*

Figure 24. *If your computer has a Sounds control panel, use it to set the sound in device, …*

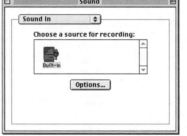

Figure 25. *…the sound out device,…*

Figure 26. *…and volume levels.*

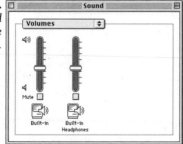

To set sound options

1. Choose Monitors & Sounds from the Control Panels submenu under the Apple menu (see **Figure 3**).

2. If necessary, click the Sound button in the Monitors & Sounds window that appears (see **Figure 23**).

3. Use the sliders to change the various volume and balance options.

4. If desired, choose options from pop-up menus to set Sound Output, Sound Input, and Sound Output Quality options.

5. To instruct your computer to listen for voice recognition commands, turn on the Listen check box.

6. Close the Monitors & Sounds window.

✔ Tips

- The options that appear in **Figure 23** vary depending on your computer model and connected devices.

- Voice recognition is a feature of Mac OS that is not included with the Mac OS 8 software. You can obtain it and instructions for using it from Apple Computer, Inc.'s Web site (*http://www.apple.com/*).

- Some computer models do not support the Monitors & Sounds control panel. If your computer doesn't, choose Sound from the Control Panels submenu under the Apple menu (see **Figure 3**). Use the pop-up menu at the top of the Sound window that appears to set Sound In (see **Figure 24**), Sound Out (see **Figure 25**), and Volumes (see **Figure 26**).

To set alert sound options

1. Choose Monitors & Sounds from the Control Panels submenu under the Apple menu (see **Figure 3**).

2. If necessary, click the Alerts button in the Monitors & Sounds window that appears (see **Figure 27**).

3. Select the sound that you would like to hear as your alert sound from the Alert Sounds list.

4. Use the System Alert Volume slider to change the volume of the alert sound.

5. Close the Monitors & Sounds window.

✔ Tips

■ You can click the Add button in the Alerts options of the Monitors & Sounds window (see **Figure 27**) to use the Recording dialog box to record your own sounds. I tell you how to use the Recording dialog box in **Chapter 6** when I tell you about SimpleSound.

■ Some computer models do not support the Monitors & Sounds control panel. If your computer doesn't, choose Sound from the Control Panels submenu under the Apple menu (see **Figure 3**). Use the pop-up menu at the top of the Sound window that appears to view and set Alert Sounds options (see **Figure 28**).

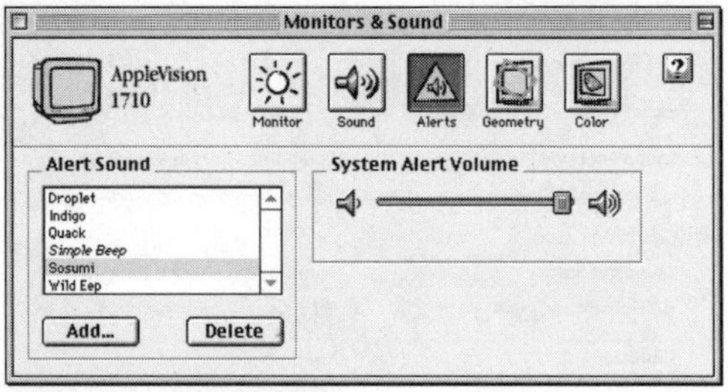

Figure 27. *Use the Alerts options in the Monitors & Sounds window to select the alert sound and set its volume.*

Figure 28. *If your computer doesn't have a monitors & Sounds control panel, use the Alert Sounds options of the Sound control panel to select an alert sound and set its volume.*

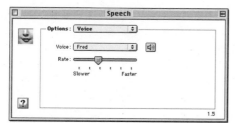

Figure 29. *The Voice options of the Speech window.*

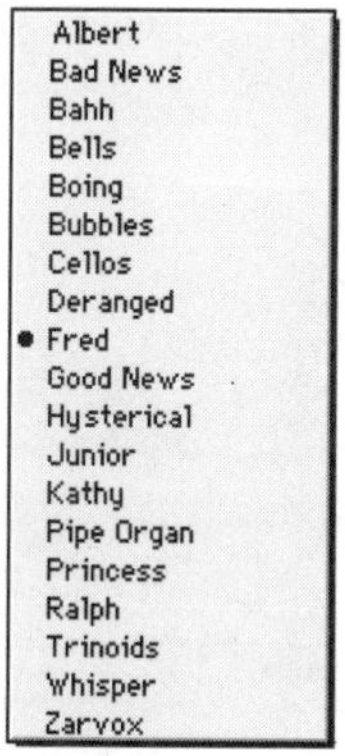

Figure 30.
Choose a voice from the Voice pop-up menu.

Albert
Bad News
Bahh
Bells
Boing
Bubbles
Cellos
Deranged
• Fred
Good News
Hysterical
Junior
Kathy
Pipe Organ
Princess
Ralph
Trinoids
Whisper
Zarvox

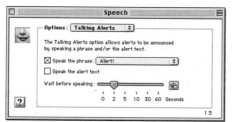

Figure 31. *The Talking Alerts options of the Speech window.*

Figure 32.
Choose a phrase from the Speak the phrase pop-up menu.

• Alert!
It's not my fault!
Blast!
Pay attention!
Oh dear!
Rats.
Yeow!
Attention!
Oh my!
Shoot!
Whoa!
Excuse me!

Next in the list
Random from the list

Edit Phrase List

To set voice options

1. Choose Speech from the Control Panels submenu under the Apple menu (see **Figure 3**).

2. If necessary, choose Voice from the Options submenu at the top of the Speech window that appears (see **Figure 29**).

3. Choose a voice from the Voice pop-up menu (see **Figure 30**).

4. If desired, use the slider to change the speaking rate.

5. Close the Speech window.

✔ Tip

■ To hear what the voice sounds like, click the speaker icon to the right of the Voice pop-up menu (see **Figure 29**).

To set talking alerts options

1. Choose Speech from the Control Panels submenu under the Apple menu (see **Figure 3**).

2. If necessary, choose Talking Alerts from the Options submenu at the top of the Speech window that appears (see **Figure 31**).

3. To hear your computer speak a phrase instead of playing an alert sound, turn on the Speak the phrase check box. Then choose a phrase from the pop-up menu (see **Figure 32**).

4. To hear your computer speak the text in alert dialog boxes, turn on the Speak the alert text check box.

5. If desired, use the Wait before speaking slider to set a delay.

6. Close the Speech window.

✔ Tip

■ To hear a demo of the talking alerts settings, click the icon beside the Wait before speaking slider (see **Figure 31**).

About Functionality Options

Many control panels can change the way your computer functions:

- **ColorSync System Profile** lets you select a color profile for your monitor so printed colors match on-screen colors.

- **Control Strip** lets you modify the appearance and functionality of the control strip on the bottom of the screen.

- **Energy Saver** lets you set options to automatically put your computer into sleep mode, start it, and shut it down.

- **General Controls** lets you change Desktop folder, folder protection, blinking, and document folder options.

- **Keyboard** lets you set the keyboard layout and sensitivity.

- **Launcher** lets you maintain a palette of buttons for launching programs and opening documents.

- **Memory** lets you set RAM management options.

- **Mouse** lets you set the way your mouse works.

- **Startup Disk** lets you select the disk from which the computer should start.

In this section, I tell you about all of these control panels.

✔ Tip

- Not all computer models support the control strip or energy saver feature. If yours doesn't, the control panel will not be installed on your system.

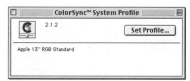

Figure 33. *The ColorSync System Profile window.*

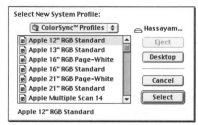

Figure 34. *Use an Open dialog box like this one to select a profile.*

Figure 35. *The Control Strip window.*

Figure 36. *If you select the Hot key to show/hide radio button, you can click Define hot key...*

Figure 37. *...to display this dialog box. Then change the hot key to show and hide the control strip.*

Figures 38 & 39. *Choose a font from the Font pop-up menu (left) and a font size from the Size pop-up menu (right).*

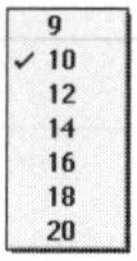

To set the ColorSync System Profile

1. Choose ColorSync System Profile from the Control Panels submenu under the Apple menu (see **Figure 3**). The ColorSync System Profile window appears (see **Figure 33**).

2. Click Set Profile.

3. Use a Open dialog box to locate and select a color profile for your monitor (see **Figure 34**). When you click Select, the profile appears in the ColorSync System Profile window.

4. Close the Color Sync System Profile window.

✔ Tip

■ ColorSync is important only if you need to match the colors on your monitor to the colors on your printer.

To set control strip options

1. Choose Control Strip from the Control Panels submenu under the Apple menu (see **Figure 3**). The Control Strip window appears (see **Figure 35**).

2. Select a radio button in the Show/Hide area. If you select Hot key to show/hide (see **Figure 36**), you can click Define hot key to display a dialog box you can use to change the hot key (see **Figure 37**).

3. Choose a font from the Font pop-up menu (see **Figure 38**).

4. Choose a font size from the Size pop-up menu (see **Figure 39**).

5. Close the Control Strip window.

✔ Tip

■ You can collapse and expand the control strip by clicking the tab at its right end.

To set automatic sleep options

1. Choose Energy Saver from the Control Panels submenu under the Apple menu (see **Figure 3**).

2. If necessary, click the Sleep Setup button at the top of the Energy Saver window that appears (see **Figure 40**).

3. Use the slider to set the amount of idle time before the computer goes to sleep.

4. To set the computer so that it shuts down instead of going into sleep mode, turn on the Shut down instead of sleeping check box.

5. To set different timing options for display (monitor) sleep and hard disk sleep, click Show details. The window expands to show two additional sliders. Turn on the check box beside the slider(s) that you want to set and set the slider (see **Figure 41**).

6. Close the Energy Saver window.

✔ Tip

■ I tell you about sleep mode and shutting down the computer in **Chapter 2**.

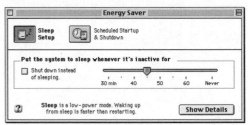

Figure 40. *The Sleep Setup options of the Energy Saver window.*

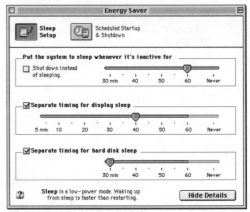

Figure 41. *Click Show Details to expand the window to show more options.*

Energy Saver
Sleep Setup
Scheduled Startup & Shutdown
Start up the computer
Weekdays
at 8:30 AM
Shut down the computer
Weekdays
at 5:30 PM

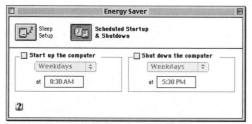

Figure 42. *The Scheduled Startup & Shutdown options of the Energy Saver window.*

Start up the computer
Weekdays
at 8:30 AM

Figure 43. *Turn on the Start up the computer check box to choose a day and time.*

✓ Weekdays
Weekends
Every Day
Monday
Tuesday
Wednesday
Thursday
Friday
Saturday
Sunday

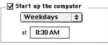

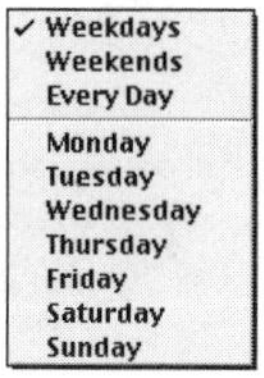

Figure 44. *Choose a day or group of days from the pop-up menu in the dialog box.*

To schedule start up and shut down times

1. Choose Energy Saver from the Control Panels submenu under the Apple menu (see **Figure 3**).
2. If necessary, click the Scheduled Startup & Shutdown button at the top of the Energy Saver window that appears (see **Figure 42**).
3. To start the computer at a specific time, turn on the Start up the computer check box (see **Figure 43**). Use the pop-up menu beneath it (see **Figure 44**) to select the day(s) on which the computer should automatically start. Enter a time in the at edit box beneath the pop-up menu.
4. To shut down the computer at a specific time, turn on the Shut down the computer check box. Use the pop-up menu beneath it (see **Figure 44**) to select the day(s) on which the computer should automatically shut down. Enter a time in the at edit box beneath the pop-up menu.
5. Close the Energy Saver window.

✔ Tips

- You can use this feature to start your computer before you arrive at work so it's waiting for you.
- You can also use this feature to automatically shut down at a certain time so you don't work too long.
- I've used this feature, along with the automatic scheduling feature of Claris Emailer, to retrieve and automatically reply to my e-mail while I'm away on vacation.

To set Desktop options

1. Choose General Controls from the Control Panels submenu under the Apple menu (see **Figure 3**). The General Controls window appears (see **Figure 45**).

2. To display the icons on your Desktop while other applications are active, turn on the Show Desktop when in background check box.

3. To automatically display the Launcher control panel when the computer starts, turn on the Show Launcher at system startup check box.

4. Close the General Controls window.

✔ Tip

■ I tell you about Launcher later in this chapter.

To set the shutdown warning option

1. Choose General Controls from the Control Panels submenu under the Apple menu (see **Figure 3**). The General Controls window appears (see **Figure 45**).

2. To have your computer inform you at start up when it was shut down improperly (see **Figure 46**), turn on the Warn me if computer was shut down improperly check box.

3. Close the General Controls window.

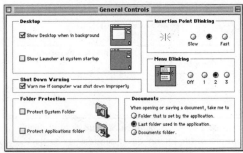

Figure 45. *The General Controls window.*

Figure 46. *This dialog box could appear if you shut down improperly.*

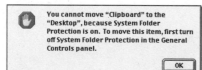

Figure 47. *With folder protection enabled, items can't be removed or renamed.*

To set folder protection

1. Choose General Controls from the Control Panels submenu under the Apple menu (see **Figure 3**). The General Controls window appears (see **Figure 45**).

2. To keep items in the System Folder or Applications folder from being renamed or removed, turn on the appropriate check box(es) in the Folder Protection area.

3. Close the General Controls window.

✔ Tips

■ You cannot change these options if file sharing is turned on. I tell you about file sharing in **Chapter 9**.

■ A dialog box like the one in **Figure 47** appears if you try to move something out of a protected folder.

To set insertion point & menu blinking options

1. Choose General Controls from the Control Panels submenu under the Apple menu (see **Figure 3**). The General Controls window appears (see **Figure 45**).

2. Select a radio button in the Insertion Point Blinking area to set the blink rate. The sample to the left of the radio buttons shows you the effect of your change.

3. Select a radio button in the Menu Blinking area to set the number of times a selected menu item should blink before the menu disappears.

4. Close the General Controls window.

To set the default save location

1. Choose General Controls from the Control Panels submenu under the Apple menu (see **Figure 3**). The General Controls window appears (see **Figure 45**).

2. Select a radio button in the Documents area to specify the default folder location in a Save As dialog box.

3. Close the General Controls window.

✔ Tips

■ If you select the Documents folder radio button but do not have a documents folder, Mac OS creates one for you on the Desktop. You can move it anywhere you like.

■ I tell you about the Save As dialog box in **Chapter 5**.

To set keyboard layout

1. Choose Keyboard from the Control Panels submenu under the Apple menu (see **Figure 3**). The Keyboard window appears (see **Figure 48**).

2. Turn on the check box to the left of each keyboard layout that you want to include on the Keyboard menu.

3. To rotate through the selected keyboard layouts by pressing ⌃⌘ Option Spacebar, turn on the check box beneath the list.

4. Close the Keyboard window.

✔ Tips

■ The Keyboard menu is displayed when WorldScript, a multi-languages feature of Mac OS, is installed. WorldScript is not automatically installed as part of a basic installation of Mac OS 8. I tell you about installing Mac OS 8 in **Chapter 1**.

Figure 48.
The Keyboard window.

■ You can use this feature to type using the keyboard layout for another language.

■ At least one keyboard layout must be selected.

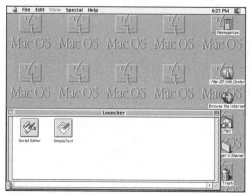

Figure 49. *The Launcher window appears at the bottom of the screen.*

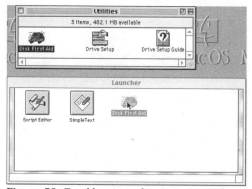

Figure 50. *To add an item, drag its icon into the Launcher window.*

Figure 51. *A button for an alias of the item is added to the Launcher window.*

To set key repeat settings

1. Choose Keyboard from the Control Panels submenu under the Apple menu (see **Figure 3**). The Keyboard window appears (see **Figure 48**).

2. Use the Key repeat rate slider to set how fast a key repeats when held down.

3. Use the Delay Until Repeat slider to set how long a key must be pressed before it starts to repeat.

4. Close the Keyboard window.

✔ Tip

■ These settings are especially useful for heavy handed typists.

To open and add items to Launcher

1. Choose Launcher from the Control Panels submenu under the Apple menu (see **Figure 3**). The Launcher window appears (see **Figure 49**).

2. Drag the icon for an item that you want to include in Launcher into the Launcher window (see **Figure 50**). When you release the mouse button, a button for the item appears in the Launcher window (see **Figure 51**). The original item remains where it was.

✔ Tips

■ To open a Launcher item, simply click its button.

■ To remove a Launcher item, hold down (Option) and drag the item to the Trash.

■ To have the Launcher automatically appear at start up, turn on the Show Launcher at system startup check box in the General Controls control panel. I tell you about General Controls earlier in this chapter.

Setting Key Repeat, Adding Launcher Items

To set memory options

1. Choose Memory from the Control Panels submenu under the Apple menu (see **Figure 3**). The Memory window appears (see **Figure 52**).

2. To set the disk cache size, click the arrows beside the Cache Size edit box to increase or decrease the value.

3. To turn virtual memory on or off, select the appropriate Virtual Memory radio button. If you select On, choose a hard disk from the pop-up menu and click the arrows beside the edit box to set the total amount of RAM that you want.

4. To turn a RAM disk on or off, select the appropriate RAM Disk radio button. If you select On, use the slider to set the RAM disk size.

5. Close the Memory window.

6. If you changed settings in the Memory window, restart your computer.

✔ Tips

- Don't change the memory options unless you know what you are doing or are following detailed instructions provided by someone who knows what he or she is doing. These are powerful options that can negatively affect your computer's performance if set improperly. When in doubt, click Use Defaults to use the default settings for your computer.

- A *disk cache* is RAM set aside for storage of frequently used computer instructions. The recommended disk cache setting is 32 kilobytes (K) of cache for each megabyte of installed RAM.

- *Virtual memory* is hard disk space used as RAM. For efficient performance on a computer with a PowerPC processor, Virtual Memory should be turned on and set to 1 megabyte (M) more than installed RAM.

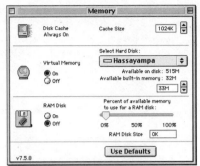

Figure 52. *The Memory window.*

Figure 53. *About this Computer tells you about the amount of RAM that is installed and in use.*

- A *RAM disk* is RAM used as disk space. If set up and used properly, it can benefit PowerBook users by reducing the computer's power consumption, thus increasing battery life.

- You can learn how much RAM is installed in your computer by choosing About this Computer from the Apple menu. A window like the one in **Figure 53** appears. It specifies the amount of installed (built-in) RAM, virtual memory, and largest unused block of RAM, as well as the amount of RAM in use by applications.

Setting Memory Options

Figure 54.
The Mouse window.

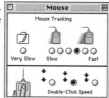

To set mouse options

1. Choose Mouse from the Control Panels submenu under the Apple menu (see **Figure 3**). The Mouse window appears (see **Figure 54**).

2. Select a Mouse Tracking radio button to set the speed of the mouse movement on your screen.

3. Select a Double-Click Speed radio button to set the amount of time between each click of a double-click. The radio button on the left is for longer time between clicks while the radio button on the right is for shorter time between clicks.

4. Close the Mouse window.

To set the startup disk

Figure 55.
The Startup Disk window shows all bootable high-capacity media.

1. Choose Startup Disk from the Control Panels submenu under the Apple menu (see **Figure 3**). The Startup Disk window appears (see **Figure 55**).

2. Select the icon for the disk that should be used as the startup disk the next time the computer is started.

3. Close the Startup Disk window.

✔ Tips

- Any *bootable disk*—a disk with a correctly configured System Folder on it—can be a startup disk.

- The Startup Disk control panel window displays all mounted bootable disks.

- To start from a bootable CD without using the Startup Disk control panel, hold down Ⓒ right after hearing the computer's startup tone. You can release it when you see the Welcome to Mac OS window.

- You don't need to use the Startup Disk control panel to start from a bootable floppy disk (like a Disk Tools disk). Just insert the disk before starting up.

Setting Mouse Options & Startup Disk

About Localization Options

There are a number of control panels you can use to set options specific to your location:

- **Date & Time** lets you set the date, time, and time zone, as well as configure the menubar clock.

- **Map** lets you set your location.

- **Numbers** lets you set number formatting, which can vary from country to country.

- **Text** lets you set text behaviors that affect sorting.

In this section, I tell you about all of these control panels.

✔ Tip

- The Date & Time control panel may be of special interest to PowerBook users who want to set time zones when they travel. I discuss other PowerBook considerations in **Chapter 11**.

To set the date & time

1. Choose Date & Time from the Control Panels submenu under the Apple menu (see **Figure 3**). The Date & Time window appears (see **Figure 56**).

2. To change the date, click the numbers that make up the date and use the arrow buttons to change them (see **Figure 57**).

3. To change the time, click the numbers that make up the time and use the arrow buttons to change them.

4. Close the Date & Time window.

Figure 56. *The Date & Time window.*

Figure 57. *Click the digits that you want to change, then click the arrow buttons to change them.*

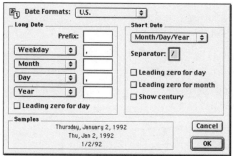

Figure 59. *The Date Formats dialog box lets you customize date formats.*

Figure 60.
Use the Date Formats, Time Format, and Number Format pop-up menus to choose one of the preconfigured date, time, and number formats.

Australian
Brasil
British
Danish
Dutch
Finnish
Flemish
French
French Canadian
German
Italian
Norwegian
Spanish
Swedish
Swiss French
Swiss German
Swiss Italian
✓ U.S.
Custom

Figure 61.
Choose a long date component from this menu:

Day
✓ Weekday
Month
Year
None

Figure 62.
Choose a short date format from this pop-up menu.

✓ Month/Day/Year
Day/Month/Year
Year/Month/Day
Year/Day/Month

Figure 63.
The Time Format dialog box lets you customize the time format.

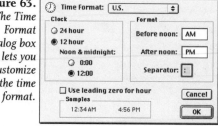

To set date & time formats

1. Choose Date & Time from the Control Panels submenu under the Apple menu (see **Figure 3**). The Date & Time window appears (see **Figure 58**).

2. To change the date format, click Date Formats. The Date Formats dialog box appears (see **Figure 59**).

3. Choose an option from the Date Formats pop-up menu (see **Figure 60**).

4. Modify the long date format by choosing options from the Long Date pop-up menus (see **Figure 61**) and entering punctuation in the edit boxes. If desired, turn on the Leading zero for day check box.

5. Choose a short date format from the Short Date pop-up menu (see **Figure 62**). If desired, change the separator character and turn on check boxes to include a leading zero for the day, a leading zero for the month, and the century as part of the year.

6. Click OK to save your changes.

7. To change the time format, click Time Formats. The Time Format dialog box appears (see **Figure 63**).

8. Choose an option from the Time Format pop-up menu (see **Figure 60**).

9. Select radio buttons in the Clock area to set clock preferences.

10. If desired, change the suffixes and separator in the Before noon, After noon, and Separator edit boxes and turn on the Use leading zero for hour check box.

11. Click OK to save your changes.

12. Close the Date & Time window.

✔ Tip

■ You can check the custom formats you create by looking at the sample area in the Date Formats and Time Format dialog boxes (see **Figures 59** and **63**).

To toggle daylight savings time

1. Choose Date & Time from the Control Panels submenu under the Apple menu (see **Figure 3**). The Date & Time window appears (see **Figure 56**).

2. Click the Daylight Savings Time check box to turn the daylight savings time setting on or off depending on the time of year and the state in which you live.

3. Close the Date & Time control panel window.

To set the time zone

1. Choose Date & Time from the Control Panels submenu under the Apple menu (see **Figure 3**). The Date & Time window appears (see **Figure 56**).

2. Click Set Time Zone. A dialog box like the one in **Figure 64** appears.

3. Locate and select a city in your time zone (preferably one that's close to you). Then click OK. The city you selected appears in the Date & Time (see **Figure 56**).

4. Close the Date & Time window.

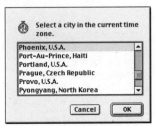

Figure 64. *Use this dialog box to select a city in your time zone.*

✔ Tip

■ You can also set your location with the Map control panel, which I tell you about a little later in this chapter.

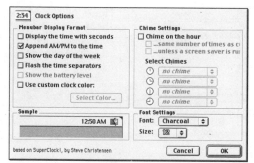

Figure 65. *Use the Clock Options dialog box to configure the menubar clock.*

Figure 66.
The menubar clock
appears at the far-right end of the menu bar, just to the left of the Application menu.

Figure 67.
You must turn on the Chime on the hour check box to set Chime Settings options.

To set menubar clock options

1. Choose Date & Time from the Control Panels submenu under the Apple menu (see **Figure 3**). The Date & Time window appears (see **Figure 56**).

2. Select a Menubar Clock radio button to display (On) or hide (Off) the menubar clock.

3. If you choose On, click the Clock Options button to display the Clock Options dialog box (see **Figure 65**). Set options as desired and click OK.

4. Close the Date & Time window.

✔ Tips

■ The menubar clock appears near the far-right end of the menu bar (see **Figure 66**).

■ If you use a program which also puts a clock in the menu bar (such as Now Up-to-Date), set the Menubar Clock option to Off in the Date & Time window (see **Figure 56**).

■ You must turn on the Chime on the hour check box in the Clock Options dialog box (see **Figure 65**) to set options in the Chime Settings area (see **Figure 67**).

■ Check the Sample area of the Clock Options dialog box (see **Figure 65**) to see the results of your changes before saving them.

Setting Menubar Clock Options

To set location with the a map

1. Choose Map from the Control Panels submenu under the Apple menu (see **Figure 3**). The Map window appears (see **Figure 68**).

2. In the edit box, type in the name of the city that you want to find. Then click Find.

3. If the city you entered is found, a flashing asterisk appears at its location on the map. Click Set to set that city as your location.

   or

   If the city you entered is not found, your computer makes an alert sound. Repeat step 2 until you find a city near you.

4. Close the Map window.

✔ Tips

■ Changing your location with the Map also changes your time zone and your system clock.

■ To add a city to the map, enter its name, longitude, latitude, and time zone in the appropriate edit boxes of the Map window (see **Figure 68**). Then click Add City.

■ If you want to know where the Middle of Nowhere is, use the Map to find it.

■ You can also use the Date & Time window to set your location. I tell you about that earlier in this chapter.

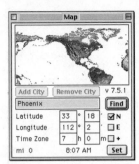

Figure 68.
The Map window offers another way to set your location or time zone.

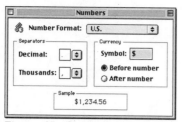

Figure 69. *The Numbers window.*

To set number formats

1. Choose Numbers from the Control Panels submenu under the Apple menu (see **Figure 3**). The Numbers window appears (see **Figure 69**).

2. Choose a format from the Number Format pop-up menu (see **Figure 60**).

3. If desired, customize the format by changing the contents of the edit boxes and selecting a different Currency radio button.

4. Close the Numbers window.

✔ Tip

■ You can check a custom number format you create by looking at the sample area in the Numbers dialog box (see **Figure 69**).

Figure 70. *The Text window.*

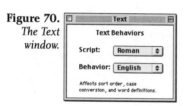

To set text behavior

1. Choose Text from the Control Panels submenu under the Apple menu (see **Figure 3**). The Text window appears (see **Figure 70**).

2. Choose an option from the Behavior pop-up menu (see **Figure 71**).

3. Close the Numbers window.

✔ Tips

■ Text behavior affects the way text is sorted. Different languages have different sorting rules.

■ The Script pop-up menu may offer options when WorldScript, a multiple language feature of Mac OS, is installed. WorldScript is not automatically installed as part of a basic installation of Mac OS 8. I tell you about installing Mac OS 8 in **Chapter 1**.

Figure 71. *Text behaviors are based on languages.*

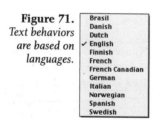

About Fonts

Fonts are typefaces that appear on screen and in printed documents. When properly installed in the Fonts folder inside the System Folder (see **Figure 72**), they appear on all Fonts menus (see **Figure 73**).

There are three kinds of fonts:

- TrueType fonts are scalable fonts that appear clear on screen and in print, no matter what size or printer you use. They come in suitcase files (see **Figure 72**).

- Bitmapped fonts are fonts are single-size fonts that appear clear on screen only when used in the correct size. They also come in suitcase files (see **Figures 72** and **74**).

- PostScript fonts are scalable fonts that appear clear in print when printed on a PostScript printer, no matter what size you use. With the help of a utility called Adobe Type Manager (ATM), PostScript fonts can also appear clear on screen and in print no matter what size or printer they use. They come in individual font files but must be accompanied by a corresponding bitmapped font (see **Figure 74**) in order to appear on Font menus.

✔ Tips

- You can open a suitcase file to the fonts inside it (see **Figures 75** and **76**). Bitmapped fonts names include numbers.

- You can open a font file to see a sample of the font's characters (see **Figures 77** and **78**). Bitmapped fonts display only one size while TrueType fonts display three sample sizes.

- If you're interested in learning more about Fonts than what's on these two pages, check out *How to Boss Your Fonts Around* or *The Macintosh Font Book, Third Edition*.

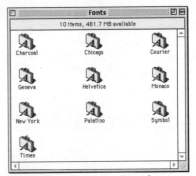

Figure 72. *The ten TrueType fonts that come with Mac OS 8 are installed in the Fonts folder.*

Figure 73. *SimpleText's Font menu is just one of the menus that list installed fonts.*

Figure 74. *Fonts can come in suitcases or as individual font files.*

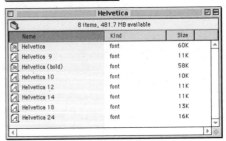

Figure 75. *This suitcase contains TrueType and bitmapped fonts...*

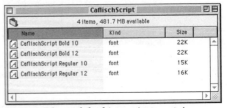

Figure 76. *...while this one just contains bitmapped fonts.*

About Fonts

Figure 77.
Open one of the font files inside a suitcase to see a sample of the font's characters. This is a bitmapped font...

Figure 78.
...and this is a TrueType font.

Figure 79. *Drag all the font's files onto the System Folder icon.*

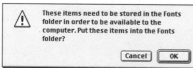

Figure 80. *Click OK when this dialog box appears.*

Figure 81.
The font you installed appears on the Font menus of your applications.

To install a font

1. Drag all suitcases and files that are part of the font onto the System Folder icon. When the System Folder becomes highlighted (see **Figure 79**), release the mouse button.

2. A dialog box like the one in **Figure 80** appears to inform you that fonts must be stored in the Fonts folder. Click OK.

✔ Tips

- You can see a freshly installed font in the Font menu of an application like SimpleText (see **Figure 81**) or your favorite word processor.

- If an application is running when you install a font, you'll have to quit the application and restart it to see the font in that application's Font menu.

To uninstall a font

1. Quit all applications.

2. Drag all suitcases and files that are part of the font out of the Fonts folder in the System Folder.

About Startup & Shutdown Items

The System Folder includes two folders you can use to automatically open items:

■ Items placed in the **Startup Items** folder automatically open when you start your computer.

■ Items placed in the **Shutdown Items** folder automatically open just before you shut down your computer.

✔ Tips

■ Need some ideas for using the Startup Items and Shutdown Items folders? Try these:

▲ Put an alias of your calendar or to-do list document in the Startup Items folder so your calendar or to-do list opens when you're ready to get to work.

▲ Put a sound file in the Startup Items folder so your computer can greet you with a recorded sound.

▲ Put an alias of your backup application in the Shutdown Items folder so you're automatically given an opportunity to back up your work before quitting for the day.

■ It's a good idea to use aliases instead of original items in the Startup Item and Shutdown Items folder. This helps keep originals where they're easy to find and back up. I tell you about aliases in **Chapter 4**.

To set an item to automatically open at start up or shut down

Drag the item (or an alias of the item) into the Startup Items or Shutdown Items folder inside your System folder.

GETTING HELP

About Getting Help

Mac OS offers several ways to get additional information and answers to questions while you work with your computer:

- **Balloon Help** identifies screen items as you point to them.
- **Mac OS Help** provides information about using Mac OS.
- **Guide help** provides information about using specific applications.
- **PC Compatibility Guide** provides information about using PC Compatibility hardware and software.
- **Application online help**, which is included in many third-party applications, provides information about the application.
- **Mac OS Info Center** provides tips and links to Internet sites with information about working with Mac OS.

In this chapter, I tell you how to access and use all these kinds of online help.

✔ Tips

- PC Compatibility Guide is only available on computers with PC compatibility hardware and software installed.
- Mac OS Help, Guide help, and PC Compatibility Guide all use Apple Guide technology, so they look and work much the same way.

About Balloon Help

Balloon Help identifies screen elements that you point to by providing information in cartoon balloon-shaped windows (see **Figures 2**, **3**, and **4**).

✔ Tips

■ Although Balloon Help might be too annoying to keep turned on all the time, you might find it useful when first starting out with Mac OS 8 or a new software application.

■ Balloon Help works in the Finder, all applications and utilities that come with Mac OS 8, and many third-party applications.

To turn on Balloon Help

Choose Show Balloons from the Help menu (see **Figure 1**).

To use Balloon Help

Point to an item for which you want more information. A cartoon balloon-shaped window appears with information about the item (see **Figures 2**, **3**, and **4**).

To turn off Balloon Help

Choose Hide Balloons from the Help menu (see **Figure 5**).

Figure 1.
To turn on Balloon Help, choose Show Balloons from the Help menu.

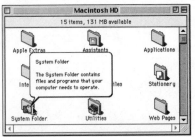

Figure 2. *Balloon Help displays a cartoon balloon-shaped window with information about items you point to.*

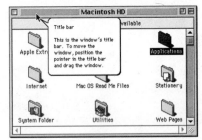

Figure 3. *With Balloon Help turned on, you can learn about almost anything on your screen, including window parts...*

Figure 4. *...and menu commands.*

Figure 5.
To turn off Balloon Help, choose Hide balloons from the Help menu.

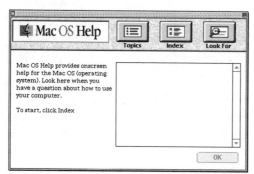

Figure 6. *Mac OS Help enables you to find information about using Mac OS.*

Figure 7. *Choose Help from the Help menu.*

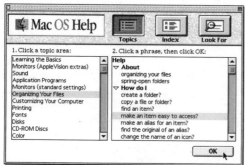

Figure 8. *When you click Topics, a list of topics appears on the left side of the Mac OS Help window. Click a topic to display corresponding phrases.*

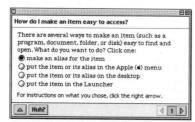

Figure 9. *Windows like this one provide explanations of key Mac OS features.*

About Mac OS Help

Mac OS Help (see **Figure 6**) offers three different ways to find information about using Mac OS:

- Browse **topics** to learn about various Mac OS features.
- Use the **index** to go right to a specific Mac OS feature.
- **Look for** explanations that contain key words you specify.

Once you've found the information you're looking for, step-by-step instructions using Apple Guide technology may also be available to walk you through a procedure.

To open Mac OS Help

Choose Help from the Help menu (see **Figure 7**).

or

Press ⌘ Shift / (or ⌘ ?).

To browse Mac OS Help topics

1. In the Mac OS Help window (see **Figure 6**), click Topics.
2. In the list of topics that appear, click a topic that interests you (see **Figure 8**).
3. In the list of help phrases that appear, click the phrase describing the explanation that you're looking for (see **Figure 8**).
4. Click OK.
5. Follow the instructions in the explanation window that appears (see **Figure 9**) to learn more about the topic.

Opening & Browsing Mac OS Help

265

To use the Mac OS Help index

1. In the Mac OS Help window (see **Figure 6**), click Index.

2. If necessary, drag the slider at the top of the index (see **Figure 10**) to display terms starting with a specific letter.

3. Click the term that interests you (see **Figure 11**).

4. Click the phrase describing the explanation that you're looking for (see **Figure 11**).

5. Click OK.

6. Follow the instructions in the explanation window that appears (see **Figure 12**) to learn more about the topic.

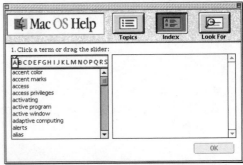

Figure 10. *When you click the Index button in the Mac OS Help window, an alphabetical list of terms appears.*

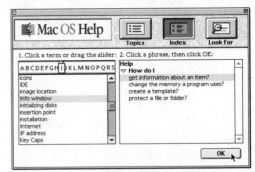

Figure 11. *Click a term in the index, then click a phrase describing the explanation that you want.*

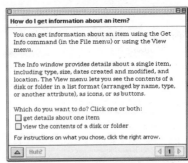

Figure 12. *Follow the instructions that appear in the explanation window to learn more about the topic.*

Figure 13. *When you click the Look For button in the Mac OS Help window, you can enter a search word or phrase.*

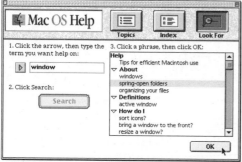

Figure 14. *Enter one or more words for the concept that interests you.*

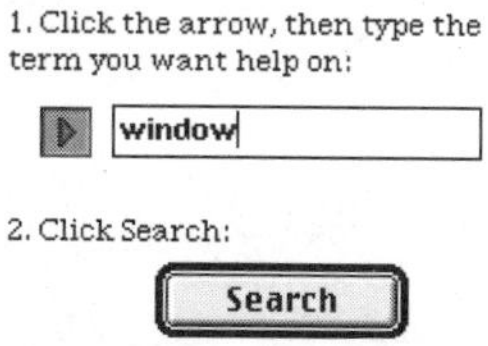

Figure 15. *Click one of the phrases in the list that appears after a successful search.*

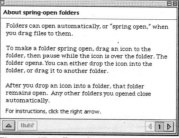

Figure 16. *If the search was unsuccessful, you'll see a message like the one in the window on the right.*

To look for key words

1. In the Mac OS Help window (see **Figure 6**), click Look For.

2. Click the blue triangle in the Mac OS Help window (see **Figure 13**) to activate the edit box beside it.

3. Enter one or more words to describe the concept that interests you (see **Figure 14**).

4. Click Search.

5. If a list of phrases appears, click the phrase that describes the explanation that you're looking for (see **Figure 15**) and click OK.

    or

    If the word cannot be found (see **Figure 16**), delete the word you entered in step 3 and repeat steps 3 through 5.

6. Click OK.

7. Follow the instructions in the explanation window that appears (see **Figure 17**) to learn more about the topic.

Figure 17. *Follow the instructions that appear in the explanation window to learn more about the topic.*

Looking for Key Words

To follow step-by-step instructions

1. Follow the instructions in the explanation windows displayed as a result of browsing, using the index, or looking for key words (see **Figures 9**, **12**, and **17**) to learn more about the topic.

2. As you advance through the windows by clicking the right-pointing triangle, instructions for completing a task may appear. As shown in **Figures 18** and **19**, instructions sometimes include red lines or underlined menu commands.

✔ Tip

■ Step-by-step instructions are created using Apple Guide technology.

To return to the main Mac OS Help window

Click the blue triangle button at the bottom of any explanation or instruction window (see **Figures 9**, **12**, and **17** through **19**).

To define a key concept

1. Click the Huh? button in any explanation or instruction window (see **Figures 9**, **12**, and **17** through **19**).

2. Read the definition in the window that appears (see **Figure 20**).

3. When you're finished with the window, click its close box.

To close Mac OS Help

Click the close box in any Mac OS help window.

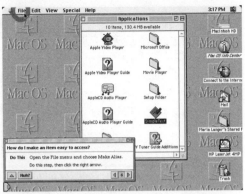

Figure 18. *Step-by-step instructions sometimes include red lines...*

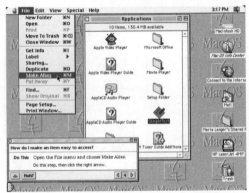

Figure 19. *...and underlined menu commands.*

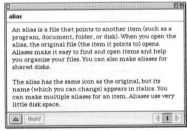

Figure 20. *Clicking the Huh? button displays information about key concepts.*

Figures 21a, 21b, & 21c.
To open Guide help for a specific application, choose Application *Guide from the Help menu. Here are the Help menus for SimpleText (top), Drive Setup (middle), and Apple CD Audio Player (bottom).*

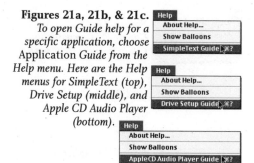

About Guide Help

Apple Guide technology also forms the basis for help within specific applications, including most applications and utilities that come with Mac OS 8. Opening an application's Guide help offers information using the same interface as Mac OS Help.

✔ Tip

■ I tell you all about Mac OS Help on the previous few pages.

To open Guide help for an application

Choose *Application* Guide from the Help menu (see **Figures 21a**, **21b**, and **21c**). The program's Guide help window appears (see **Figures 22a**, **22b**, and **22c**).

✔ Tip

■ As shown in **Figures 21a**, **21b**, and **21c**, the exact name of the command to open Apple Guide depends on the application name.

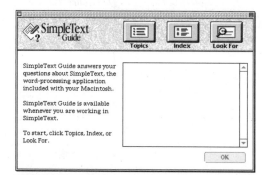

To use Guide help

Guide help works just like Mac OS Help, which I discuss on the previous few pages. Follow the instructions there.

✔ Tip

■ If a Guide help window does not include Topics, Index, and Look For buttons (see **Figure 22c**), you can only browse topics—you can't use the index or search features.

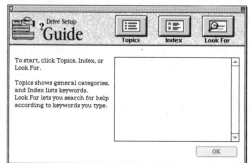

Figures 22a, 22b, & 22c.
Here are the corresponding Guide Help windows: SimpleText Guide (top), Drive Setup Guide (middle), and AppleCD Audio Player Guide (bottom).

About PC Compatibility Guide

If you have PC compatibility hardware and software installed in your computer, you can also take advantage of Apple Guide technology to learn about PC compatibility features.

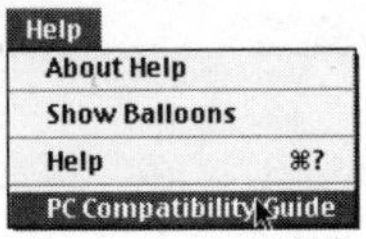

✔ Tip

■ I tell you about PC Compatibility hardware and software in **Chapter 7**.

To open PC Compatibility Guide

Choose PC Compatibility Guide from the Help menu (see **Figure 23**). The PC Compatibility Guide window appears (see **Figure 24**).

✔ Tip

■ The PC Compatibility Guide command will not appear on your Help menu unless you have PC Compatibility hardware and software installed.

To use PC Compatibility Guide

Guide help works very much like Mac OS Help, which I discuss earlier in this chapter. The main difference is the lack of Topics, Index, and Look For buttons. As a result, you can only browse topics—you can't use the index or search features. Check the appropriate instructions in the Mac OS Help section of this chapter for more information.

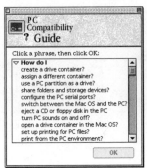

Figure 23.
Choose PC Compatibility Guide from the Help menu.

Figure 24.
PC Compatibility Guide works very much like Mac OS Help to provide information.

Click a phrase, then click OK:

▽ **How do I**
create a drive container?
assign a different container?
use a PC partition as a drive?
share folders and storage devices?
configure the PC serial ports?
switch between the Mac OS and the PC?
eject a CD or floppy disk in the PC
turn PC sounds on and off?
open a drive container in the Mac OS?
set up printing for PC files?
print from the PC environment?

OK

Using PC Compatibility Guide

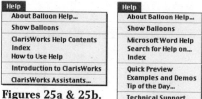

Figures 25a & 25b.
*The Help menus for
ClarisWorks (left) and Microsoft Word
(right) offer a variety of online help options.*

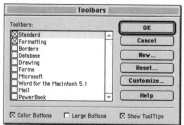

Figure 26. *Some dialog boxes, like
this one from Microsoft Word, include
a Help button you can click to get
contextual help.*

About Application Help

Many applications include extensive online
help. The help features of various applications look and work differently so I can't
cover them in detail here. I can, however,
tell you how to access help in other applications and assure you that most online
help features are easy to use.

✔ Tips

■ Some applications, like the Microsoft
Office suite of products, include an
entire online manual that is searchable
and printable. The only drawback to
Office's online manual is that the
Microsoft Office CD must be inserted
in order to use it.

■ Not all applications include online
help. If you can't locate an online help
feature for an application, check the
documentation that came with the
application to see if it has one and how
you can access it.

To access an application's online help

Choose a command from the Help menu
within that application (see **Figures 25a**
and **25b**).

or

Click a Help button within a dialog box
(see **Figure 26**).

Accessing an Application's Online Help

About Mac OS Info Center

Mac OS Info Center (see **Figure 27**) uses a Web browser interface to provide:

- Information and tips for using Mac OS 8.
- Links to sites with additional information and tips for using Mac OS 8.

✔ Tips

- You do not need an Internet connection to get information from Mac OS Info Center. You do, however, need an Internet connection to follow links to other sites on the Internet.
- I tell you more about using a Web browser in **Chapter 10**.

To open Mac OS Info Center

Double-click the Mac OS Info Center Icon on your Desktop.

or

Select the Mac OS Info Center Icon on your Desktop and choose Open from the File menu or press ⌘O.

To get information

1. Click one of the three big buttons on the Mac OS Info Center's main window (see **Figure 27**):

   ▲ **Show Me What I Can Do** provides information and links for what you can do with Mac OS (see **Figure 28**).

   ▲ **Help Me Solve a Problem** provides information and links for troubleshooting and getting technical information (see **Figure 29**).

   ▲ **Help Me Explore the Internet** provides information and links for getting connected to and "surfing" the Internet (see **Figure 30**).

2. Click underlined links to get the information that you want.

Figure 27. *The main menu for Mac OS Info Center.*

Figure 28. *Information is available in three categories: Discovering What You Can do,...*

Figure 29. *...Solving Problems,...*

Figure 30. *...and Exploring the Internet.*

MENUS & KEYBOARD COMMANDS

About Menus & Keyboard Commands

This appendix illustrates all of the Mac OS 8 Finder's menus—both Simple Finder (left) and standard Finder (right)—and provides a list of keyboard commands you can use with the Mac OS 8 Finder.

To use a keyboard command, hold down the modifier key (usually ⌘), while pressing the keyboard key corresponding to the command. It's important to note that the only keyboard command that works when Simple Finder is turned on is ⌘ Shift / (Help).

I tell you all about using menus and keyboard commands in **Chapter 2**.

File Menu

⌘ N	New Folder
⌘ O	Open
⌘ P	Print
⌘ Delete	Move to Trash
⌘ W	Close Window
⌘ Option W	Close All Windows
⌘ I	Get Info
⌘ D	Duplicate
⌘ M	Make Alias
⌘ Y	Put Away
⌘ F	Find
⌘ R	Show Original

File (Simple Finder)

- New Folder
- Open
- Close Window
- Duplicate
- Find...

File (Standard Finder)

New Folder	⌘N
Open	⌘O
Print	⌘P
Move To Trash	⌘⌫
Close Window	⌘W
Get Info	⌘I
Label	▶
Sharing...	
Duplicate	⌘D
Make Alias	⌘M
Put Away	⌘Y
Find...	⌘F
Show Original	⌘R
Page Setup...	
Print Desktop...	

Label submenu

- ✓ None
- Essential
- Hot
- In Progress
- Cool
- Personal
- Project 1
- Project 2

Edit menu

⌘Z	Undo	
⌘X	Cut	
⌘C	Copy	
⌘V	Paste	
⌘A	Select All	

View Menu

(no command keys)

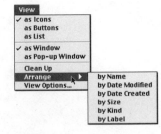

Special Menu

⌘E   Eject

Help Menu

⌘ Shift /   Help

Other Command Keys

⌘ Shift 1	Eject diskette
⌘ Shift 3	Create picture of screen
⌘ Shift /	Create picture of selection

Edit, View, Special, & Help Menus

Index